Broken Altars

Broken Altars

Secularist Violence in Modern History

Thomas Albert Howard

Yale
UNIVERSITY PRESS
NEW HAVEN & LONDON

Published with assistance from the Louis Stern Memorial Fund.

Yale University Press books may be purchased in quantity for
educational, business, or promotional use. For information, please email
sales.press@yale.edu (U.S. office) or sales@yaleup.co.uk (U.K. office).

Set in Spectral type by Newgen North America.
Printed in the United States of America.

Library of Congress Control Number: 2024942762
ISBN 978-0-300-26361-9 (hardcover : alk. paper)

A catalogue record for this book is available from the British Library.

This paper meets the requirements of
ANSI/NISO Z39.48-1992 (Permanence of Paper).

10 9 8 7 6 5 4 3 2 1

This book is dedicated to Brittany and Lindsey
and to the memory of our grandparents

They had faith in violence as the only means of knocking the future into shape.

—Raymond Aron

Contents

Broken Altars

INTRODUCTION

Things are not always what they seem.
—Aesop

IN THE PAST SEVERAL DECADES, AND ESPECIALLY AFTER 9/11, "religion" has become a white-hot topic in the world of culture, ideas, and journalism. One sees this in books, articles, and blogs; in the burgeoning of "post-secular studies" in the academy; and in a veritable industry of programs and institutions promoting interreligious or interfaith dialogue.[1] In the mix, fresh and sometimes compelling attention has been paid to the relationship between religion and violence. In the academic world, see, for example, Arizona State University's Center for the Study of Religion and Conflict or the University of Groningen's Centre for Religion, Conflict and Globalization. The *Journal of Religion and Violence* aims to study the topic in depth. Weighty tomes such as the *Blackwell Companion to Religion and Violence* (2011) and the *Oxford Handbook of Religion and Violence* (2013) reflect the trend, as do numerous conferences and symposia held on the topic.

One should welcome these developments as they engage matters often shortchanged in the past. Still, one wonders if the complex realities under consideration are adequately captured by the frequently deployed phrase "religious violence." One need not look hard, moreover, to discover that the recent interest frequently stems from the debatable, Enlightenment-derived commonplace that religion is inherently irrational and violent and must always be countermanded by political secularism.

Popular books, such as Hector Avalos's *Fighting Words: The Origins of Religious Violence*, reinforce the commonplace: "Religion is inherently prone to violence."[2] Not all that long ago, so-called new atheists—Sam Harris, Richard Dawkins, Daniel Dennett, and Christopher Hitchens—argued that deeply held religious convictions invariably reflect ignorance and aim for social domination.[3] Margaret Atwood's *Handmaid's Tale* and its popular television adaptation fantasizes about what such a theocracy might look like if troglodyte religionists finally got their way. Not least, the U.N. General Assembly in 2019 established August 22 as "the international day commemorating the victims of acts of violence based on religion or belief."[4]

In short, for many educated Westerners, the idea that religion promotes violence and secularism ameliorates the problem is a settled certainty, a *doxa,* an unstated premise of right thinking. "[Assuming] that religion has a tendency to cause violence is part of the conventional wisdom of Western societies, and it underlies many of our institutions and policies," observes the theologian William Cavanaugh.[5] "The idea that secularism is the best response to religious violence is part of the progress narrative that organizes modernity," adds the social scientist Janet R. Jakobsen. "In this story, progress is marked by an advance from religious faith to secular reason. Secularism is an advance over religion because [secular] reason provides a means of resolving conflict without violence."[6]

This book raises questions about this conventional wisdom. By no means do I deny that religious energies—particularly when tied up with ethnic identities and economic scarcity—can be turned toward destructive ends, especially by unscrupulous politicians in times of crisis and uncertainty. Think of the Balkans, Kashmir, or the Middle East. The list is familiar, although Jonathan Swift might have said more than he realized when he quipped that often we "have just enough religion to make us hate, but not enough to make us love one another." Nonetheless, concentration on or simply assuming religion's inclination toward violence insouciantly glides past a glaring reality of the twentieth century: namely, that regimes committed to secularism have not infrequently possessed just as much capacity for violence as, and often much more than, those tied to religious identity. Twentieth-century secularist ideologies bear as an ignominious hallmark, moreover, systematic attacks against religious communities. In terms of sheer numbers, the misery, deaths, and destruction visited on religious communities by secularist regimes in the twentieth century vastly exceed the violence committed during early modern European wars of religion, which are routinely invoked to legitimize the necessity of the modern secular nation-state.

Violence tied to religious belief invites ongoing inquiry, to be sure. This is not disputed. But might attentiveness to violence committed under a secularist aegis bring needed nuance and perspective to this complex, often fraught topic? Such attentiveness is the purpose of this book.

SECULARISMS

Of course, not all forms of secularism foster violence. Distinctions are necessary. But at least two kinds have done so, and it is worth pondering why and in what way. Doing so will take us in chapter 1 back to the ideological ferment of the nineteenth century, when many modern political ideas and narratives about the meaning of modernity first took shape.[7] In the wake of the French Revolution and the Napoleonic Wars (1789–1815), debates about the appropriate relationship between religion and a modern polity became pointed and acrimonious across Europe and the West more broadly. Confronted by a Restorationist order after 1815 intent to reassert the time-honored relationship between throne and altar, or crown and church, characteristic of the ancien régime, leading proponents of modernity offered three principal ways of making sense of and indeed solving the religiopolitical dilemma: what we might categorize as *passive secularism, combative secularism,* and *eliminationist secularism.*[8] This book focuses on violence under the aegis of the latter two, but the first one, as a foil, merits some attention as well.

While most citizens of the United States would not recognize a term like *passive secularism,* they know from experience the political-religious arrangements it describes, for, broadly speaking, this is the solution offered by the U.S. Constitution's First Amendment (1791): the national government should neither establish a religion nor meddle with citizens' free exercise of their faith. In the brief period before the French Revolution's radical turn, something comparable held sway in France. The Belgian Constitution of 1831 exemplifies it as well. In the nineteenth century, well-known liberals such as Benjamin Constant, Alexis de Tocqueville, John Stuart Mill, Félicité de Lamennais, Charles de Montalembert, and Lord Acton, among others, laudably theorized and endorsed versions of passive secularism and its familiar cognates: freedom of conscience or freedom of religion, combined, too, with freedom of speech and assembly.[9] The deeper roots of this officially secular but religion-accommodating arrangement lay in the thought of

John Locke, especially his *Letter Concerning Toleration* (1689), conceived as a pragmatic solution to the religiopolitical turpitude that convulsed Britain in the seventeenth century. Long skeptical of secularism in whatever form, the Catholic Church at the Second Vatican Council (1962–65) endorsed a modified form of passive secularism. Not a few modern constitutions espouse some version of it, as does the U.N. Universal Declaration of Human Rights (1948).[10] While regarding the state as secular, this solution, even if seldom perfectly implemented, does not raise questions concerning violence as pointedly as the other two.[11] Too often, however, Western scholars, pundits, and journalists myopically equate this form of secularism with secularism as a whole. Historically speaking, this is far from the case. This point becomes especially apparent when one adopts a more expansive global frame of reference, "provincializing" Western Europe and the North Atlantic world, as this book attempts to do.[12]

Combative secularism, more problematically, descends from the Jacobin stages of the French Revolution after 1792. At this time, the anticlerical sentiment of the French Enlightenment (remember Voltaire's *écrasez l'infâme*—crush the loathsome thing, that is, the Catholic Church) gained an outlet for political expression.[13] This resulted in extensive measures of *déchristianisation:* the shuttering and destruction of churches and monasteries, erasure of the Christian calendar, rampant iconoclasm, guillotining of clergy, and a genocidal response to Catholic opposition to revolutionary excesses in the Vendée region of western France.[14] Often if not always tempering its early capacity for violence, this form of secularism—later tagged as *laïcité* (secularism, laicism)—grew apace throughout the nineteenth century, coming to expression in the European-wide revolutions of 1830 and 1848 and in the short-lived Paris Commune of 1871; it found a congenial (and eventually more moderate) political home in France's Third Republic (1871–1940). In the late nineteenth century, this version of secularism derived major intellectual support from August Comte's theory of stadial civilizational development, which posited theological and then philosophical stages of human history inexorably giving way to a purely "positivist" one—an age of science and strictly immanent conceptions of well-being.[15] The Third Republic politician Léon Gambetta embodied combative secularism, sloganeering *le cléricalisme, voilà l'ennemi* (clericalism, that's the enemy!) throughout much of his career. For Gambetta and other committed anticlericals (within and beyond France), the church assumed the role of a "mythic enemy," the antithesis of revolution, reason, and progress, according to Joseph Moody; "the function of the myth . . . simplified beliefs [and] gave a single satisfactory object to passions that otherwise would be tempered by contradictory data."[16] Such assertive laïcité was institutionalized in various "laic" laws in the late nineteenth century, especially the well-known French Law on the Separation of the Church and State (1905), which effectively crushed the Catholic Church's role in public life, asserting the political order, the state, as the locus of social solidarity. The outcome in France invited imitation from other republican-anticlerical polities.[17] In the twentieth century, revolutionary Mexico, republican Spain, and Kemalist Turkey embraced and adapted versions of combative secularism, ratcheting up its anticlerical hostility and capacity for violence. I profile these instances of combative secularism in chapter 2.

Finally, *eliminationist secularism* designates a political solution gestated and shaped by Europe's Far Left—by Karl Marx, Friedrich Engels, Pierre-Joseph Proudhon, Mikhail Bakunin, and other socialist intellectuals, anarchists, and syndicalists operating within the swelling Communist cells and political movements of the mid- and late nineteenth century.[18] Despite sharp disagreements among them, they tended to see religion itself as wrongheaded and reactionary. "The first duty of a free and intelligent mind," Proudhon once wrote, "is to chase the idea of God out of his mind incessantly."[19] Despite Marx's well-known phrase about religion serving as "the opiate of the masses," he wrote little on religion per se, concentrating on political and economic matters. But religion's place in his thought is crucial and became globally influential in the twentieth century. In brief, Marx saw religious belief as a species of "false consciousness," a compensatory delusion reflecting unjust social conditions. Once the proletarian revolution overcame these conditions and modernized society, achieving this-worldly well-being, religion would simply be eliminated, becoming a curious relic of humanity's pre-socialist past.[20] As Marx's intellectual heir Leon Trotsky once quipped, the Russia of "icons and cockroaches" would necessarily pass into oblivion.[21]

Implicit in this view, however, is a major problem for a Marxist regime once it attains power: what if religion fails to follow its assigned script and wither away? And what if it even puts up stiff resistance, obstructing the "historical process"? What, too, if the paradise on earth promised by dialectical materialism falls woefully short? This reality confronted many socialist regimes in the twentieth century: the persistence of religion became therefore a major embarrassment, a worrisome sign of the failure of theory, not to mention a rival source of moral judgment and a breeding ground for political dissent.[22] To save appearances, socialist regimes resorted to extensive measures in the Soviet era to persecute, repress, and/or control religious elements in society. What Lenin and Stalin began in the 1920s and 1930s, dictators like China's Mao Zedong and Albania's Enver Hoxha, among others, continued during the Cold War. Exploring trajectories of eliminationist secularism in the twentieth century, starting with the Soviet Union, begins in chapter 3.

Despite their differences, both combative secularism and eliminationist secularism are the offspring of the Enlightenment's progressive wing—what the intellectual historian Jonathan Israel has called the Radical Enlightenment. They descended from the belief that reason should everywhere supplant tradition and "superstition" and that an individual or group's religious convictions ought to take a back seat to collective immanent social progress.[23] Surveying the Communist onslaught against religious communities in the twentieth century inclines one to understand not only Voltaire's "écrasez l'infâme" but also Diderot's well-known quip that "men will never be free until the last king is strangled with the entrails of the last priest" not as instances of rhetorical excess but as prescriptive desiderata. As the philosopher and dissident from Communist Poland Leszek Kolakowski once wrote: "The rationalism, contempt for tradition, and hatred of the mythological layer of culture to which the Enlightenment gave birth developed, under Communism, into the brutal persecution of religion, but also into the principle that human beings are expendable: that individual lives count only as instruments of the 'greater whole' or the 'higher cause,' i.e., the state, for no rational grounds exist for attributing to them any special, non-instrumental status."[24] The historical record lends credence to Kolakowski's judgment.

Finally, both combative secularism and eliminationist secularism have abetted violence not only by what secularist regimes have afflicted on their own populations but also by the forms of determined backlash that they have often inspired by their intrusive overreach.[25] While rank-and-file believers have often sympathized with the *political* objectives promoted by modernizing secularist regimes (equality, literacy, redistribution of wealth), they have often found themselves driven into the arms of the regimes' adversaries by their disagreement over the harsh treatment of the religious sector of society or by the fact that a state-imposed secularism did not accompany genuine democratization and freedom, as was often promised.[26] Zealous (political) secularism, in other words, has ironically sometimes begotten a zealous (religious or religiopolitical) counterreaction, and thus the former deserves at least an honorable mention in the causal chain leading to the latter. This sub-argument surfaces at several points in the upcoming chapters. But it plays second fiddle to the main argument, which might be summarized in two parts: that (1) certain ways toward or types of modern secularism (the combative and eliminationist varieties) have contributed to extraordinary violence by regimes that adopted them, not only but notably directed at religious communities and their leaders—and their material culture as well; and that (2) this reality should give us reason to think more critically (and historically and globally) about the unreflective bromide that religion promotes violence and that secularism is the self-evident solution.

DIFFICULT WORDS, COMPLEX REALITIES

"Religion," "secularism," and "violence" resist simple definitions. How ought one, then, to think lucidly about them and the complicated realities that they aim to represent? The foregoing taxonomy of secularism is a helpful start, but it is important to push ahead farther.

"Religion" poses especially thorny challenges. Ever since Wilfred Cantwell Smith's groundbreaking *The Meaning and End of Religion* (1962), one cannot assume that the word is a straightforward descriptor of identifiable historical phenomena and an obvious domain of universal human experience that exists neatly apart from other social domains such as culture, law, or politics.[27] With great erudition, Smith demonstrated that the term's modern meaning is largely a creation of the post-Enlightenment, colonialist West, lacking clear-cut equivalents in other languages and cultures. Even in Europe, prior to the modern era, *religio* meant something more akin to piety or devotion; it was regarded as a component of the virtue of justice in the thought of Thomas Aquinas—that is, what one owed to God.[28] Beginning roughly in the eighteenth century, assisted by the classificatory sensibilities of the Enlightenment and Europe's overseas expansion, scholars, missionaries, and colonial bureaucrats began using the term differently, adapting it to denote a putative genus with particular "ism" species (Hinduism, Buddhism, and so on)—many of these "isms" coined for the first time only by

Western scholars—that possessed nonetheless some vague, common sub-strate.[29] Religion's modern meaning, in other words, reflects Westerners' attempts to make sense of, classify, and even control the great heterogeneity of beliefs, practices, and deities that they encountered beyond their shores. Other languages have simply lacked the term in the sense of a common genus comprising diverse species, only adopting it, or cognate versions of it, in the modern era. Pushing Smith's argument to the limit, the scholar of religion Jonathan Z. Smith has even argued that "religion is solely the creation of the scholar's study. . . . Religion has no independent existence apart from the academy."[30] Nevertheless, writing in the nineteenth century, Karl Marx and like-minded social critics anchored their social analysis in this peculiar etymological development, assuming its universal epistemic validity and durability. "Religious violence" theorists often assume it as well, despite profound theoretical difficulties in isolating "religion" as the "smoking gun" from other social variables contributing to violence.

Expanding on Wilfred Smith's work, the anthropologist Talal Asad has shown how the terms "religion" and "secularism" have conceptually developed in tandem, both reflecting the attempt in the West after the Protestant Reformation to demarcate a separate religious sphere from a (profane) political one. In earlier periods of history, the "secular" (*saeculum*) simply meant the realm of this world, the present age, used many times as such in the Latin Vulgate and in early and medieval Christian thought.

"Secularization" (*saecularisatio*) at first denoted the change from monastic life (*regularis*) to the life of canons (*saecularis*) within a bishop's jurisdiction. After the Reformation, secularization came to refer to the transfer of ecclesiastical property from the hands of the church to the state or private owners.[31] It retained its connection to political and legal realities until the nineteenth century, at which time it expanded to indicate a view of the world—an outlook, an episteme—specifically irreligious in orientation and one keen to curb religious involvement in statecraft and society generally.

In roughly this sense, the word "secularism" first appeared in English in George Holyoake's *English Secularism: A Statement of Belief* (1851). By this time, though, the concept had long existed *avant la lettre,* advanced forcefully by thinkers carrying forward the tradition of the Radical Enlightenment.[32] While some scholars persist in associating secularism with mere neutrality, more compelling recent scholarship has pointed out how secularism's manifestations in history, along with its aspirations toward epistemic and moral certainty, betray a specific, often fraught genealogy that complicates any attempt to universalize it straightforwardly as a transcultural human value. Echoing what the philosopher Charles Taylor has called "subtraction theory," the social theorist Saba Mahmood has argued that secularism cannot be conceived of as a neutral umpire of religious difference, some supra-ideological leftover after the "modern state's retreat from religion"; it is rather itself "a historical product" with its own commitments and "with specific epistemological, political, and moral entailments."[33] Put differently, secularism usually carries normative assumptions and frames of reference, reflecting the specific historical conditions of its provenance, and it should not be regarded simply as preexisting neutrality/rationality awaiting the "subtraction" of encrusted religious obscurantism.

Because of the terms' deep and specific ties to the West's passage into modernity, some scholars have registered insightful concerns about the applicability of "religious" and "secular" and the implied binary distinction between them to non-Western lands. William Cavanaugh, for instance, has argued that the religious-secular distinction, regularly presented as "embedded in the immutable state of things," is in fact a much more contingent, problematic reality, "part of the legitimating conceptual apparatus of the modern Western nation-state." To mix religion and secular public life, from this ideological perspective, is to court irrationality, violence, and sectarianism. The two must therefore assiduously be kept apart.

The problem with this view, however, is that most non-Western parts of the world, for most of their history, have simply not thought about or ordered society in such a manner. More often, politics has possessed a sacral character, and beliefs about transcendence have pervasively colored both public and private life. The extent to which the binary religious-secular distinction has become a global reality or at least a global aspiration is the result of colonization and Westernization and the global intellectual transformations, transfusions, and disruptions that these processes have wrought in the modern era. Consequently, according to Cavanaugh, "violence that is labeled religious" comes to be seen as peculiarly virulent, atavistic, and reprehensible. But "violence that is labeled secular" hardly counts as violence at all, since it, not born of "religion," is inherently peacemaking and often necessary to quell religious passions.[34] But this still begs the question—made acute by the rise of modern political ideologies—of what exactly counts as "religious" and what as "secular." And how, too, can one appropriately attach the word "violence" to either?

In efforts to navigate through the terminological and conceptual complexities identified by Asad, Cavanaugh, and others, some scholars have turned to the concepts "secular religion" and "political religion" to describe modern political ideologies such as nationalism, fascism, socialism, and Communism. The tradition of deploying such terminology has a venerable pedigree, going back at least as far as Eric Voeglin's *Political Religions* (Vienna, 1938). It includes the works of such thinkers as Nicolas Berdyaev, Raymond Aron, and Hans-Joachim Schoeps, among others, arguably culminating in the subtle and sophisticated work by the Italian historian of modern fascism Emilio Gentile.[35] Many things recommend this point of view, especially as it pertains to nationalism. In the eyes of political-religion theorists, as Philippe Burrin has summarized, nationalist movements regularly seek to merge with, rather than attack, the religious sphere; they "use the religious culture of their society in order to elevate the political to a supreme and all-encompassing sphere," thereby effecting a dual process: "the sacralization of the political on the one hand and the politicization of elements of the inherited [religious] culture on the other."[36] Though differing in some respects, this rings true of Mussolini's Italy, Franco's Spain, Salazar's Portugal, and, today, Narendra Modi's India, among other regimes. In strongly nationalist societies, the border between the political and the religious becomes blurred, the latter enchanting the former with an aura of sacredness eliciting a response of devotion and absolute duty.

This blurring of boundaries should not surprise, according to Benedict Anderson, who connected the early stirrings of nationalism with "religious modes of thought" in his influential *Imagined Communities: Reflections on the Origins and Spread of Nationalism*. Indeed, for Anderson, nationalism in many respects bears a "strong affinity for religious imaginings" and draws from the preexisting "religious community" to fashion another community that revolves around the modern nation-state—a historical formation Western in origin but today global in scope.[37] But this does not necessarily imply a zero-sum game, in which the energies from one (religious) community are simply channeled into those of an ersatz (national) political community. Rather, the domain of piety (*religio*) is expanded: a multifaceted sacralization of the political occurs. The whole process often gains legitimation from the extant religious powers, even if some prophets might arise worrying about political idolatry corrupting the purity of the religious community. For all these reasons, and recognizing that every form of nationalism might not exactly fit this model, I am less inclined to frown on applying the concept "political religion" to nationalist ideologies and movements. It is also for this reason that I have not made nationalism per se a focus of this book. At the same time, I recognize that more often than not twentieth-century secularist violence took place *within* the territorial borders of particular nation-states—despite the internationalist rhetoric of global Communism— mixing sometimes with nationalist rhetoric as well as ethnic identity in the process. The standing *raisons d'état* of nation-states and the loyalties that they inspire, whether conceived of as quasi-religious or not, should thus be understood as an abiding contextual factor for grasping the foci of this book. In this context, secularist ideologies often provided leaders with a bracing, sophisticated-sounding ideological élan, permitting one to appeal to the march of progress, science, and historical inevitability to help justify more visceral (national) political motivations.

Yet the notion of political religion sits more uneasily with secularism as such, particularly with the two forms that I have identified as combative secularism (growing out of the Enlightenment-Comtean tradition) and eliminationist secularism (especially as it has appeared under Marxist-Leninist regimes). It might be helpful, furthermore, to regard both forms of secularism as exhibiting characteristics of *exclusive humanism,* a term first employed by Henri de Lubac and then Charles Taylor in their studies of modernity, even if we recognize that combative secularism, historically speaking, has veered more in an *anticlerical* direction (and in its more moderate forms has evinced laudable concern for religious minorities), while eliminationist secularism has proven to be more comprehensively *anti-religious.*[38] But in both cases, the modus operandi of the secularist regime has led it to confront traditional religious actors, drastically curtail their authority and scope of operation, degrade their material culture, and/or intimidate them into quietism and public insignificance—with some among the religious incentivized to acquiesce and cooperate—by employing the various carrots and especially sticks at the state's disposal. Moreover, unlike right-wing forms of nationalism, which often evince a nostalgic view of history and seek the retrieval of a mythic past, the twentieth century's violent secularisms have tended to possess a future-oriented, progressive, stadial, and/or purely immanent understanding of the historical process—instigated by an (revolutionary) overcoming of the superstitious/authoritarian/feudal past. Champions of secularism in possession of this kind of "historical stadial consciousness," notes the social theorist José Casanova, have in turn contributed to a global situation, at least among educated elites, that "turn[s] the particular . . . [Western] historical process of secularization into a universal teleological process of [global] human development from belief to unbelief, from primitive irrational or metaphysical religion to modern rational postmetaphysical secular consciousness."[39] This outlook and the seemingly axiomatic character of the assumptions informing it among many modern state-builders and intellectual classes are factors that have impeded wider recognition of the relationship between modern ideological secularism and violence, which this book seeks to elucidate.

In such an immanent vision, "religion"—an abstraction that secularist ideologues as diverse as Vladimir Lenin, Kemal Atatürk, and Mao Zedong, among others, have found politically expedient despite its specifically Western provenance—is regularly regarded as an obstructing, reactionary force, meriting confrontation, controlling, debilitating, and/or possible elimination, either sooner or later. In this vein, as the historian Philippe Burrin has noted, regimes inclined toward exclusive humanism tend to

> collide with religion and . . . the antagonism, declared or veiled, engendered by their politics by far exceeds the classic disputes over the distribution of the respective powers of God and Caesar. In fact, they can only regard institutionalized religion as a disturbing force, not only because it obstructs their goal of conquering minds, but also . . . [because] religion is an internalized tradition that engages the human being more profoundly than political opinions. Christianity, which was one of the most formidable forces for reducing heterogeneity that has been known in Western history, now [under secularist regimes] emerges as an element of heterogeneity intolerable to political phenomenon that were no less obsessed than itself with [a new, state-defined] unity and homogeneity.[40]

This is a mouthful, to be sure, but the essential point is that secularist regimes, committed to an exclusively immanent flourishing (and even if paying lip service to the notion "freedom of conscience" or more often a restrictive "freedom of worship") have frequently found pockets of religious opposition—harboring transcendent visions of human destiny and powerful non-statist mechanisms of community building and moral formation—more deeply rooted in the social fabric than the regimes had originally anticipated.

From the synoptic of the centralizing modern secularist state, therefore, religious communities have often appeared as hatcheries of disloyalty—hoary, cunning, obstinate competitors for the hearts and minds of citizens. Speaking of the Soviet Union but with applicability to other twentieth-century regimes, Kolakowski observed that "[o]nce the state had become the appanage of the party with its anti-religious philosophy, this separation [of church and state] was impossible. The party's ideology became that of the state, and all forms of religious life perforce became anti-state activity."[41]

Furthermore, some secularist regimes have defined themselves against religious communities with respect to claims about rationality and ontology, further discouraging conceptualizing them as purveyors of political religion. Many religious traditions, not least Christianity, prize understanding the world as a mystery, the numinous expression of divine volition and creativity that can never exhaustively be appreciated or explained by rational or empirical means.[42] Eastern Orthodox strains of Christianity even delight in "the apophatic," the view that humankind's limited epistemological and linguistic capacities permit one to say better what God is not than what he is. From this perspective, the divine inhabits a transcendent realm, shrouded in inaccessible light, intimated perhaps by the ontological realities around us but never fully disclosed by them. Comparable judgments appear in other religious traditions, especially within their mystical, contemplative strains—for example, Sufism, Vedanta, Hasidism.[43]

By stark contrast, exclusive humanism, epitomized in Marxist-Leninist historical materialism but also apparent in Comtean positivism and in other immanent strains of post-Enlightenment stadial historical thought, rests on a conception of reality that is irreducibly unmysterious. The raw data of the empirical world, understood by the scientific method, mastered by political will and technocratic planning, is presented as *the* only way forward for human understanding and social progress. The divine is simply not part of the ontological economy in any meaningful sense. "I hate all gods," Marx wrote, quoting Aeschylus, as an epigraph for his dissertation on materialism in the ancient world.[44] For Russia to have a future, "[one] must be a materialist," as Lenin bluntly put it: "an enemy of religion."[45] For the historical materialist, to quote Kolakowski once again, "there is no other hidden reality behind it [the world]; the world as we see it is the Ultimum; it does not try to convey a message to anything else."[46] In such a world, time understood as the Greek *kairos* (auspicious, sacred time) becomes simply *chronos*—"homogenous, empty time," to use Walter Benjamin's locution: time understood as chronological succession shorn of divine sanction or religious mystery.[47] Or, in Max Weber's well-known language, the march of time leads inexorably to "disenchantment," the evacuation of all gods from human consciousness and institutions and the pursuit of a future indifferent to prophets and priests.[48] As we shall see, the abrupt abolition of time-honored holy days—the dismantling of kairos, as it were—became routine practice among many modern secularist regimes, whether in France, Mexico, the Soviet Union, Czechoslovakia, Albania, China, or elsewhere.

With respect to social philosophy, exclusive humanism presents three additional counterpoints to traditional religiosity. First, in place of the church (or synagogue, mosque, temple) or local community, the (national) state becomes the locus of individual and communal action and the driving engine of human history. Modernity often appears as a "centralizing rather than a liberating force," as the social anthropologist Ernest Gellner once put it.[49] The roots of such a reality go back to political theorists such as Thomas Hobbes and Jean-Jacques Rousseau, among others, and it manifested itself politically before the modern era in the centralizing and Erastian reforms of so-called enlightened despots such as Joseph II of Austria and Frederick the Great of Prussia, both of whom draconianly increased the purview and authority of the state at the expense of other institutions, church bodies and economic guilds preeminently. The French Revolution and Napoleon expanded on what these enlightened despots had begun in practice, as Hegelian thought did in the realm of theory, and it is common knowledge that the incremental expansion of the state over other intermediary social bodies is one of the major themes of nineteenth-century history.[50] Combative- and eliminationist-secularist regimes in the twentieth century built atop this ideological and institutional inheritance.

Second, in contrast to the Jewish and Christian notion that each individual person is created in God's image (*imago Dei*) and is thus sacrosanct by divine association, exclusive humanism has veered strongly in the direction of making the *immanent collective* the paramount focus of social thought and moral reasoning: achieving the ideal of the "nation" or even "humanity," not personal blessedness or the acquisition of merely private rights and freedoms, looms larger than other considerations.[51]

Finally, at least rhetorically, "equality" emerged as an almost absolute value in exclusive humanism in ways that it had not in the European old regime or in classical liberal thought. "Equals know neither God nor the devil," as the French socialist and materialist Jean-Jacques Pillot pithily put it.[52] From a modern perspective, traditional religiosities have permitted disconcerting levels of hierarchy—lamas over monks, priests and rabbis over laity, men over women, older generations over younger ones—while defending the prerogatives of non-state corporative bodies against forces of state centralization to retain sufficient freedom to define communal norms and traditions in their own terms. The setting-up and legitimation of a polity charting a course toward unprecedented egalitarianism—as a redress of past injustice but also as a tool to actualize statist ambitions—served as a powerful selling point for secularist regimes, Marxist-Leninist ones preeminently, even if it also helped justify harsh policies of repression and retaliation against "backward" or "feudal" elements of the old order distressed by the new agenda. "Enemies of the people," Robespierre called them in "On Political Morality." But once the new regime was in place, some people turned out to be more equal than others, to paraphrase George Orwell's *Animal Farm.*

For all the above reasons, we should be wary of speaking of exclusive humanism as a political religion. Insofar as all human thought grows out of and is usually compared to what precedes it, we may concede that some elements in new ideologies resemble faith traditions—tight-knit Marxist parties have long been likened to churches, for example. Other similarities could be adduced, and in what follows I sometimes draw material from scholars inclined to think in these categories. Still, we should not be so smitten by our analogies between past and present that we fail to see those elements in history that merit being regarded as genuinely discontinuous from what came before and therefore require different terms and modes of analysis. The secularist ideological currents treated in this book ought to be appraised as what they are: relative novelties in the grand scheme of things. Simply labeling them "religious" or "ersatz religious" restricts insight and reinforces the wanting religion-always-leads-to-violence conceit.

Finally, we turn to the question of "violence," candidly acknowledging that few terms have been more saturated in explanation and analysis.[53] Among numerous works, the philosopher Hannah Arendt's short classic *On Violence* is most applicable to this book in its concern to understand state-sponsored violence within a given polity. For Arendt, power and violence are antithetical to each other. A government exhibiting genuine power—authority might have been a better word for her to have chosen—does not need to resort to violence, because it commands the allegiance of the governed. It possesses legitimacy. By contrast, when governments are not in possession of power or when this power is fragile and contested (say, during or immediately after a revolution or civil war, or when facing an insurrection), violence is employed in an intrastate fashion even if this is fraught with problematic, often unintended consequences. In Arendt's own words: "Power and violence are opposites; where the one rules absolutely, the other is absent. Violence appears where power is in jeopardy, but left to its own course it ends in power's disappearance." And again: "Rule by sheer violence comes into play where power is being lost. . . . To substitute violence for power can bring victory, but the price is very high; for it is not only paid by the vanquished, it is also paid by the victor in terms of [eroding] his own power."[54] Protracted recourse to violence by a regime, in other words, tends to undermine the regime's claim to legitimacy, even if the violence originally aimed to establish or maintain legitimacy.

Repeatedly, we shall see how the persistence of religious communities posed threats, whether real or imagined, to secularist governments inclined philosophically toward exclusive humanism. What resulted was often the subtle forfeiture of power and the resort to violence. This violence patently affected religious communities, but it also drained legitimacy from the governments that administered it, provoking many of them to resort to terror to maintain control. And "terror" is precisely the name that Arendt gives regimes, bereft of genuine authority, that feel compelled to resort to violence on a continual basis to maintain themselves: "Terror is not the same as violence; it is, rather, the form of government that comes into being when violence, having destroyed all power, does not abdicate but . . . remains in full control. It has often been noticed that the effectiveness of terror depends almost entirely on the degree of social atomization. Every kind of organized opposition [not least religious ones] must disappear before the full force of the terror can be let loose."[55] This does not describe every regime engaged in repression of religion treated in this inquiry. But it does describe the efforts of some.

In the twentieth century, the actual administration of violence took many forms: the sudden abolition of long-standing religious practices, institutions, and holy days; confiscation of religious property; destruction of religious art, sacred objects, manuscripts, and architecture; requiring oaths of political allegiance; repurposing sacred sites for mundane uses; censorship;

requirements to inventory sacred valuables; secret-police surveillance and the employment of civilian informants; banning or politically dominating seminaries and other institutions of religious education; coercing believers into psychiatric institutions; insistence on cumbersome forms of official registration; travel bans and restrictions; public ridicule; exhuming the dead and destroying cemeteries; denying educational opportunities and job promotions; banning public religious proclamation; promoting schisms within and between religious communities; the production of anti-religious propaganda; punitive taxation and fees; and other forms of excessive and arbitrary bureaucratic regulation in addition to show trials, imprisonment, deportation, forced labor, reeducation camps, struggle sessions, torture, and execution.

Military and police forces, party apparatchiks, local cadres, politicized young people, government informants, bureaucrats, the judiciary, and, not least, executive leadership and ideologically compliant citizens—including at times compromised and co-opted fellow believers—constituted the principal human agents of repression. Sometimes violence was furious and sensational; often it was banal, bureaucratic, and persistent. Sometimes it yielded submission; quite often it did not, as religious actors defied authorities, dispersing their activities into underground and dissident channels.[56]

Mao Zedong famously quipped in "Problems of War and Strategy" that "political power grows out of the barrel of a gun." Following Arendt's lead, my book seeks to question this view, for the reliance on violence quite often compromised the authority of a government in the eyes of the governed while, ironically, inducing comparably extreme forms of religiopolitical opposition. In the twentieth century, religious communities faced historic and often unrecognized levels of violence from secularist, putatively enlightened governments. Their fates bear witness to efforts of maintaining ideological and political control and to the unraveling of these efforts, as well as to the more general recurrences, complexities, and unforeseen outcomes of human history. The sheer scope of twentieth-century anticlerical and anti-religious repression, however, should give one pause when encountering the platitude that religion is inherently violent and in need of secular containment. Religious traditions have been complicit in violence, to be sure. The historical record on this is clear and invites ongoing inquiry. But the fact that secularism too has been complicit—and on a massive scale— should make us puzzle over the reliability of our assumptions, narratives, and vocabulary in thinking perspicaciously about these complicated matters. Which secularism, whose religion, under what circumstances, and combined with what other factors, we might more probingly ask. In the final analysis, anyone inclined to invoke modern secularism indiscriminately as an antidote to religious violence might speak well but not wisely, handicapped by potent historical amnesia.

CHAPTER ONE

Three Ways

Clericalism, that's the enemy!
—Léon Gambetta

Even the most refined, most well-intentioned,
defense or justification of the idea of god is
a justification of reaction.
—Vladimir Lenin

ON 23 SEPTEMBER 1823, THE DEACON OF THE COLLEGE OF
Cardinals, Fabrizio Ruffo, appeared on the balcony of the Quirinal Palace
in Rome to announce the election of a new pope: "I give you tidings of a
great joy; we have as pope the most eminent and reverend Lord, Hannibal
Cardinal of the Holy Roman Church della Ganga, priest of the title of Saint
Mary's beyond the Tiber, who has assumed the name of Leo XII."[1]

Present at the announcement, Britain's Cardinal Nicholas Wiseman
(1802–65) later observed that "the election is of a prince as well as a pontiff,
and that serious diversities of opinion may be held, relative to the civil polity
most conducive to the welfare of subjects, and the peace even of the world."[2]
For progressive critics of the old regime, Leo XII's election represented a
disaster with respect to the office of prince and pontiff, that is, the pope's
temporal and spiritual rule. A sickly man with ulcerated legs, elected by
a show of strength from the most traditionalist cardinals, the *zelanti*, Leo
lasted only seven years in office—far too long in the eyes of his detractors.
His election came at the height of the Restoration in Europe, when conservative statesmen and intellectuals outbid one another to consign the events
of the French Revolution and Napoleonic era (1789–1815) to the ash heap
of history and to revive a social unity based on the Constantinian recipe of
"throne and altar" that had characterized the ancien régime.[3] A stickler for
decorum, ruling the Papal States in central Italy as a temporal monarch, Leo

valued confessional unity and supported the dynastic principle of monarchy throughout Europe, including in France, where the restored Bourbon monarchy regarded the Revolution as Luciferian in origins and as nightmarish in results.

For reform-minded observers, Leo's views symbolized everything that was wrong with the old regime with respect to religion and statecraft but that, due to Napoleon's defeat, had been spared from perdition by diplomats at the Congress of Vienna (1814–15), presided over by Austria's arch-conservative, Prince Klemens von Metternich. Yet many forces of state expansionism—effected by eighteenth-century absolutist rulers, the Revolution, and Napoleon alike—remained in place, now pressed into the service of reactionary goals.[4] Nonetheless, the "ideas of 1789" (liberty, fraternity, and equality) and before that the example of the American Revolution, with its outgrowth the Constitution's First Amendment (1791) chartering freedom of conscience, simply could not be forgotten. Despite a string of conservative victories after 1815, many sharp minds felt that a better solution, a *secular* solution, to the state-church question remained a desideratum, one that would grant the political sphere autonomy from religious influence or at least protection from excessive religious influence. But as Cardinal Wiseman observed, "serious diversities of opinion" existed over exactly how to go about this, and not only in the Papal States and France but across Europe and in its colonial holdings.

For those convinced that the age-old throne-and-altar recipe amounted to a nostalgic throwback, three principal ways or options for removing religious power from the state presented themselves in the course of the long nineteenth century: what I have called *passive secularism, combative secularism,* and *eliminationist secularism.* Each in its own way aimed to achieve a secular polity, but their means and ends differed markedly. Proponents of passive secularism sought to achieve a cordial modus vivendi between a neutral government advancing political liberty and religious communities, convinced that a climate of freedom, while politically desirable, might also benefit religious life. By contrast, channeling Voltairean anticlericalism, combative secularists villainized organized religion and sought to achieve an assertive, more comprehensive statist secularism, at once conflicting with and seeking to control inherited traditions. Finally, eliminationist secularism, apotheosized after the century's end by Marxism-Leninism, entertained a still more sweeping anti-religious vision, best realized above the grave of all traditional faiths, which its proponents either intended to dig themselves or await the dialectical exigencies of history to dig on their behalf. In either case, religion deserved elimination, once and for all.

PASSIVE SECULARISM

Broadly speaking, passive secularism reflects the church-state solution offered by the First Amendment of the U.S. Constitution, which forbade the federal government to establish a state church but protected the "free exercise" of religious life, thus creating a historically unprecedented voluntary religious domain. The example was not lost on the Old World. Before the French Revolution's Jacobin turn, something comparable held sway in France during the Revolution's first, moderate phase (1789–92), and such later state foundations as the Belgian Constitution of 1831 bear witness to its vitality in postrevolutionary Europe. Many nineteenth-century thinkers who regarded themselves as "liberals" adopted some version of passive secularism. Tracing its intellectual genealogy fully would return one to the likes of John Locke and Moses Mendelssohn in the Old World and William Penn, Roger Williams, and James Madison in the New, among others. Wary of secularism in whatever form well into the twentieth century, the Catholic Church came to endorse a modified form of passive secularism during the Second Vatican Council (1962–65), and by then it had already received laudable expression in the U.N. Universal Declaration of Human Rights (1948).

To examine the appeal of passive secularism—and to see its distinction from combative and eliminationist secularism and their capacity for anti-religious violence—the thought of the French priest and scholar Félicité de Lamennais (1782–1854) and the Belgian Constitution of 1831 merit spotlighting.

Born in 1782, ordained as a priest in 1817, Lamennais cuts a remarkable figure in modern history. Shocked by the excesses of the French Revolution and Napoleon's top-down rule, he moved in a decidedly ultramontane (literally "over the mountains," the Alps, toward papal authority) direction early in his career, championing the authority of Rome against both secularists and Gallicans, that is, fellow Frenchmen who looked to the French ecclesiastical hierarchy, not Rome, for leadership. Lamennais's first work, *On the Tradition of the Church under the Institution of Bishops* (1814), in fact condemned Gallicanism and the interference of the state in the church's affairs. His second work, *An Essay on Indifference in Religious Matters* (1817), established his European-wide reputation. In it, he doubled down on an ultramontane viewpoint, while also arguing that the state could not be indifferent to religious matters and that modernity's intellectual malaise owed its origins to Protestant heresies and Cartesian philosophy. Broadly speaking, until about 1825, Lamennais passed as a fairly typical Catholic traditionalist, distressed by the legacy of the French Revolution and looking to the past for a social recipe to restore church-state unity. Pope Leo XII esteemed his views and tried (unsuccessfully) to persuade him to join the College of Cardinals.[5]

But changes in Lamennais's outlook were afoot. He despised the heavy-handed statism of post-Napoleonic higher education in France. The Restorationist principle of monarchical legitimism, moreover, began to irk him, in large part because Catholic minorities often received poor treatment from "legitimate" non-Catholic rulers. This held true in the case of Ireland, which stood under British authority; in Poland, which stood under Russian and Prussian control; and in nearby Belgium, which stood under Dutch control within the United Kingdom of the Netherlands, a political confection of the Congress of Vienna.[6] In each case, the principle of dynastic (and putatively Christian) legitimism prevailed, but to the detriment of Catholic minorities, Lamennais maintained. He thus began to wonder if Catholicism might fare better if ties between church and state were abrogated in favor of a more general religious liberty.[7] His thoughts dovetailed with those of Engelbert Sterckx, vicar-general to the archbishop of Malines and later archbishop himself, and an advocate of Belgian independence from the (largely Protestant) Netherlands—which came about in 1830–31, a time of renewed revolutionary palpitations across Europe.

Galvanized into action by developments in the Low Countries, in 1831 Lamennais—along with two other notable liberal Catholic scholars, Charles de Montalembert and Henri Lacordaire—founded the journal *L'Avenir* ("The Future"), which had as its motto "God and Liberty." As short-lived as it was prescient, the journal advanced stridently liberal points of view: separation of church and state; democracy; freedom of conscience; and freedom of the press.[8] "Each day," the journal editorialized in August 1831, "one understands more and more that political liberty is bound inseparably to religious liberty. It has its root in it and cannot be affirmed and developed other than through it."[9] With the help of Montalembert, Lamennais also founded the Agency for the Defense of Religious Liberty, the first organization of its kind, which monitored and recorded violations of religious freedom in France. Threatened by his superiors for holding wrongheaded views, Lamennais attempted an end-run around the local hierarchy and took his case directly to the pope, then Gregory XVI (r. 1831–46). With Lacordaire and Montalembert in tow, Lamennais journeyed to Rome in December 1831, convinced that the newly elected pope might smile on his views if he could just explain himself directly.

Things turned out otherwise. After months of waiting, the Frenchmen were granted an audience with the pope lasting all of fifteen minutes. The short conversation yielded little of substance. To add insult to injury, on his return home, Lamennais received word that a papal encyclical—*Mirari vos* (1832), presumably being prepared during his stay in Rome—had been issued, directly challenging his notions of democracy, freedom of conscience, and separation of church and state. Demoralized, Lamennais felt that the church had closed its ears to good sense.

But history has many surprise twists. While papal documents echoed *Mirari vos* throughout the nineteenth century, most notably in Pius IX's well-known "Syllabus of Errors" (1864), an itemized list of modernity's errors, Lamennais had successfully planted seeds eventually reaped at the Second Vatican Council (1962–65).[10]

In his lifetime, Lamennais's ideas enjoyed more success in shaping the Belgian Constitution of 1831. In 1830, Belgian liberals and Catholics joined forces to throw off the Protestant Dutch yoke and draft a constitution that upheld liberal principles while avoiding excessive hostility in religious matters.[11] "Religious liberty and freedom of public worship, as well as liberty to express opinions in all matters, are guaranteed," as article 14 of the constitution states.[12] Inspired by English constitutional principles, the pre-Jacobin French Constitution of 1791, and the American First Amendment model, the Belgian Constitution became a beacon of light for liberals and constitutionalists all over Europe—"the most liberal governing document in Europe," according to the legal scholar George Athan Billias.[13] Historians have traced its influence on the Spanish Constitution of 1833, the Greek Constitutions of 1834 and 1864, the Luxembourg Constitution of 1848, the Danish Constitution of 1849, and the Prussian Constitution of 1850, among others.[14]

It also set a precedent for twentieth-century developments. Skirting other constitutional realities in individual countries, arguably no single development rivals in importance the drafting of the U.N. Universal Declaration of Human Rights after the Second World War. In the words of the constitutional scholar Linde Lindkvist, this process resulted in one of the "the most influential statements on religious freedom in human history."[15] Completed and adopted in 1948, the declaration proclaims that "everyone has the right to freedom of thought, conscience and religion; this right includes freedom to change his religion or belief, and freedom, either alone or in community with others and in public or private, to manifest his religion or belief in teaching, practice, worship and observance."[16] Since the declaration's promulgation after the Second World War, these words have rallied defenders of passive secularism in the West and throughout the world, even if some U.N. member states have only paid it lip service.[17]

Throughout the nineteenth century and into the twentieth, Catholic teaching and practice remained firmly hostile to secularism in any form, often labeling it "indifferentism." But as discourse about religious freedom expanded in the twentieth century, some Catholics came to believe that the church might have missed an opportunity with the Lamennais affair and required a do-over. By the 1940s, the French philosopher Jacques Maritain and the American Jesuit John Courtney Murray, in particular, argued that the church should abandon its anti-modern stance toward religious liberty and adopt a version of passive secularism on the basis of innate human dignity—a topic of recurrent discussion in the then-ascendant personalist and neo-Thomist philosophical movements.[18] This dignity, they argued, implied that human conscience should never be coerced and that a climate of religious freedom helped make this possible. Through many twists and turns, and despite vocal old-guard criticism that tended to resent all of modernity as the fiendish offspring of Voltaire, the Second Vatican Council vindicated the cause of religious liberty in the conciliar decree *Dignitatis humanae* (1965).[19] It declares that "the human person has a right to religious freedom. This freedom means that all men are to be immune from coercion on the part of individuals. . . . [N]o one is to be forced to act in a manner contrary to his own beliefs, whether privately or publicly, whether alone or in association with others, within due limits." This right, furthermore, "has its foundation in the very dignity of the human person."[20] With kinship ties to the American and Belgian Constitutions, and other precedents, *Dignitatis humanae* and the clauses on religious freedom in the U.N. Declaration of Human Rights, despite minor differences, represent clear articulations of what I am calling passive secularism, a commendable achievement in human affairs.

Specifically, they attempt to eschew a substantive conception of secularism or a secularist conception of the good. Rather, they aim to remove the religious question from the purview of the state and place it in the realm of human freedom and civil society, asking that the state neither establish its own hegemonic religion nor trespass on the consciences and religious practices of its citizens. In a word and although often implemented imperfectly, these documents strive for passivity with respect to governmental authorities and institutions on the one hand and religion on the other. Such a conception of "passive secularism," in the words of the political scientist Ahmet Kuru, "demands that the state play a 'passive' role by allowing the public visibility of religion. . . . [It] prioritizes state neutrality toward such [religious] doctrines."[21] Put differently, passive secularism permits religious individuals and institutions a wide berth in articulating and living out the convictions of their faith traditions within a democratic polity that neither endorses them nor seeks to advance its own religion.

While passive secularism has played a large role in modern discussions about religion and politics, and although it is the conception of secularism most closely associated with classical liberal political principles, it does not exhaustively speak for modern secularism. Nor has it been universally influential or universally implemented. From the perspective of this book, then, the other two views, combative and eliminationist secularism, rank higher in significance. One might even call the former secular, the latter two secular*ist*—the "ist" capturing their ideologically anticlerical and/or anti-religious dimensions.

COMBATIVE SECULARISM

Combative secularism, then, represents another answer to the religion-politics, church-state question as it developed after the French Revolution. Anticlerical and progressive in orientation, it gained expression in postrevolutionary Europe and found an especially hospitable home in France's Third Republic (1871–1940), during which leading intellectuals and republican politicians advanced a stridently secularizing agenda against the Catholic Church, which had grown increasingly ultramontane in the course of the nineteenth century. But in fact combative secularism erupted episodically throughout Catholic Europe in the nineteenth century, and across the Atlantic in Latin America as well, usually developing, as in France, in dialectical counterpoint to forces of religious traditionalism and political reaction.[22] Its export to and adoption in post-Ottoman Turkey in the early twentieth century—with the French term "laïcité" (secularism) rendered in Turkish as *laiklik*—represents an arresting example of the transfusion of this militant version of Western modernity eastward and the sudden, draconian top-down secularization of a Muslim society.[23]

While combative secularism first dramatically burst on the scene in the radical, anticlerical phases of the French Revolution after 1792, it in fact possesses deeper roots in the intellectual and political sediment of the eighteenth century, among anticlerical *philosophes* and in the policies of the "enlightened despots" of that era, eager to aggrandize state power over ecclesiastical authority and inherited tradition.

To be sure, many intellectual currents during "the century of light" fostered needed church reforms and tolerance, and eighteenth-century religious voices in no way uniformly stood against the Enlightenment.[24] Nonetheless, vitriol against traditional religiosity, against the Catholic Church in particular, stands out as a marked legacy of the time. Voltaire's well-known line "écrasez l'infâme" ("crush the infamous thing," that is, the church) is thus one well-known example of what Alexis de Tocqueville called the eighteenth century's "studious ferocity" against organized religion.[25]

Whether through satire, humor, or ridicule, Voltaire left little room to doubt his attitude toward Christianity. "Every sensible man, every honorable man, must hold the Christian sect in horror," he once opined; "it is a tree that has only borne rotten fruit."[26] His views on Judaism and Islam were equally disparaging, Moses and Mohammed being, in his judgment, blatantly pious frauds.[27] To Diderot, Voltaire confided that organized religion "must be destroyed among respectable people."[28] In France, he advocated for the full submission of ecclesiastical to civil laws, the abolition of clerical celibacy, the secularization of priests' salaries, and the shuttering of monasteries—most of which came about during the Revolution. Not incidentally was Voltaire's body reverentially exhumed by the revolutionaries and given an elaborate state burial in Paris's imposing Pantheon—originally intended as a church dedicated to Saint Genevieve, the city's patron saint, but turned into a secular mausoleum during the Revolution. Voltaire's "écrasez l'infâme," as the historian Peter Gay once summed up, meant straightforwardly "that one must destroy Christianity before one could build a rational society."[29]

One hears echoes of Voltaire's sentiments among other radically inclined *philosophes* such as Julien La Mettrie, Claude Helvétius, Paul d'Holbach, Jean Le Rond d'Alembert, Marquis de Condorcet, and Denis Diderot. La Mettrie's *Man a Machine* (1742) and Holbach's *System of Nature* (1770) offered thoroughly materialist accounts of reality that sought to expose religious traditions as the work of charlatans and dupes. Diderot, who excoriated convent life in his novel *The Nun*, infamously opined that "mankind would never be free until the last king is strangled with the entrails of the last priest." "Superstition" and "fanaticism" recur as the preferred charges against the church, while religious orders—especially contemplative ones—embodied the epitome of religious idiocy and social impracticality. Most *philosophes* were not outright atheists; they acknowledged a general "supreme being" and desired some sort of secular civic religion to supersede traditional faith. Condorcet's influential stadial conception of history, which saw a teleological progression from ancient barbarism through medieval obscurantism toward modern enlightenment, summarizes influential tracts of *le siècle des Lumières.* Furthermore, *philosophes* looked to the state, not the church or other social bodies, as the means of enlightenment; "the Church, formerly the chief authority in society . . . [was] replaced by the State," according to the historian Charles A. Gliozzo, as the guide for "morality and virtue."[30]

Not surprisingly, many eighteenth-century rulers warmed to ideas supporting the expansion of state power. The centralized role of the state, as Tocqueville incisively recognized, stands out as an often overlooked element of continuity between the late ancien régime and the Revolution. Prussia's Frederick the Great (patron of Voltaire) and Russia's Catherine the Great (patron of Diderot) are two well-known examples who combined patronage of Enlightenment ideas of rationalism and progress with extensive efforts to centralize power by restricting and co-opting ecclesiastical privileges.[31]

But perhaps the clearest example of what we might call proto-combative secularism in the eighteenth century came in an international event: the suppression of the Society of Jesus, or the Jesuits. In Portugal, the Marquis de Pombal—the "Voltaire of Portugal," as he has been called—set the process in motion by accusing the Jesuits of fomenting lawlessness and rebellion in their South American missions and then by expelling them from

Portugal and its colonies in 1759, after duly confiscating their wealth for the royal treasury.

Widespread anti-Jesuit sentiment, even among reform-minded Catholics, along with admiration of Portugal's bold precedent produced similar scenarios in France, Spain, and smaller Italian states in the following years. The *philosophe* d'Alembert nudged the process along in his *Sur la destruction des Jésuites en France* (1765).[32] Jesuits encouraged insubordination to the state's authority and had too much influence in education, so Pombal, d'Alembert, and like-minded critics argued; and the church had better rein them in. Complaints about Jesuit power and manipulation from other statesmen and enlightened opinion added pressure on Rome. Feeling as if he had little choice but to sever a limb to save the body, Pope Clement XIV (r. 1769–74) reluctantly suppressed the Jesuits in Western Europe in 1773, a momentous event in itself and a harbinger of a much more extensive assault on religious orders during the French Revolution and the Napoleonic era.[33]

Another portent of combative secularism appeared in the church policies of Austria's Emperor Joseph II (r. 1780–90), or what came to be called "Josephism." Building on reforms of his Hapsburg mother, Maria Theresa, Joseph set about remaking the church according to his own image with a mandate that it should "contribute to a tangible secular purpose."[34] He closed the houses of many contemplative orders, deeming them not useful to society; revamped the diocesan system; abolished most confraternities (lay religious organizations); imposed a state-run system of education for clergy; and enacted measures to curb the church's wealth. In many respects, his reforms in Christian Europe presaged the top-down reforms of Islam by Kemal Mustafa in Turkey in the 1920s, as we shall see. With the papacy greatly weakened after the suppression of the Jesuits, Pope Pius VI (r. 1775–99) voiced concerns about Joseph's actions, paying a rare visit outside Italy to chide him in person. Joseph patiently listened to the pope's concerns before continuing to do exactly as he pleased, with the pope, revealingly, choosing not to reprimand him. "The French revolutionaries [later] took comfort from the pope's acquiescence in Joseph's reforms," as the historian Derek Beales perceptively points out.[35]

Of course, the French Revolution looms largest in shaping the ideology, substance, and trajectory of combative secularism. Unlike the more passive secularism of the American and Belgian Revolutions, which sought freedom *of* religion, the French Revolution, especially during its radical stages, sought something more akin to freedom *from* religion—or at least from the entrenched dominance of the Catholic Church.[36] Yet already before the extensive de-Christianizing measures of 1793-94, the church had received many blows, even as Protestants and Jews had gained rights. The abolition of tithes and fees in August of 1789 paved the way for the nationalization and selling-off of church properties in November of the same year. In February 1790, the National Assembly abolished monastic vows and began to close contemplative religious houses, with their wealth and property, redefined as "national goods" (*biens nationaux*), winding up in state or private coffers.[37] On 12 July 1790 the assembly passed the epochal Civil Constitution of the Clergy, forcing priests to take an oath of loyalty to the state and thus effectively dividing the clergy in France between those willing to take the oath (jurors) and those who felt that it violated their conscience (non-jurors). Furious about the oath, Pope Pius VI, whose effigy was burned by revolutionaries, lashed out at events in Paris in several encyclicals in 1791, blaming the Revolution for declaring "war against the Catholic religion."[38]

But then things truly went south for the church as the Revolution lurched in a more generally anti-Christian direction, especially during the Reign of Terror (1793-94). The National Convention, which replaced the National Assembly in August 1792, outlawed the Christian-Gregorian calendar, substituting a calendar of the convention's own making—one that abolished Sundays, saints' days, and even Christmas. Streets and places bearing royal or ecclesiastical references were renamed. Anticlerical events and parades mocked the church hierarchy in bitterly polemical, sometimes scatological terms. Non-juring priests were forced into exile, persecuted, or slain— including three bishops and 183 clergy in the September Massacres of 1792 and about three thousand in total in the course of the Revolution.[39] Examples exist of dispossessed female religious, charged with "fanaticism," guillotined for privately adoring the Eucharist.[40] The historic papal lands in Avignon and Comtat Venaissin, summarily annexed to France, were legally incorporated into the state. Churches and monasteries were looted and pillaged, as others, notably the Cathedral of Notre Dame in the heart of Paris, briefly became "temples of reason," holding services glorifying reason, the "supreme being," and republican virtues in the spirit of Jean-Jacques Rousseau, who had emphasized the need to establish some sort of popular civic religion. Not least, the government violently suppressed a popular uprising against the Revolution in the Vendée region of western France led by non-juring priests—a truly devastating, bloody event that some histo-rians plausibly regard as Europe's first genocide.[41] By late 1794, only 150 of France's some forty thousand pre-Revolution parishes openly celebrated Mass. Most prerevolutionary bishops had fled; ten were dead, six on the scaffold. Radicals and church loyalists alike interpreted the Revolution as a zero-sum game between revolutionary ideology and the church. At the height of Jacobinism, the Revolution, in the words of Tocqueville, "seemed even to aim at dethroning God himself . . . and nothing did more to shock contemporaries."[42]

The regime of the French Directory (1795–99), which followed the Ter-ror, and that of Napoleon (1799–1815) moderated the anti-religious course of the Revolution, Napoleon through his 1801 Concordat with Rome, which regulated church-state relations in France throughout the nineteenth cen-tury. Even so, Napoleon's legacy, too, contributed to the shaping of combat-ive secularism by expanding the state apparatus and the statist philosophy that nourished it. The Concordat—along with the Organic Articles uni-laterally appended to it by Napoleon in 1802 (acquiesced to if never offi-cially embraced by the church)—recognized the primacy of Catholicism in France, but it effectively made the church a dependency of the state; bishops were nominated by the government; papal encyclicals were not to be pub-lished without state approval; and a Ministry of Public Worship pinioned the church more generally to French officialdom. In all these measures, Napoleon offers a classic example of what the political scientist Timothy Samuel Shah and his coauthors helpfully call *conflictual integration,* whereby a modern regime evinces antipathy toward and distrust of society's religious sphere while simultaneously seeking to incorporate it into that state and thus render it more pliable, often employing the rhetoric of the necessity of paternal protection.[43]

Furthermore, wherever Napoleon's armies went across Europe, mon-asteries and churches were looted, plundered, and closed down; priceless works of ecclesiastical art, "relics of superstition," were shipped to Paris, forming the basis of the Louvre and other French museums.[44] Napoleon ridiculed monks as "worms" and "madmen."[45] In 1806, he presided over the demise of the Holy Roman Empire and, earlier, through the so-called Imperial Decree or *Reischsdeputationshauptschluß* (1803) in central Europe, dissolved centuries-old monasteries, bishoprics, and other ecclesiastical principalities—their properties and wealth absorbed by newly minted central European states in thrall to and attempting to imitate Napoleonic France.[46] After French forces invaded the Papal States in 1809, Napoleon had Pope Pius VII kidnapped, imprisoning him at first in Savona, near Genoa, and then in 1812 unceremoniously hauling the Vicar of Christ to France, where Napoleon remonstrated with him personally until his release in 1814. Few actions outraged pious sentiment more, hardening it against revolutionary ideals and stoking an ultramontane backlash—a harbinger of other forms of religious backlash in the late nineteenth and twentieth centuries. And in all of this, no mention has been made of Napoleon's Russian campaign and its vast despoliation of Orthodox Christianity. In Moscow and its surroundings alone, twenty-two of twenty-four monasteries were sacked and desecrated; 252 of 323 churches.[47]

Napoleon's defeat and the Congress of Vienna (1814–15) brought a measure of stability to Europe, but "the ideas of 1789" were around to stay. They provided fuel for the revolutionary imagination as it combated reactionary, and increasingly ultramontane, forces throughout the nineteenth century. Revolutionary anticlericalism spiked in the French July Revolution of 1830, in the European-wide revolutions of 1848, and—mixing with still more radical elements—in the Paris Commune of 1871, during which the archbishop of Paris, Georges Darboy, and several other clergymen, held as hostages by the Communards, were gratuitously murdered as symbols of reaction and thrown into a common grave.[48] Communards also vandalized churches and tried to revive the revolutionary calendar. In more moderate form, anticlericalism found a congenial home in France's Third Republic and formed the basis of the official government policy throughout the era. The church did not simply acquiesce in this arrangement. Conflict between the Catholic and anticlerical forces became so severe during the Third Republic that historians frequently speak of "the war of two Frances": France as "the eldest daughter of the church" versus France as the birthplace of "la révolution."[49]

Nineteenth-century combative secularism, it should be clear, drew from the heritage of Enlightenment and revolutionary-era anticlericalism, and from the specific memory of Voltaire, Diderot, Condorcet, and other intellectual heroes—many of whom were honored with public statues and other laudatory remembrances during the Third Republic.[50] But it also drew inspiration from nineteenth-century thinkers, among whom none looms larger than Auguste Comte (1798–1857).[51] A rapt admirer of Condorcet, Comte created an intellectual system, "positivism," that exerted tremendous influence throughout the late nineteenth century; some have even called it the official ideology of the Third Republic.[52] In Comte's view, the French Revolution represented a necessary cataclysmic purgation of the old order. The task of the future, Comte argued, was to supply a new social order, one based not on faith and religious authority but on science, progress, and order. He took on this task himself in his monumental *Cours de philosophie positive* (*Course on Positivist Philosophy*), in which he developed a stadial theory of historical development made up of three parts. First, humankind existed in a "theological" phase, the state of the world prior to the early modern era. Second, the Scientific Revolution and the Enlightenment ushered in the "philosophical" or metaphysical stage of human history, an awakening from the religious stupor of the past and the birth of critical reason. The final "scientific" or "positivist" phase of human history, coming into its own in the nineteenth century and indeed in Comte's own writings, promised to deliver humanity entirely from its benighted past. "Essentially," as the historian Michael Burleigh has summarized, "Comte sought a new unifying social doctrine to replace theology and the church."[53]

Comte did not labor alone in providing intellectual guidance for the Third Republic. Jules Michelet (1798–1874) arguably served as the Republic's founding historian. His *Histoire de la Révolution française,* aptly described as the "Bible of the Third Republic," painted a picture of two clashing world-historical forces in nineteenth-century Europe: Christianity and the Revolution. The latter ought to triumph over the former, which Michelet regarded as morally compromised beyond redemption.[54] Ernest Renan (1823–92), a committed Comtean and skeptic, also provided ideological direction for the Third Republic. His sensational *Vie de Jésus* (1863) portrayed Jesus not as divine but as an exemplary ethical person who had upended obscurantist Judaism to lead humanity to a higher moral plane, though his legacy had been hijacked by the church. Another diehard Comtean, Émile Zola (1840–1902), waged a bitter war against clerical forces in his literary works, which are replete with debauched priests, conniving monks, and greedy bishops. Going beyond typical republican anticlericalism, "Zola marks the apex of a campaign against Christianity," according to the literary critic Joseph N. Moody. "He gathered up most of the anti-religious themes that had circulated for two centuries and expressed them with a cogency and passion unmatched by any major writer."[55]

With other kindred spirits, these intellectuals shaped a political milieu in France conducive to the realization of combative secularism and the scuttling of the compromising Napoleonic Concordat. Beginning in 1879, when republican and other leftist forces first fully dominated the republic's Senate and Chamber of Deputies, a wide-ranging anticlerical program was carried out. "Sunday rest" restrictions were abolished, divorce legalized, and the confessional character of cemeteries ended. Sympathetic municipalities removed religious iconography from public places, banned religious processions, and renamed streets previously named after saints.[56]

Education emerged as the arena of the bitterest church-state struggles, with anticlerical legislation and degrees emerging victorious in the early 1880s, guided by the positivist and anticlerical minister of education and later prime minister Jules Ferry and championed by secularist organizations such as the Ligue de l'enseignement (Educational League, f. 1866).[57] In 1880, laws forbade Catholic institutions of higher education from using the word "university" and closed all publicly funded theological faculties. Concurrently, the government ended episcopal influence in the administration of public education at lower levels and dissolved many religious orders, including the Jesuits—their second suppression in France. Police and gendarme forces forcibly entered many religious houses, overcoming barricades and evicting priests. In Tarascon, a regiment of infantry and five squadrons of dragoons undertook a four-day siege to evict thirty-seven noncompliant monks. In total, in 1880, 261 teaching religious houses and 5,643 members were suppressed.[58] Additional legislation in 1882 made secular primary education free and compulsory and exchanged religious instruction for a "universal" civic moral code. In 1886, all remaining teachers belonging to religious orders were replaced: "In public schools of every kind instruction is to be given only by lay personnel," the law reads.[59]

Pope Leo XIII (r. 1878–1903) tried to moderate tensions in the 1890s, but to no avail. Further anticlerical legislation came in the early 1900s, during and following the infamous Dreyfus Affair, which compromised many Catholics through anti-Semitism and ham-fisted royalist reaction. The upshot of the affair shifted French politics in a more dramatically secularist direction.[60] In July 1901, under Prime Minister Pierre Waldeck-Rousseau, the so-called Law of Associations stepped up measures against religious orders, mandating that *all* orders had to receive governmental authorization, closing many which refused, denying the applications of others, and categorically forbidding all of them to teach. This law resulted in the shuttering of more religious houses, including southern France's storied eleventh-century Grande Chartreuse monastery, where governmental gendarmes forcibly removed the brothers from their choir stalls, driving many into exile.[61] In 1904 the Chamber of Deputies severed ties with the Vatican and removed Paris's papal nuncio, Benedetto Lorenzelli. By this time, thousands of religious schools had been closed and thousands of religious driven into exile.

The coup de grâce came in the Law on Separation of 9 December 1905. Formulated by the Chamber of Deputies member Aristide Briand, and passed under the direction of Prime Minister Émile Combes, a former seminarian turned pugnacious anticlerical, this statute finished off the Napoleonic religious settlement and represents a high-water mark of French anticlericalism and laïcité. Boards of lay trustees known as "worship associations" (*associations cultuelles*) under governmental watch were set up to oversee and administer ecclesiastical properties. The law required all religious symbols removed from public places, the discontinuance of all clerical salaries, and a ban on priests serving on municipal councils. Prison, it made clear, awaited any priest who so much as insulted a public official.[62] "Every religious person is sick," as the prominent leftist legislator and French Socialist Party leader Jean Jaurès summed up the law's rationale: "We are fighting the church and Christianity because they are the negation of human rights and contain the source of intellectual bondage."[63]

Although some have seen these measures as the triumph of liberalism and tolerance, several things countermand this interpretation. First, the 1905 law specifically targeted the Catholic Church through the worship associations, effectively creating a publicly recognized counter-authority to the Catholic hierarchy in administering its own parishes. Second, the law unilaterally abolished the Concordat, a recognized international treaty, without consulting Rome. Third, churches and other religious buildings functioning before 1905 were, at the stroke of a pen, permanently seized and turned into public property; thereafter the faithful needed state authorization to use what customarily they had understood to be their own buildings.[64] Finally, anticlerical legislation massively favored the word "worship," or *culte* (used sixty-one times), over "religion" (never used), suggesting that the law sought to limit religious freedom strictly to private worship and to discourage its general public exercise.[65]

Finally, implementing all the laws often required extreme measures, including coercion and violence. In Paris and throughout the provinces, five thousand instances of recourse to armed force were recorded as the government's gendarmes breached church doors to inventory valuables, as article 3 of the law required. In one arresting case, the priest and parishioners in a small village in the Pyrenees, Cominac, placed circus bears at the church's entrance to impede the gendarmes' efforts (figure 1)![66] For the same purposes of resistance, other churches utilized wooden barricades, brick walls, tree trunks, and even active beehives. Lay demonstrators, chanting and singing hymns, regularly showed up at churches to demonstrate against the gendarmes. Altogether, in the "turmoil of the inventories" (*la tourmente des inventaires*), as it has been called, 295 demonstrators were imprisoned, fifty-five noncompliant officials or military personnel disciplined, and 108 local magistrates either resigned or had their offices suspended or revoked.

Figure 1. Postcard from around 1906 showing a scene from Cominac, France, of a priest and villagers with two circus bears trying to prevent the inventorying of their church by government gendarmes. Photographed by Patrice Cartier. Image © Tallandier / Bridgeman Images.

Not least, two men—André Régis of Montregard and Géry Ghysel of Boeschepe—were slain in altercations defending their churches, becoming martyrs in the eyes of the pious.[67]

For all these reasons, according to the distinguished historian of French secularism Jean Baubérot, the immediate effect of the 1905 law was emphatically *not* widespread agreement about religious freedom and tolerance but a bitter, nationwide social "fracture" reminiscent of the one that had followed the Civil Constitution of the Clergy of 1790.[68] French secularism from this era, echoes the scholar Olivier Roy, "is historically a matter of dispute between the republican state and the Catholic Church. It is [thus best described] as combative *laïcité* marked by verbal violence and anathema."[69]

Images from the era shed light on combative secularism. The anticlerical magazine *La Calotte* captured the ethos behind the laic laws when, on a cover from 1908, it showed an obese priest squatting and defecating on all of Europe. Another magazine, *La Lanterne,* depicted a clergyman appearing as a menacing vampire hovering over Paris's Basilica of the Sacred Heart—a church constructed as an act of national penance after the Commune and thus deplored by secularists (figure 2). A photograph from 1906 shows gendarmes in the village of Yssingeaux in southern France using battering rams to break down locked church doors to inventory the valuables inside, while a cartoon from the time shows a state official holding a club with smashed valuables at his feet and shocked clergy members looking on; the caption reads "La liberté, c'est moi." ("Liberty, that is me").[70] Finally, a postcard entitled "la separation," printed in 1905, allegorized the Law on Separation with two figures: one, a woman symbolizing France, dressed in a white toga and proudly holding the French flag; the other, a downcast Catholic seminarian dressed in a black cassock, being escorted off cloistered premises with the figure of France guardedly looking on.[71]

To be sure, the laïcité tradition in France, along with kindred intellectual and political currents in other countries, has been given more moderate interpretations, gaining distance from its stridently Voltairean, revolutionary, and Comtean roots, moving more toward a "Lockean" sensibility of passive secularism.[72] But in at least three cases in the twentieth century—Mexico, Spain, and Turkey, all profiled in chapter 2—its violent potential, sometimes mixing with more radical, nationalist, and authoritarian political elements, found historical circumstances conducive for its realization.

Figure 2. Image of a clergyman made to look like a vampire above Paris's Sacré-Coeur on the cover of the anticlerical journal *La Lanterne* (1902). Artwork by Eugène Ogé. Courtesy of Wikimedia Commons.

ELIMINATIONIST SECULARISM

Eliminationist secularism, the third way or category in this book's typology of secularisms, captures a range of solutions by Europe's Far Left to the postrevolutionary dilemma concerning politics and religion; it gained strength during the second half of the nineteenth century. It too possessed a stadial understanding of historical development. But if combative secularists focused their antipathy and criticism largely on ecclesiastical authorities and institutions, eliminationist secularists offered a more sweeping solution: the eviction of religiosity as such from human consciousness and society and an orientation toward wholly immanent schemes of human improvement. The religious impulse itself, not just clericalism and church privilege, signaled a disease that the appropriate form of social analysis and political action could cure.

With its headwaters in the Enlightenment and the French Revolution as well, this secularist vision more particularly originated in early nineteenth-century socialist thought, in the ideas of anarchists and freethinkers such as Pierre-Joseph Proudhon and Mikhail Bakunin, and in Hegelian philosophy, particularly as advanced by so-called Young or Left Hegelians, including Ludwig Feuerbach, who greatly influenced Karl Marx and Friedrich Engels. In the nineteenth century, the sheer novelty of eliminationist secularism worked against its translation into law or policy. But many late nineteenth-century radicals embraced it, and ultimately Vladimir Lenin and the Bolshevik Party in Russia made a version of it integral to their ideology in the early 1900s. With the rise of the Soviet Union after 1917, it improbably passed from theory into practice, becoming intertwined with the Marxist-Leninist conception of the good society and, as such, among the most destructive anti-religious forces in human history.

Pioneer socialist thinkers such as Henri de Saint-Simon, Charles Fourier, and Robert Owen—disparaged as "utopian socialists" by Marx and Engels, who nonetheless owed a considerable intellectual debt to them—paved the way. Like Comte, they both admired and found wanting the French Revolution. They admired it because, in their view, it had cleared away much that was oppressive and irrational in the old regime and opened the future to more just and equitable development. But they also viewed the Revolution as a hulking half-measure that had left humanity bereft of a higher harmony that the church had previously supplied. They, therefore, sought to supply this harmony—what Saint-Simon called a "universal harmony" based on science and reason. Furthermore, utopian socialists tended to think that the Revolution's three ideals—liberty, equality, and fraternity—were essentially incompatible. In their view, liberty—the ideal most emphasized by Europe's nascent bourgeois classes—demonstrably led to anarchy and exploitation: a society atomized by individuals' pursuit of wealth, status, and pleasure. They thus stressed equality and fraternity, which entailed the abolition of private property, schemes for more equitable and rational labor practices, and communal forms of living.[73] In the past, at least in theory, church teachings had conferred dignity on all, and the church itself had fostered community. But after the Revolution, the church stood compromised by its untoward attachment to the old regime and its wanting attitude toward modern science. The goal of the modern intellectual and social activist was thus to theorize anew a sense of social harmony and legitimize it through post-Christian commitments to science, progress, and secular communalism. While frequently having recourse to religious terms and phrases, early socialists nonetheless theorized an incipiently secularist vision of human solidarity.[74] "For most of these secular thinkers," as the critic D. G. Charlton has summed up, "the very starting-point of their religious quest was the conviction that there is no personal God and that an acceptable creed must be rational and scientifically based."[75]

Whether labeled anarchists or freethinkers, figures such as Proudhon and the Russian émigré Bakunin, despite their differences, pursued similar lines of inquiry, emphasizing the dereliction of postrevolutionary society and adding hatred of the very idea of God—interpreted in their view as a time-honored excuse for social injustice.[76] Welcoming the political furies that buffeted the church during the Revolution, Proudhon once noted, "The supreme work of the Revolution in the nineteenth century is to eradicate it [Catholicism]," before prophesying that "not a half century [will be] . . . passed before the priest is prosecuted as a thief for exercising his ministry."[77] While drawn to the Gospels' ethical ideals, and even expressing indebtedness to them in his own immanent vision of justice, Proudhon sought to consign Christianity and the concept of God to the dustbin of history. "The first duty of a free and intelligent mind," he proclaimed, "is to chase the idea of God out of his mind incessantly."[78]

Bakunin—who once rivaled Marx for the leadership of international Communism—advocated for militant atheism as well. "The heaven of religion," he wrote in *God and the State*, "is nothing but a mirage in which man, uplifted by ignorance, rediscovers his own image, but magnified and transposed."[79] The society of the future, Bakunin repeatedly thundered, must spare no effort in demolishing every form of religious belief and church authority—come what may. His atheism was absorbed into the Russian intelligentsia's anarchist and nihilist circles in the second half of the nineteenth century, particularly as seen in the thought of Nikolay Chernyshevsky, Nikolay Dobrolyubov, and Dmitry Pisarev, all of whom in turn left their mark on the development of Russian radical thought.[80] "And if the future lay in the fragmentation and the explosion of your present universe into a new form of existence," as Isaiah Berlin once described the demolitionist attitude of many nineteenth-century Russian intellectuals, "it would be foolish not to collaborate with this violent and inevitable process."[81]

Both Bakunin and Marx, as well as like-minded peers, owed a significant debt to mid-nineteenth-century Hegelian ideas and especially to the thought of Ludwig Feuerbach.[82] When Hegel died in 1831, he had devoted followers throughout Europe. In their eyes, Hegel had managed to reconcile traditional Christian teachings with post-Kantian philosophy. Through his "dialectical method," furthermore, Hegel appeared to divine the very direction of human history: occasional setbacks notwithstanding, the inexorable march of the modern world toward greater realizations of reason, progress, and freedom superintended by the modern state. In his own time, the "thesis" of the French Revolution (and its anticlericalism) had been countered by the "antithesis" of political reaction (and its clericalism), which led in turn to the "synthesis" of the present, circa 1830, which was being worked out admirably enough by the Prussian government, Hegel's employer in Berlin, and the Prussian state church. At least Hegel's more conservative followers advanced such an interpretation of his thought.[83]

But another, more radical branch of Hegelian thought surfaced in the 1830s, the intellectual fruit of which captivated Marx and left its mark on his influential conception of religion as "the opium of the masses."[84] In his *Life of Jesus* (1835), the biblical critic and Hegelian devotee David Friedrich Strauss argued that the upshot of Hegelian thought, when married to modern historical criticism of the Bible, did not support but in fact vitiated traditional Christianity; conservative defenses of the faith stood out as hopelessly anachronistic, Hegelian influenced, simply disingenuous—subtle and sophisticated perhaps, but false. Strauss shared much in common with another radical Hegelian, Bruno Bauer, who intensified the anti-Christian implications of Hegelian thought in an 1841 book that cleverly exhibited how atheistic Hegel's teaching must appear to naive but pious Christians.[85]

The literary review the *Hallische Jahrbücher für deutsche Wissenschaft und Kunst* (The Halle Yearbook of German Science and Art) and its successor, *Deutsch Jahrbücher* (German Yearbook), were the chief organs that disseminated Left Hegelian thought. The increased political radicalism of the latter in the 1840s made it suspect in the eyes of the Prussian censors, forcing it to move its literary offices from Prussia to Saxony and eventually to Paris, where, under the new title *Deutsch-französische Jahrbücher* (German-French Yearbook), it expired after just one issue under the joint editorship of Arnold Ruge and Karl Marx.[86]

For understanding Marx and subsequent Marxist approaches to religion, however, all roads lead to Ludwig Feuerbach. A native of Bavaria who studied under Hegel in Berlin in the 1820s, Feuerbach soon began criticizing his teacher, finding common cause with Young Hegelians such as Strauss and Bauer. Claiming later to have "inverted" the Hegelian method, Feuerbach argued that Hegel's focus on grand ideals such as freedom, mind, and reason, traveling purposefully through history, said less about these ideals and more about the human subject investigating them. The same held true for religion and the concept of God, according to Feuerbach's best-known work, *The Essence of Christianity* (1841). "The divine being," he wrote, "is nothing else than the human being, or, rather, the human nature purified, freed from the limits of the individual man, made objective—i.e., contemplated and revered as another, a distinct being." When theologians or philosophers spoke of God—or the "Absolute Spirit," to borrow from the lexicon of German idealism—they in fact were "projecting outward," (*entäussert*) and really speaking about humankind: "The Absolute Spirit is nothing other than the finite spirit, abstracted, self-estranged (*von sich selbst gesonderte*); just as the infinite Being of Theology [God] is nothing other than an abstract and finite being."[87] Put most directly, if one wrenched open the door of Hegelian mystifications, theology all along was really about anthropology; assuming otherwise alienated humankind from its true essence. Traditional religiosity had perverted truth, blinded the masses, projected human attributes onto a nonexistent abstract being, and prevented human beings from grasping their own high, nontheistic destiny. Both Christianity and Hegelianism thus merited crumpling and tossing into the trash bin in preparation for a more exclusively human-centered, fundamentally atheist social analysis, but one that in large part kept intact an Enlightenment/Hegelian stadial approach to history.

Or at least something like this was what Marx and Engels derived from Feuerbach's thought. "We are all Feuerbachians now," as Engels later expressed the influence of Feuerbach on Marx and himself.[88] "There is no other road . . . to truth and freedom," wrote the young Marx, "except through the fiery brook," a play on Feuerbach's name, which literally means fiery stream or brook.[89] Or, as the scholar Traugott Koch has written: "From Feuerbach's criticism of religion, Marx formed a more general critical theory of society," connecting it with insights from utopian socialists and from his deep reading in classical economic theory and modern history since the French Revolution.[90] In Marx's judgment, the French Revolution amounted to a "bourgeois" revolution, a half-measure that had nonetheless laid the groundwork for the more epochal socialist revolution of the future, if industrial workers, "the proletariat," could transcend their national (and religious) differences and realize their common interests as a "class."

While Marx's analysis of religion borrows much from Feuerbach's, it possesses additional dimensions and draws its pugnacious energy from Marx's own atheism, manifested in his youthful dissertation on materialism in the ancient world. Marx follows Feuerbach in regarding religion as the "externalization" onto the idea of God humankind's highest ideals, thus resulting in human "alienation." The source of this alienation, however, resides not in the human psyche or in the realm of ideas, as it did for Feuerbach, but in the socioeconomic environment, the frequent misery of which induces people to embrace socially fabricated heavenly consolations. Put differently, Marx saw religion less as a cause than as a symptom of social malaise—the "pus of a sick world," as one critic has pithily put it.[91] Both the Feuerbachian inheritance and Marx's initial efforts to modify it are summed up at the beginning of his dense *Contribution to the Critique of Hegel's Philosophy of Right* (1843), in a passage destined for vast global influence among twentieth-century Communist regimes. Permit a lengthy quote:

> For Germany the *criticism of religion* [by the Young Hegelians] is for the most part complete, and criticism of religion is the premise of all criticism. . . .
>
> The basis of irreligious criticism is: *man makes religion*, religion does not make man. In other words, religion is the self-consciousness and self-feeling of man who has either not yet found himself or has already lost himself again. But *man* is no abstract being squatting outside the world. Man is *the world of man*, the state, society. This state, this society produces religion, *a reversed*

world-consciousness, because they are a reversed world. . . . It is a fantastic realization of the human essence because the human essence has no true reality. The struggle against religion is therefore . . . the fight against *the other world* of which religion is the spiritual *aroma.*

Religious misery is at the same time the *expression* of real misery and the *protest* against real misery. Religion is the sigh of the oppressed creature, the heart of a heartless world, just as it is the spirit of a spiritless situation. It is the *opium* of the people.

The abolition of religion as the *illusory* happiness of the people is required for their *real* happiness. The demand to give up the illusions about its condition is the *demand to give up a condition which needs illusions.*[92]

To overcome alienation and achieve this-worldly happiness, as Marx understood it, religion must be eliminated by transforming the social conditions that made religion seemingly desirable in the first place.

Attempting to overcome these conditions by liberal political means alone did not pass muster with Marx. So-called bourgeois revolutions, along the American and French models, demonstrably failed to usher in a better, religionless world, according to Marx's *On the Jewish Question* (1843). In this difficult but revealing work, the young Marx contends that liberal notions of freedom of conscience come up short in light of the deeper need for full-scale socialist emancipation. Drawing from Tocqueville, he profiles the United States in particular, arguing that the persistence of revivalist religiosity across the Atlantic after the American Revolution ipso facto reveals the limitations of bourgeois liberation alone. "North America," he writes, "is pre-eminently the country of religiosity. . . . However, the states of North America only serve as an example. The question is: what is the relation between *complete* political emancipation and religion? If we find in the country which has attained full [bourgeois] political emancipation, that religion not only continues to *exist* but is *fresh* and *vigorous,* this is proof that the existence of religion is not at all opposed to the [bourgeois] perfection of the state. But since the existence of religion is the existence of a defect, the source of this defect must be sought in the *nature* of the state itself."[93] In essence, Marx equates the decline of religion with the success of genuine political emancipation, and he criticizes the United States—and by implication other bourgeois societies—for falling short. He furthermore draws the lesson that polemicizing against religion has its limits; one must focus on overthrowing the entire bourgeois order. If it falls, religion or "superstition" will necessarily ebb as liberal political structures collapse before the tide of class revolt and socialist revolution.

Marx worked out his theory of religion in subsequent publications. In *The Holy Family* (1845), he and Engels augment Feuerbachian conclusions about religion by discussing skeptical and materialist currents of thought in the eighteenth century, noting in particular Pierre Bayle, who showed that "it is not by atheism but by superstition [religion] and idolatry that man debases himself." In his *Theses on Feuerbach* (1845), Marx praises Feuerbach for dissolving the "religious world into its secular basis" even as he criticizes him for not going far enough with respect to social action and thus for remaining stuck in "contemplative materialism." Thought deserves translation into action: "The philosophers have only interpreted the world in various ways; the point, however, is to change it," as he famously put it—words with which East German Communist authorities during the Cold War saw fit to adorn the entrance of the famous Humboldt University of Berlin.[94]

In *The German Ideology,* written in the nineteenth century but first published in the Soviet Union only in 1932, Marx (with Engels) presents the clearest case for what came to be called "historical materialism" or "dialectical materialism"—the pillar of Soviet psychology and social science, mandatorily taught in classrooms throughout the Communist world in the twentieth century.[95] Ideas, ideals, beliefs, culture, religion—everything that makes up human consciousness and culture—appear in this work as the mere surface expression ("superstructure") of the underlying material circumstances of life ("base"). "It is not consciousness that determines life, but life that determines consciousness," as Marx succinctly put it, equating "life" with socioeconomic conditions made possible by one's "means of subsistence." Or more fully: "Morals, religion, metaphysics and other forms of ideology and the forms of consciousness corresponding to them, [because of historical materialism] no longer retain their apparent independence. They have no history, they have no development, but men, developing their material production and their material intercourse, with this, their reality, their thinking and the products of their thinking also change."[96] From such a standpoint, simply preaching atheism and denouncing clergy possessed limited value; if one truly desired the elimination of "the opium of the masses," one had to transform the material circumstances that gave birth to it in the first place. Overcome feudal and bourgeois privilege, dispense with socioeconomic misery, and, as a happy consequence, achieve the extinction of religion too. Importantly, Marx and Engels (and later countless Communist commissars) felt that this conception of history possessed *universal* value applicable to all human societies, the religious elements of which expressed a uniform phenomenon predictably inclined to align with reactionary forces with socially harmful effects.

By the time *The Communist Manifesto* (1848) appeared, Marx's views on religion—mostly corroborated by those of Engels—were essentially complete.[97] For the remainder of his life, Marx focused more on political and economic matters and advocacy for socialist revolution. But religion continued to occupy a crucial place in his thought. It stood out as a particularly salient and revealing manifestation of human alienation (*Entfremdung* or *Entäusserung*—terms borrowed from Feuerbach and increasingly important for Marx from the 1840s onward).[98] Confronted with socioeconomic misery, the downtrodden turned to illusory beliefs for consolation, forfeiting a true understanding of themselves and a chance to remake history through revolution. But if the realities enforcing these conditions could be changed and workers convinced as a "class" to become the charioteers of their own destiny, then religion, according to this theory, would necessarily peter out.

As Marx's ideas spread, and as socialist political agitation and organization took off in the mid- and late nineteenth century in the form of the First (1864–76) and Second International (1889–1916), Marxist analysis of religion figured in the ideological mix. But it was far from a forgone conclusion that the dominant, globally influential strain of revolutionary socialism in the twentieth century—Marxism-Leninism—would evince the pungently anti-religious character that turned out to be the case. In the middle decades of the nineteenth century, not a few churches had in fact gravitated toward socialist ideals and politics as an expression of the Gospels' ethics.[99] In his social encyclical *Rerum novarum* (1891), Pope Leo XIII smiled on some socialist ideas in an effort to address the "worker question," breathing life into Catholic efforts to speak to urban workers, even as the pope also blasted the godlessness and heavy-handed statism of Marxist socialism.[100] Britain's Labour Party (f. 1900), finally, heartily welcomed the presence of religious beliefs, especially from British nonconformist faith traditions, offering a clear alternative to atheist socialism.[101]

But on the Continent—in part from the perceived merit of secularist ideas, in part because of churches' alliance with reactionary forces after the debacle of the Paris Commune (1871)—anti-religious elements found more fertile ground in socialist circles.[102] In the late 1870s, Marxism became the official creed of Germany's Social Democratic Party (SPD), Europe's largest and most influential socialist party. In Berlin, the socialist Johann Most led a vocal exit of socialists from churches (*Kirchenausbetrittsbewegung*).[103] "Religion is the most powerful enemy of socialism," the German socialist Albert Dulk thundered in the socialist organ *Vorwärts* in 1878; "religion is the main bastion of antisocialism, of reaction, [and] the breeding ground of all social evil."[104] Although the SPD's official platforms in 1875 and 1891—respectively, the "Gotha" and "Erfurt" programs—regarded religion as a private matter (*Privatsache*), and although the SPD sometimes formed alliances with the Catholic Center Party, these should be seen more as tactical measures than as a compromise of party principle, since most key leaders—August Bebel (1840–1913), Eduard Bernstein (1850–1932), Karl Kautsky (1854–1938), and Rosa Luxemburg (1871–1919)—had adopted the Marxist line that religion was bound to die out, often throwing in "Darwin" and "modern science" as well to reinforce their conclusions.[105] Engels spoke for many when, advising the SPD against overheated statements against religion, he tartly observed that "the only service that can be rendered to God today is to declare atheism a compulsory article of faith."[106] In the same vein, the bedrock conviction of party leadership, as August Bebel once summarized in an exchange of letters with Wilhelm Hohoff, a priest sympathetic to socialism, was a conviction that saw "the relationship between Christianity and socialism as one between fire and water," the former standing out as "inimical to humanity."[107]

While avant-garde thinkers across Europe attentively followed and oriented themselves in relation to Germany's SPD, one cannot understand the shaping of Marxism-Leninism vis-à-vis religion as it played out in revolutionary Russia without considering Russia's own radical political and intellectual traditions—memorably and critically depicted in Turgenev's *Fathers and Sons* and Dostoyevsky's *The Possessed*—and customarily subdivided into populist, anarchist, nihilist, and socialist factions, with often porous borders between the various groups (along with much infighting) and many willing to embrace extremist and violent tactics.[108] To be sure, religious sentiments were not altogether missing from Russian radicalism. In fact, some voices felt that faith traditions, if in a drastically redefined form, had a place in a future society so long as they were purged of authoritarianism and bourgeois self-interest. Even in the early twentieth century one sees this line of reasoning surfacing in Anatoly Lunacharsky's *Religion and Socialism* (2 vols., 1908, 1911). Lunarcharsky and other "God-builders," as Lenin derisively called them, who included for a time the writers Maxim Gorky and Vladimir Bazarov, proposed the idea that instead of hastening its end, socialism should shape religion into some higher form, one somehow compatible with radical ideas and politics.[109]

But Lenin would have none of it, once insisting to Gorky that "even the most refined, most well-intentioned, defense or justification of the idea of god is a justification of reaction."[110] Lenin's polemical war against the "God-builders" culminated in what many regard as his only philosophical work, *Materialism and Empirio-criticism* (1909), in which he fiercely insists on undiluted historical materialism, scientific empiricism, and uncompromising secularism as the only way forward. This work and Lenin's general activity at the time suggest that, in addition to Marx and Engels, Lenin's predecessors in the Russian radical tradition were especially those who took their cues from the atheism of Bakunin, with whom Lenin has frequently been compared.[111] In their view, the Orthodox Church in Russia was an antiquated prop of a diseased social order, deserving perdition, the sooner the better. These intellectuals included Nikolay Chernyshevsky, who championed the eradication of all gods in a famous essay, "The Anthropological Principle in Philosophy," and Dmitry Pisarev, hailed as "the teacher of atheism" by later Bolsheviks. "What can be smashed [in Russia's traditional society] must be smashed," as Pisarev once delicately put it.[112]

And what of Lenin's own utterances on religion prior to 1917? They combine a Marxist criticism of religion with the strident anti-religiosity and demolitionist panache of Russian radicalism. But they also evince a concern to carve out a position at once different from the "God-builders," as mentioned above, and from what Lenin called "false bourgeois anticlericalism" (the laïcité tradition, broadly understood). He also rejected what he regarded as the excessive accommodation to religious freedom present in the SPD's "Erfurt Program." In "Socialism and Religion" (1905), for instance, Lenin made it clear that religion amounts to "oppression, which everywhere weighs heavily on the popular masses. . . . [I]t is a sort of spiritual booze, in which the slaves of capital drown the image of man and their demand for a life more or less worthy of human begins."[113] It followed that confiscating monastic and ecclesiastical property, as done in the French Revolution, should be heartily embraced by socialists too.[114] In an address, "The Attitude of the Workers' Party to Religion" (1909), Lenin recognized that even if the state, in the interest of governance, might at times make some strategic concessions to religious freedom, the party should remain fully committed to the elimination of religion.

Lenin recognized, however, that unlike Western Europe, which had experienced the Enlightenment and a bourgeois revolution, Russia presented more retrograde historical conditions. This made it necessary, Lenin felt, for the workers' party, and not necessarily liberal ones, to spearhead the effort in combating religious traditions. "In Russia, conditions are quite different," he wrote: "The proletariat is the leader of our bourgeois-democratic revolution. Its party [therefore] must be the ideological leader in the struggle against all forms of medievalism, including the old official religion and every attempt to refurbish it or make out a new, different case for it."[115] "Marxism is materialism," he added, and "is . . . relentlessly hostile to religion. . . . [Combating religion] must be linked up with the concrete practice of the class movement, which aims at eliminating the social roots of religion."[116]

Finally, in the aforementioned letter rebuking the "God-builder" Gorky, Lenin additionally insisted that the idea of God in any form "has always lulled to sleep and dulled 'social sentiments,' substituting dead for living things, always being an idea of slavery." Religion, he added, "tied down the oppressed classes with faith in the divine character of the oppressors," while later contending that all religious organizations should be "regarded by Marxism as organs . . . [of] reaction serving to define exploitation and to stupefy the working class." Any attempt to reform religion, however well intended, would only produce a "new, refined subtle poison for the oppressed masses"; religion was rather like an "infection," not to be coddled or refined but eliminated.[117]

A foil to passive secularism, more militant, theoretically sophisticated, and globally influential than combative secularism, the eliminationist secularism of Marxism-Leninism came into its own politically after the Bolshevik Revolution of 1917 and, amalgamating with other social variables, again farther east after the Chinese Revolution of 1949.

CHAPTER TWO

Secularist Onslaughts

Father Domingo was a very good man. But we had to kill all the priests.
—Aragonese anticlerical after the Spanish Civil War

FRANCE'S 1905 LAW ON THE SEPARATION OF CHURCH AND
State represents a decisive moment in French history, to be sure. But like
the earlier French Revolution, it also marks an international event, as
reformers and opinion shapers from other countries in Europe and the
New World had long looked to France for intellectual and moral leadership.
Put differently, the 1905 law represents a major flashpoint in the "culture
wars" that had raged between liberal and progressive secularists, on the one
hand, and advocates for church statism and traditionalism, on the other,
throughout the nineteenth century.[1] The former, especially those in majority Catholic countries, showed particular interest in the 1905 law, because it
had appeared that France's combative secularism had triumphed decisively
over its opponents and thereby set a precedent and a possible blueprint for
other lands.

This rings true of Mexico and its colonial mother, Spain, both of which
had chafed under clay-footed clericalist regimes and possessed a long history of clerical-anticlerical struggles during the previous century. In these
struggles, anticlericals regularly exhibited what Wolfram Kaiser has called
"a binary vision with a clear friend-foe scheme: on one side, the enlightened
defenders of economic and cultural progress and of the 'modern world'—
on the other, the exponents of an obsolete, retrograde oligarchic order, in
which a small clerical elite instrumentalized sheep-like believers."[2] Both
countries, moreover, experienced political turbulence and revolutionary
upheaval in the first half of the twentieth century, marked by extraordinary
levels of anti-ecclesial violence legitimized in part by secularist ideologies.
This chapter seeks to explain why and how.

But the analysis is extended to another country on Europe's doorstep: Turkey. In the twilight decades of the Ottoman Empire, reformist intellectuals—the so-called Young Turks—had become increasingly smitten with Western-style secularism and nationalism, French varieties in particular. Since no word existed for secularism in Turkish, they even had to adapt the French term "laïcité" in the late imperial period, rendering it in Turkish as "laiklik." Through various twists and turns, this strand of combative secularism became fundamental to the ideology of Kemalism, as the Ottoman Empire collapsed and gave way to the modern nation-state of Turkey in the years following World War I. The rapid modernization of Turkish identity at this time, presided over by Mustafa Kemal, came with extraordinarily harsh and authoritarian treatment of traditional Islamic culture and practices, and the repression of several ethnic and religious minorities, not least the Armenians, who did not fit the ascendant "Turkish" nation-state template. This all stood in sharp contrast to the bygone Ottoman *millet* system, which, though not without its own blemishes, had granted considerable toleration to religious minorities so long as they stayed in their own enclaves (*millets*) and paid the requisite tax (*jizya*).

To sum up, this chapter profiles three cases of national modernization and secularization in the early twentieth century: Mexico, Spain, and Turkey. In each case, species of combative ideological secularism inherited from the previous century and typified by Third Republic France made significant contributions to episodes of political violence directed against religious communities, their leadership, and their material culture. Despite the violence that took place, it would be going too far to characterize these episodes as eliminationist secularism in the fullest sense—a term more applicable, as we shall see, to the Soviet Union and Communist China. At the same time, combative secularism during the Mexican Revolution (1910–30) and the Spanish Civil War (1936–39) sometimes went beyond anticlericalism alone, tipping into a broader anti-religious animus. Still, it was principally the Western European variety of laïcité—*laicismo* or *laicidad* in Spanish, *laiklik* in Turkish—that occupied the driver's seat. Mixing freely with other ideological elements, adapting itself pragmatically to local conditions, and faced with an assertive reactionary opposition that enjoyed significant levels of popular support, combative secularism constituted a significant ingredient in the violent assault on traditional religious life in all three countries.

MEXICO

The Mexican Revolution began in 1910 as a social movement against the long-standing strongman rule of Porfirio Díaz (r. 1876–1911), who was forced to resign in May 1911 after a public outcry over electoral fraud. But its course turned increasingly chaotic and radical, eventuating in protracted infighting, intrigue, regional splinter movements, and the most brutal persecution of the Catholic Church ever seen in the Western Hemisphere. The worst of it took place under the fiercely anticlerical presidency of Plutarco Elías Calles (r. 1924–28) and shortly thereafter, claiming the lives of numerous priests and tens of thousands of Mexican citizens, to say nothing of extensive iconoclasm, censorship, police actions, ruined vocations, and the closure or destruction of churches, monasteries, and seminaries. Founder of the National Revolutionary Party, which dominated Mexican politics in one-party fashion throughout the twentieth century, Calles succeeded the short-lived presidencies of Venustiano Carranza (1917–20) and Álvaro Obregón (1920–24), both of whom had prepared the way for Calles, the former overseeing the constitutional convention that produced the Mexican Constitution of 1917.

Echoing the 1905 Law on the Separation of the Church and State in France, the 1917 Constitution also took its cue from the Mexican Constitution of 1857, requiring civil marriage, the disamortization of church property, and the barring of clergy from running for office. But it went even further, refusing to grant the church any corporate legal status and banning public displays of religiosity beyond church buildings. In addition, it denied clergy the right to vote and own property, refused to recognize foreign-born clergy, outlawed monastic orders, forbade priests and religious periodicals from commenting on political matters, criminalized the wearing of clerical garb in public, allowed individual states to regulate the number of clergy, and sought to ensure that "education shall be maintained entirely apart from any religious doctrine and, based on scientific progress; [education] shall strive against ignorance, . . . fanaticism, and prejudices."[3] The latter clause provided a fillip for the so-called defanaticization (*desfanatización*) campaigns in the 1920s and 1930s that sought to intimidate the clergy and encourage unbelief. Recognizing the difficulty that these laws posed for Mexico's pious population, however, President Carranza only selectively enforced them, as Porfirio Díaz had done in the past with anticlerical elements in the 1857 constitution. But this approach changed dramatically in the 1920s once Calles came to power.[4]

But to understand the spirit of the constitution and its harsh enforcement, one must step back and take stock of the assertive forms of laicismo that, paralleling and echoing developments in France, had taken shape intellectually in Latin America in the mid- and late nineteenth century.[5] This secularism, exercised by both liberal and more authoritarian regimes and advocated by many elites, built on numerous prior church-state conflicts in which newly independent national states sought to expropriate church wealth, exercise a say in selecting bishops, stanch the influence of religious orders (not least the Jesuits), and limit the power that the church wielded over rural, often very pious populations. Sometimes these conflicts remained verbal, in the domain of the press and legislatures, but sometimes they turned messy and violent. This happened frequently in Mexico between 1858 and 1860 over disputes about the 1857 Constitution until the liberal government's victory and the decision to ban male religious orders and nationalize much church property.[6]

Yet perhaps the best-known example of the church-state violence occurred in Colombia during the presidency of Tomás Cipriano de Mosquera (r. 1861–64), who sought to bring the clergy to heel by demanding their silence on political matters, sequestering church lands not used explicitly for worship, and mandating state licensure based on an oath to the new Constitution of 1863. Excommunicated by Pope Pius IX, Mosquera threatened bishops and priests with physical violence if they did not swear on the constitution. Some did, but many did not, the latter taking refuge in rural Antioquia—sometimes referred to as Colombia's "Vendée"—where they preached and administered sacraments clandestinely as a protracted Catholic insurgency resisted the central government. But the government only doubled down on anticlericalism and counterattack, fanning the flames of conflict into the 1870s and 1880s until, finally, Rome negotiated a concordat with a much-secularized Colombian state in 1887.[7]

As these events transpired in Colombia, progressive European ideologies such as anarchism, socialism, and Comtean positivism gained greater currency in Latin America, fusing with preexisting forms of anticlericalism growing out of the Enlightenment and French revolutionary traditions.[8] Influenced by freemasonry as well, leading intellectuals and officials argued that education should become strictly "scientific," that the religious stages of humanity belonged in the past, and that governments ought to hasten religion's obsolescence.[9] The Peruvian anarchist-positivist Manuel González Prada (1844–1918) embodied the new spirit of the age— one that the historian Jeffrey Klaiber has aptly characterized as "antireligious anticlericalism," for priests in Prada's view bore witness to a deeper malady: religion itself. A Francophile who had immersed himself in au courant literature during travels in Europe, Prada took liberals to task for their continued support of church-state unions (or holdovers thereof), for not seeing religion itself as the problem, and for hypocritically sending their children to parochial schools. Women, children, and Indigenous peoples in particular, he felt, were "slaves" to the Catholic Church and in need of liberation. "As far as religions go," he once averred, "they are like diseases: none is good."[10] If a slaughter bench of history was necessary to liberate humanity, so be it: "Everywhere revolutions are painful yet fruitful gestations of a people: they shed blood but create light, they eliminate men but elaborate ideas."[11]

That intellectual gains might require the elimination of people was something that Mexican revolutionaries understood quite well. After Díaz left the political stage and fled the country in 1911, Mexico sputtered under the short-lived presidency of Francisco Madero until he faced a coup d'état and subsequent assassination in February of 1913 on the orders of the military strongman Victoriano Huerta, whose brief grasp of power encountered immediate opposition from Venustiano Carranza and the "constitutional army" loyal to him—not to mention from a colorful, unruly faction in the south led by Emiliano Zapata and one in the north led by Pancho Villa. Confronted with threats of its extirpation, the church had moved sharply rightward in its outlook, seeming to some an "enemy of the people" after Madero's assassination. Several politicians in congress defamed priests as "vermin," "foul and treacherous vampires," and much worse. As revolution and civil war spread in 1913 and 1914, many clergymen and religious were jailed or sent into exile. Caudillos loyal to the revolutionary cause roughed up priests, seized church property, vandalized churches, and burned confessionals. The National Catholic Party (founded only in 1912, modeled on the German Center Party) practically ceased to function.[12] The church's opponents regarded it as a Trojan horse hell-bent on the clericalist domination of society. In a premonition of things to come, the regional leader in Yucatán, the "Jacobin" Salvador Alvarado, expelled priests, confiscated church valuables, and abolished confession and public rituals.[13] The government of Jalisco instigated comparable actions.

Given the shape of things, it is not surprising that Catholicism did not fare well in the constitution of 1917, drafted and ratified once Carranza's constitutional army had bested Huerta's federal army and brought a modicum of peace to the country. Since Mexican bishops voiced reservations about the constitution, repression of Catholics did not entirely abate. What is more, the constitution had put them in a much weaker place, legally and politically. Articles 27 and 130 in particular contained a raft of anticlerical provisions, as itemized earlier.[14] Were it not for the fact that Carranza tried to steer a moderate course and relax enforcing many aspects of the constitution, all-out conflict might have begun much earlier.

But this fragile truce between the government and the church fizzled once Carranza fell from office in 1920, succeeded by Obregón, who began to pivot away from Carranza's moderate course. Obregón, for instance, deported the papal nuncio Ernesto Filippi in 1923 for conducting an open-air religious service—illegal according to the constitution. Obregón once opined, "[Priests] will do nothing for our afflicted nation, which will curse them forever. A malignant tumor has never benefitted the patient who suffers from it."[15] Yet things worsened precipitously for the church once Calles succeeded Obregón in 1924. A revolutionary's revolutionary, an active freemason, and a committed atheist with a visceral hatred of the Catholic Church, Calles set out to extirpate "superstition" from Mexican soil in the context of a major land-redistribution scheme. Within weeks of his coming to power, 73 religious houses, 92 churches, and 129 religious colleges were shuttered.[16] In the summer of 1926, Calles presided over new legislation, the so-called Calles Law, that promoted active enforcement of anticlerical elements of the constitution, criminalized offenders, and required state licensure for all clergy. Through this law and other directives, Calles encouraged regional caudillos to make the lives of priests and the faithful miserable, subjecting them to fines, searches, interrogation, church closures, and worse. Ridding education of Catholic influences constituted one of Calles's top priorities: "We must enter and take possession of the consciences of the children, of the consciences of the young, because they do belong, and should belong to the revolution," as he once put it. Some states went so far as to mandate pledges from teachers, such as the following: "I declare that I am an atheist, an irreconcilable enemy of the Catholic, Apostolic, Roman religion, that I will endeavor to destroy it, detaching consciences from the bonds of religious worship, and that I am ready to fight against the clergy anywhere and wherever it may be necessary."[17]

In response, Catholics, enjoying a renaissance in social thought under the influence of Pope Leo XIII's encyclical *Rerum novarum* (1891), went on the offensive. In 1925, several activist Catholic groups came together to form the National League for the Defense of Religious Liberty, demanding the cessation of persecution and opposition to the anticlerical legislation. For their part, bishops with Rome's support attempted something never undertaken in the history of the church, calling essentially for a religious boycott in July 1926. Beginning on Sunday, 1 August 1926, no priest celebrated Mass in Mexico or dispensed other sacraments publicly. But these measures could not stem the tide of events. Looking askance at Rome and the majority of Mexican bishops' counsel of patience and long-suffering, fed-up Catholics, especially in rural regions populated by Indigenous and mestizo peoples, began to agitate for armed resistance, setting in motion the chain of events that led to the popular uprising known as the Cristero War, or La Cristiada (1926–29). Resulting in roughly seventy thousand lives lost, it took place principally in the central-western states of Jalisco, Zacatecas, Guanajuato, Colima, and Michoacán. Claiming the Lady of Guadalupe as their protector and rallying around the cry *Viva Cristo Rey!* (Long live Christ the King!), Cristeros waged an impossible guerrilla war that lasted until 1929, when the U.S. ambassador, Dwight Morrow, intervened to negotiate a truce. But in truth anti-Catholic violence continued well into the 1930s under the presidency of Lázaro Cárdenas, not completely ceasing until the election of Manuel Ávila Camacho, a practicing Catholic, in 1940.[18] From 1929 to 1935, in fact, the federal army undertook a systematic manhunt against Cristero leaders, ultimately killing around five thousand people and driving thousands more into exile.[19]

Because the Cristeros were recognized as political rebels, not innocent lambs, violence against Catholics took various forms in the 1920s and 1930s, some of it captured literarily in Graham Greene's travelogue *The Lawless Roads: A Mexican Journey* (1939) and in his novel *The Power and the Glory* (1940). Although hardly any priests actively engaged in violence themselves, they became reviled as symbols of opposition and consequently were attacked, jailed, exiled, or slain in large numbers. At least ninety priests met their maker during the war or shortly afterward, the most famous being the Jesuit

Miguel Pro, a man known for his piety and largeheartedness. Arrested on false charges of having participated in an assassination attempt against President Obregón, Pro was executed without trial on 23 November 1927, declining a blindfold and holding a crucifix in one hand and a rosary in the other (figure 3). When the initial shots of the firing squad failed to kill him, a rifleman administered the coup de grâce at point-blank range. Calles thought that circulating photographs of Pro's execution would deter the Cristeros. The opposite took place: many soldiers thereafter carried newspaper pictures of the new martyr into battle, vowing revenge.[20] And thousands followed him to the grave. As active agents of anticlericalism and the anti-religious struggle, federal troops, *federales*, sometimes went out of their way to make a point, executing people in an especially gruesome manner; in several instances they displayed slain, decomposing bodies of Cristeros on utility poles alongside railroad tracks in an effort to deter further rebellion.[21] Other well-known priests slain by government forces at this time include Luis Bátiz Sainz, Rodrigo Aguilar Alemán, Agustín Caloca Cortés, Román Adame Rosales, Atilano Cruz Alvarado, and Miguel de la Mora. (Pope John Paul II canonized these priests and several others in 2000.)

Figure 3. The Jesuit Miguel Pro before his execution in Mexico City by a firing squad, 23 November 1927. Photographer unknown. Courtesy of Wikimedia Commons.

An assault on church buildings and holy images constituted another means of repression during the "religious conflict" (*conflicto religioso*), as these years are sometimes called. Many churches were completely destroyed. In Veracruz alone, pro-government partisans—often the local police, inspectors, and teachers—burned or dynamited twenty churches. Many other churches were converted into school buildings, government offices, union headquarters, dance halls, or granaries. In several states, church doors were simply bolted shut, often for years.[22]

The predominant form of iconoclasm, however, was the burning of saints' images, although hacking them to pieces took place too. Such actions violated the religious sensibilities of poorer, Indigenous Catholics in particular, who practically identified the image of the saint with the saint him- or herself. The dreaded revolutionary "saint burners" (*quemasantos*) attacked the "idols" or "fetishes," as they called them, in the states of Sonora, Tabasco, Michoacán, Chiapas, Veracruz, Aguascalientes, Guanajuato, and elsewhere. After being hauled into a town's public square, images were often ceremoniously incinerated to the accompaniment of revolutionary hymns, such as the Socialist Internationale, the Marseillaise, and the Mexican National Anthem. Sometimes the reviled figures received a mock trial before destruction.

Revolutionaries focused on images associated with miracles, healing, and pilgrimages.[23] As early as 1922, an image of the Virgin of Guadalupe, the most widely venerated saint in the Americas, barely survived a bombing attempt. In Huejutla, Hidalgo, on 3 June 1935, inspector Francisco Zárate and his aides carried out a massive revolutionary auto-da-fé, burning hundreds of holy objects. The celebrated Black Christ of Otatitlán in Veracruz witnessed the lethal shooting of several pilgrims trying to defend it from anticlerical attack. Eventually, the assailants succeeded in burning and decapitating the venerated statue, the cult of which had been outlawed. Another celebrated case took place in Magdalena in Sonora involving its patron saint, Francis Xavier, believed to work miracles for the local community. Pro-revolutionary forces stormed the church, burning most of its images. They extracted the large statue of the saint and had it incinerated at a local brewery. Remarkably, for many days thereafter pilgrims traveled to the site, gathering ashes in small pouches for veneration. To offer a final example: a large Cross of Pardon on the road from San Miguel de Allende to Atotonilco, Guanajuato, was toppled from its pedestal and hacked to pieces by local pro-revolutionary forces.[24] Numerous comparable instances could be cataloged.

Such actions represented part of the government-decreed defanaticization campaigns that took off under Calles in the 1920s, continuing into the
1930s. Although these affected practically all of Mexico, they were particularly pronounced in the southern state of Tabasco, presided over by Calles's
regional alter ego, Tomás Garrido Canabal, a committed revolutionary who
fancied himself "the personal enemy of God." In an effort to free Tabasco
from "clerical opium," he established a youthful corps of "Red Shirts" to
do his bidding, which included forbidding the ringing of church bells, the
naming of places after saints, the wearing of crucifixes, and even bidding
farewell to others with the traditional "adios," since this word referenced
God. His Red Shirts bore responsibility for torching the church of Santa
Cruz in Villahermosa, destroying the cathedral there, and demolishing
the towers of the church in Cunduacán. In this "godless state," as Graham
Greene labeled Tabasco, contrived secular festivals, such as the "Fiesta
of the Banana Flower," replaced traditional religious holidays. Here and
elsewhere, Sundays, too, were abolished as a holy day of religious rest and
rebranded as "Cultural Sunday," a day to visit museums, listen to music,
and the like. Tabasco marked the Feast of the Virgin Mary (12 December)
by publicly incinerating two thousand Marian "fetishes."[25] Garrido, furthermore, required that all priests marry on pain of exile or death. Some in fact
met these fates; others were driven into hiding like the "whiskey priest"
in Greene's *Power and the Glory,* in which the character of "the governor,"
modeled on Garrido, is "infuriated to think that there were still people in the
state who believed in a loving and merciful God."[26] In his encyclical *Acerba
animi* (1932), Pope Pius XI compared the situation in Tabasco to the persecutions under Stalin "raging in the unhappy borders of Russia."[27] Garrido,
incidentally, named one of his children Lenin.

Tabasco represents an extreme example of a countrywide reality. In
numerous states, priests faced arrest for minor reasons, such as adorning
churches, ringing church bells, or organizing processions. The defanaticization campaign in Sonora included outlawing Mass, prayer, and the celebration of religious feasts; penalized violators faced hefty fines and even
imprisonment. Workers, soldiers, and the police raided a secret 1935 Easter
celebration at the house of one Ricardo Durazo in Magdalena, arresting
forty of the two hundred people in attendance and saddling many with
fines.[28] At the local level, pro-revolutionary soldiers, policemen, union leaders, and teachers led the anticlerical charge, receiving support from a host

of anticlerical organizations, such as the Vanguard Antireligious Bloc of Jalapa, Veracruz; the Anticlerical and Antireligious League of Ciudad Guzmán, Jalisco; the Mexican Anticlerical Group of Salvatierra, Guanajuato; Tabasco's League of Atheist Teachers; among others.[29]

In the 1930s, many states took aggressive actions to secularize the classroom, pitting "science" against "religion" in a crude zero-sum game, comparable to concurrent actions in the Soviet Union. Germán List Arzubide's *Practice of Irreligious Education* circulated widely and informed numerous curricula. In several states, so-called purge committees (*comités de depuración*) were set up to carry out campaigns of ideological purity (*depuración ideológica*). Many teachers had to sign statements making clear their secularist and revolutionary bona fides. Evaluations of teachers sometimes rested on a multipoint rating system that took into account ideological commitments. An estimated 35 percent of teachers in Sonora received pink slips due to these measures: "[They] do not consider themselves sincerely and honestly capable of undertaking this task . . . due to their ideology in religious matters," one government circular colorlessly put it. In Guanajuato, a purge expelled 150 teachers.[30]

Across Mexico, finally, the federal government granted states the right to limit the number of priests as they saw fit and encouraged policies that resulted in the dramatic reduction in the number of clergy. All bishops and foreign-born priests were either summarily exiled or driven into hiding in the 1920s after Calles began enforcing the constitution's anticlerical elements. Whereas forty-five hundred priests had served the Mexican people before the Cristero War, only 334 remained afterward, licensed by the government to serve fifteen million people—the rest having been eliminated by emigration, expulsion, or assassination.[31] All the while, the exclaustration of religious orders proceeded apace with vacated monasteries often converted to other purposes. By 1935, due to the draconian enforcement of laws, seventeen states (out of thirty-two) had no officially recognized priest at all.[32] To dramatize a point, the state of Colima stipulated that it could have a single priest, but he had to be older than fifty and was required to be married![33]

To be sure, much religious life went underground during these years, and the government received considerable pushback from a distraught and often traumatized faithful. Even so, the 1930s did not witness anything quite like the Cristero rebellion of the late 1920s, despite ongoing episodic violence that some scholars nonetheless refer to as *la Segunda,* or the Second Cristero

War. In 1940, motivated by recent events, Catholics turned to the ballot box in droves, electing Manuel Ávila Camacho, who relaxed enforcement of anti-clerical laws as Carranza had done before him. If anything, the repressions of the 1920s and 1930s, ironically, appeared to embolden the energies of popular Catholicism in Mexico.

In retrospect, the many complexities of these years notwithstanding, what Mexico experienced in the 1920s and 1930s bears witness to combative secularism's potential for violence—a violence that evinced both anticlerical and, if to a lesser degree, more general anti-religious dimensions. "The revolutionary elite," the historian Adrian Bantjes explains, "deemed it impossible to forge new Mexicans without eradicating . . . [the] influence of the Church. They targeted not merely the clergy, but religiosity as well. The seriousness of this effort is demonstrated by the wide array of cultural techniques used, including iconoclasm, the closure of churches, the banishment of priests, the prohibition of religious practices, and the often violent persecution of Catholics."[34] The suppression of Catholicism, consequently, reached an unprecedented extent by the mid-1930s, at which point, the historian Donald Mabry summarizes, the church in Mexico "legally had no corporate existence, no real estate, no schools, no monasteries or convents, no foreign priests, no right to defend itself publicly or in the courts, and no hope that its legal and actual situation would improve. Its clergy were forbidden to wear clerical garb, to vote, [and] to celebrate public religious ceremonies."[35]

Loitering in Tabasco on a Sunday at a time when the government had prohibited church services and religious holidays, Graham Greene evocatively captured a sliver of this same reality: the erasure of sacred time. "The anonymity of Sunday seems peculiarly unnatural in Mexico; a man going hunting in the marshes with his dog and his gun; a young people's fiesta, shops closing after noon—nothing else to divide this day from all the other days, no bells to ring."[36]

SPAIN

Turning from the New World to the Old, due to the victory of General Franco and the Nationalist side in the Spanish Civil War (1936–39) and the enormities committed by his repressive regime, it is tempting to reduce to a footnote the atrocities committed in Republican areas under a secularist aegis in the mid-1930s. But historical veracity requires attention to arguably the most vicious and intense attack against clergy and church institutions in modern European history—rivaling and often surpassing that seen during the French Revolution. With most of the atrocities committed in the second half of 1936, the final reckoning astounds: the killing of thirteen bishops, 4,172 diocesan priests and seminarians, 2,364 monks, and 283 nuns.[37] Accompanying these deaths were thousands of mock trials, torture, vandalism, iconoclasm, coercion to blasphemy, ritual humiliations, and even (recalling Nero's Rome) death by animal attack, as several priests met their end by assault while confined in a bullring.[38] Church burnings, or what has been called *incendiary anticlericalism,* occurred on a large scale as well.

Making sense of the onslaught requires recognition of the complexity and highly polarized nature of the Spanish situation and of the fact that many legitimate grievances against the restored Bourbon monarchy (1874–1931) had, by the early twentieth century, metastasized into an all-encompassing effort by oppositional political forces to demonize the church (the destiny of which had long been entwined with that of the crown) as the root and symbol of all contemporary evils. The Tridentine baroque religiosity in this overwhelmingly Catholic state appeared to have simply outlived its expiration date, or so many believed, having in their eyes willfully and benightedly embraced forces of political reaction.[39] A similar reality had taken shape in Portugal, though resulting in less if still considerable violence there as well.[40]

Drawing freely from the Radical Enlightenment tradition, spiked with socialist and anarchist elements as well, Spanish anticlericals in the nineteenth century, not unlike their counterparts in other Catholic countries and in the New World, had fashioned a formidable tradition of combative secularism or laicismo, contributing to numerous church-state clashes that erupted into violence on several occasions (notably in 1822–23, 1834–35, 1868, and 1873) and resulted in numerous cases of arson and the deaths of an estimated 235 clerics.[41] Spanish anticlericals had also been unusually successful in taking advantage of long-standing popular grievances to gain support for their outlook, especially in cities and in the south of the country, convincing many lower-class Spaniards that the clergy amounted to little more than avaricious, gluttonous, and lustful hypocrites. Although the foundation for the short-lived First Republic in 1873 seemed to herald a new age, the quick restoration of the monarchy a year later enraged republicans and anticlericals, setting in motion future conflicts that simmered and sometimes raged in the late nineteenth century.[42] A premonition of things to come took place in July 1909 during the so-called Tragic Week (*la semana trágica*), during which eighty religious buildings were torched in Barcelona and nearby villages as a means of protesting certain policy decisions of the government.[43] Things quieted down thereafter, but the left-wing and especially anarchist press continued to propagate harsh, often violent anticlerical messages leading up to the founding of the Second Republic in 1931, at which time a republican-reformist coalition came to power with the opportunity to enshrine its views in a new constitution.

Imitating in many respects the 1905 law in France, the religious provisions of the 1931 constitution went beyond the mere separation of church and state, seeking to crush the Catholic Church as a public entity.[44] Itemized in article 26, the new foundational document secularized public education, legalized civil marriage and divorce, forbade confessional cemeteries, cut all religious funding from the budget, dissolved the Jesuit Order, and forbade members of religious orders to teach. Religious processions, moreover, were banned and many church properties confiscated and placed under government control. Subsequent decrees and enforcement measures prevented the ringing of church bells, removed all religious symbols from classrooms, and placed onerous taxes on clergy and Catholic charities. In some areas, people were forbidden to wear crucifixes and other religious insignia. "Spain has ceased to be Catholic," as the Second Republic's Prime Minister Manuel Azaña crowed about the new order.[45] Not surprisingly, all of this did not sit well with the Catholic Church, beginning with Pope Pius XI, who condemned the legislation in his encyclical *Dilectissima nobis* (1933).[46] Some liberals, such as the philosopher José Ortega y Gasset, also felt that in light of Spain's deeply religious history, the constitution gratuitously offended pious sensibilities and portended national fragmentation.

Howls of protest and defiance from Spanish Catholics in the early republic triggered reprisals from the government and anticlerical partisans. Swept up in the moment, Azaña infamously thundered that "all the convents of Spain [were] not worth the life of a single republican" after a spate of riots and torching of churches in and around Madrid in 1931.[47] More burnings followed in 1932. The radical weekly *La Traca* depicted on its cover of February 1932 a guillotine placed near a group of frightened priests, nuns, and pious laity with the caption: "This [guillotine] working for two hours a day for a month would free Spain of all the evil rubbish which wants to make the Republic a failure" (figure 4).[48] This was not atypical in the radical press.

Figure 4. Cover of the Spanish anticlerical magazine *La Traca* (20 February 1932) suggesting the guillotining of the clergy and their supporters as a solution to Spain's troubles. Artwork by staff of *La Traca*. From the author's collection.

"The Church must disappear forever, the churches must never again be used for the most squalid pimping. . . . We've finished with holy water stoups," thundered another newspaper in favor of the church burnings.[49]

Tensions mounted in 1934 in Asturias, a mining region in northern Spain, when local officials and anticlerical partisans lashed out at Lasallean brothers and a Passionist priest in the city of Turón for failing to abide by the constitution's anticlerical provisions by teaching in the local schools. In the context of an election setback and an uprising in favor of a more militant revolution, agents of the local government and their supporters entered the brothers' monastery on the pretext of looking for concealed weapons. Before evening Mass on the night of 4 October, nine brothers were taken and held without trial before being summarily shot in a local cemetery—the first act of violence that soon spread elsewhere in Asturias, resulting in the death of thirty-seven priests and the destruction of fifty-eight churches, before the mayhem was suppressed by General Franco and the Spanish Foreign Legion.[50]

This whole episode set the country on edge, dividing people into two highly polarized if internally diverse camps. The Republican faction, organized politically by early 1936 into the Popular Front, was made up of an assortment of liberals, republicans, socialists, trade unionists, communists, and anarchists—most regarding the church as a pillar of reaction. They faced off against a Nationalist coalition, a comparably large collection of right-wing, monarchist, fascist, and traditionalist parties, some of whom were given to demonizing the republic as a tool of freemasonry, Jewish intrigue, and international Bolshevism. After the Popular Front narrowly won the 1936 election and began to form a government under Manuel Azaña, several military leaders, led by Franco and General Emilio Mola, took matters into their own hands, instigating a coup d'état in July 1936. Since the church hierarchy had voiced disapproval of the Republic, clergy immediately became execrable symbols of the old regime trying to reassert itself and thus an inviting, helpless target for retaliatory political violence. The anarchist *Solidaridad Obrera* on 15 August 1836 was not alone in insisting, "The Church has to disappear forever. . . . The priest, the friar, the Jesuit have dominated Spain; we must extirpate them. The religious orders must be dissolved; the bishops and cardinals must be shot; and church property must be expropriated." Or, as the Trotskyite-inclined paper *La Batalla* put it four days later: "It should not be a question of burning churches or of executing priests, but of destroying the Church as a social institution."[51] As the guns of war rumbled to life, officials in Republican-held areas, with some notable exceptions, either turned a blind eye to the assaults or actively participated in an orgy of violence against the clergy.

The violence went beyond simple retaliation, although this certainly played a role. Rather, it had roots in what the historian Julius Ruiz has called an "exterminatory discourse" against clergy that preceded the attempted coup and was endemic in militant circles.[52] Recall the church burnings and priestly deaths from the nineteenth century. Note, too, that church hierarchs did not formally support the Nationalist side until 1937. "According to recent analyses," as the historian Manuel Pérez Ledesma elaborates, "rather than political reprisals . . . we should talk about genuine 'religious persecution.' Religious, not political, as it was not in response to the Catholic Church's support of the 'nationalist' side, but rather preceded any ecclesiastic declaration in this respect." It was also religious, he continues, "because, in addition to the indiscriminate murder of members of the clergy, often accompanied by torture and humiliation, the sacrophobic actions were directed against anything related to the Church and its beliefs."[53]

The violence took diverse forms. Sometimes a mock trial took place before killings, sometimes not. Many victims were simply "taken for a ride," as the expression went, and never came back, winding up instead suffocated, burned to death, or shot. Others were hanged, buried alive, drowned, or dragged through the streets. Mockery, forced blasphemy, beatings, mutilation of the body, and other forms of torture not infrequently preceded death. Thirteen bishops met their end—those of Lérida, Cuenca, Barbastro, Segorbe, Jaén, Tarragona, Ciudad Real, Almería, Guadix, Barcelona, Teruel, Sigüenza, and Orihuela. Some dioceses lost almost all of their clergy; Barbastro in Aragón, for example, lost 123 out of 140 priests, or 88 percent, while Lérida lost 66 percent; Tortosa, 61 percent; Segorbe, 55 percent; Madrid, 30 percent; Barcelona, 22 percent; and Valencia, 27 percent. Mutilations inflicted on the bodies revealed a morbid fixation on genitals, understandable in the context of traditional anticlerical obsession with the sexuality of priests, monks, and nuns.[54] Amid the general carnage, some truly heartbreaking cases stand out, such as the twenty-three nuns belonging to the order of Adoratrices taken to a cemetery near Madrid and shot on the morning of 10 November 1936. Or the wanton killing of members of the Brothers of Saint John of God, who cared for the mentally ill in asylums outside Madrid.[55] Finally, sometimes an eerie rationality about the killing process prevailed, as captured in this after-the-fact interview with an Aragonese anticlerical:

> Interviewee: I killed, among others, Father Domingo at Alcañiz [Aragon].
>
> Interviewer: Dear me! Why did you kill him?
>
> Interviewee: It's quite simple. Because he was a priest.
>
> Interviewer: But then, did Father Domingo meddle in politics or have personal enemies?
>
> Interviewee: No sir, Father Domingo was a very good man. But we had to kill all the priests.[56]

Death did not spare one from the anticlerical wrath. Across Republican-held areas, exhumations took place followed by the macabre public display of long-buried corpses of priests, monks, and nuns, some naturally mummified by the dry Spanish heat. Such incidents occurred in Madrid, Barcelona, Batea, Belchite, Canet lo Roig, Fuenteovejuna, Minorca, Orihuela, Oropesa, Valencia, Toledo, Almería, Peralta de la Sal, Vich, and elsewhere. In Madrid, Republican partisans dressed as clowns adorned the main altar of the Carmelite church with skulls and body parts and masqueraded around it. In Barcelona, in a notorious instance, nineteen nuns' corpses, disinterred from a convent cemetery attached to La Enseñanza Church, were exhibited on the street for passersby to see. Cedric Salter, a correspondent for London's *Daily Telegraph,* described the scene: "The poor, centuries-old bodies of the nuns were exposed and what flesh still clung to the bones was slowly blackening in the hot sun. Fresh coffins were excavated from the convent burial ground and a peseta was being charged for the hire of a long stick with which to strike or insult with unnamable obscenities these sightless, shrunken relics."[57] At the Church of San Antonio de la Florida in Madrid, a mob played soccer with the patron saint's skull.[58]

Exhumations in gravesites constitute one element in the attacks on holy sites. According to one recent study, 957 attacks on ecclesiastical property took place during the early phase of the Spanish Civil War, including 325 cases of the total or partial burning of churches. By the end of the war, thousands of churches, monasteries, and convents had been affected. Spared buildings still often lost benches, confessionals, liturgical items, and other interior furnishings to destruction. Pillaging of libraries and looting occurred as well, as did the toppling and defacing of statues. Among the most well-known images from the time is a picture of Republican militiamen shooting at the statue of the Sacred Heart of Jesus atop the Cerro de los Ángeles just outside Madrid. In several instances, iconoclasts even demanded that private devotional objects of town inhabitants be retrieved from homes and placed on public bonfires.[59] Both priest and church perished together in many cases, as recorded in Barcelona by Salter of the *Daily Telegraph:* "On my way...I passed a burning church.... Flames were licking up round the altar, on which stood two beautiful wrought silver candlesticks gleaming through the clouds of black smoke. From the high carved stone pulpit an elderly priest swung very slowly to and fro by his sickeningly elongated neck."[60] Such realities drove religious expression underground in Republican-held areas. Masses took place in secret. Priests concealed their identity in civilian dress. Others fled to safer areas or left the country.

The anticlerical fury found its way into literature as writers reported reality and wrote fiction imitating it. In his *Homage to Catalonia* (1938), George Orwell offers an account of an Aragonese anticlerical chiseling out crosses and other religious symbols in a local cemetery.[61] In José María Gironella's *Cypresses Believe in God,* arguably the greatest work of Spanish literature from the Civil War era, Republican partisans destroy church images, desecrate elements of the Mass, topple statues, and set churches and monasteries aflame. One vivid passage describes how they took down an immense crucifix from a church and hurled it from an embankment to the ground below, where "the wooden arms of the cross pointed pathetically in all directions. The image rested head-down, like St. Peter." Meanwhile, inside the church, "the struggle of man against matter was at its height. Everything was of such good quality that there was no choice but to employ fire. . . . Professor Morales [a character in the book] had not realized that it was so easy to destroy things that were centuries old."[62] In spite of his own left-wing sympathies, Robert Jordan, a character in Ernest Hemingway's *For Whom the Bell Tolls,* experiences pangs of conscience when he remembers the anticlerical violence: "I've always known about the other [atrocities], he thought. What we did to them at the start [of the Civil War]. I've always known and hated it and I have heard it mentioned shamelessly and shamefully, bragged of, boasted of, defended, explained, and denied."[63]

Accounting for Spanish anticlerical violence in the 1930s requires careful judgment. It was certainly not, as some Nationalists claimed, centrally planned or executed by agents of international Communism, although Stalin backed the Madrid regime, and more than a few "reds" numbered among the foreign brigades who traveled to Spain to aid the Republican cause. But neither is the violence reducible to an aggregation of isolated, irrational outbursts committed only by so-called uncontrollables, as defenders of the Republic claimed after the Civil War. Surveying the recent historiography of the republic during the war, the historian Maria Thomas makes clear that despite the fragmentation of power "terror was as integral to the Republic's war effort as it was to Franco's" and that, while not directly responsible for all the violence in every instance, "the state remained firmly in control of its machinery of coercion"; the violence itself displayed "a coherent logic firmly grounded in the radical remaking of social relations."[64] Furthermore, scant evidence has shown that the clergy actively aided the military uprising of July 1936 or that houses of worship served as rebel arms dumps.[65] While some clergymen made broadcasts supporting the uprising, no clear evidence exists to support the idea that hordes of sharpshooting priests took potshots at Republicans from their belfries, as some later claimed.[66] Certainly, the wartime revolutionary atmosphere had a lot to do with the violence, given the fearmongering and demonization that took place on both sides and the tendency of each side to cast the other as a repugnant "enemy from within." But this should be understood as existing in addition to the pervasive con-ditioning power exerted by preexisting laicist and anticlerical traditions. As the historian Julio de la Cueva has nicely summed up: "They [acts of violence] were the consequence of a long tradition of . . . anticlericalism . . . which had considered the vicious clergy the main cause of the country's ills and had proposed elimination—either legal or physical—of the former as a solution to the latter." In 1936, in the extraordinary circumstances brought on at the beginning of the war, "revolutionaries were simply putting con-sistently into effect what they already knew: that they had to eradicate the clergy if they wanted a new, better, unpolluted society."[67] Or as one Repub-lican later said about the church burnings: "Those buildings had lasted long enough. . . . [They were] anachronisms, weighty and obstructing, casting a jailhouse stench over the city. The times condemned them to death and the people carried out the execution of justice. These burnings were the *auto da fé* necessary for the progress of civilization."[68]

Finally, it merits pointing out that the outcome of the Spanish Civil War was never a foregone conclusion and that anti-Republican forces were often disorganized and given to factionalism and infighting. The extremity of aggression against churches and clergy, in this context, appeared as a pure gift to Franco, providing him with an emotionally charged, unifying rally cry to defend "Christian civilization" against mayhem and destruction.[69] Thus, a speculative counterfactual presents itself: what might the outcome of the Civil War have looked like had so much anticlerical violence not taken place in the first place? One could imagine a better or at least more moderate outcome. Which is not to say that the ugly repressions of the ensuing Franco regime were caused by Republican assaults, but perhaps in their incipience they were crucially abetted by combative secularist overreach.

TURKEY

The phrase "secularist overreach" might well describe the rise of modern Turkey (f. 1923) after the collapse of the Ottoman Empire—an event long in the making but wrought suddenly as a consequence of the Great War's outcome. Although certainly a religiously different patch of earth from Mexico or Spain, the Anatolian Peninsula witnessed draconian and sometimes violent measures of state-imposed secularization in the 1920s, 1930s, and beyond. As with Mexican and Spanish reformers and militants, Turkish revolutionaries—the decorated-general-turned-nationalist-strongman Mustafa Kemal foremost among them—latched on to the French-revolutionary tradition of laïcité—adapted into Turkish as laiklik—as a polestar for transitioning the Ottoman heartland from the seat of a decrepit and defeated empire into a modern, Westernized nation-state. "His [Kemal's] archetype was France's Troisième République. . . which he viewed as the most successful regime in the history of human kind," as Kemal's biographer Şükrü Hanioğlu has noted; "he approved official France's militant anti-clericalism, its pugnacious laïcité."[70] The epochal changes wrought in these decades affected not only the Turkish people but the entire Muslim world, with global ripple effects lasting until the present.[71] At their core stands the question of combative secularism and the complexities and ironies entailed in applying it suddenly and ruthlessly to a profoundly devout society, one in which what counted as "religion" and what counted as "politics" arguably interpenetrated in far more complex and comprehensive ways than in the Christian West. Viewed as a whole, the ideology driving the changes—customarily spoken of as "Kemalism"—possessed two principal, seemingly contradictory aspects with respect to religion. On the one hand, it aimed to bring about the disestablishment of religion, mirroring the legal template of many Western nations. But on the other, it sought to control religion in an authoritarian manner, forcing it to submit to the bureaucratic machinery of the newly minted state; one might therefore think of this as Turkish "Josephism," to invoke a European analogue. Religious opposition to these measures, not surprisingly, was often intense, but it ultimately proved no match for the iron will of Atatürk (the "father of the Turks," as he was honorifically called after 1934), his fellow reformers, and the powerful state apparatus that they forged.

Of course, in history no change occurs apart from a particular background and possible antecedents. With respect to early republican Turkey, several considerations merit mentioning. First, in the decades before World War I, nationalist ideologies unleashed potent and destructive forces in the Balkans and the greater Middle East, practically all of which stood at one time under Ottoman suzerainty. For a declining multireligious, multiethnic empire, "the sick man of Europe" as the expression went, this was bad news. This reality merits keeping in mind, because what might ostensibly look like "religious violence" at this time—say, in the Balkan Wars of 1912–13, the Turkish massacre of Armenians beginning in 1915, or the Greco-Turkish War (1919–22) on the heels of World War I—is more accurately understood as the political manipulation of religious and ethnic identities in uncertain times and their being put at the mercy of modern nationalist ambitions amid a tumultuous, postimperial scramble to create uniethnic states.[72] The consequent bloodshed in fact stands in stark contrast to the earlier, fundamentally Qur'anic Ottoman millet system, which permitted non-Muslim "people of the book," principally Jews and Christians, to live relatively tranquilly in their own communities so long as they did not disturb the general peace and paid the required poll tax (jizya) to Istanbul.[73] Second, alongside nationalism, proto-secularist currents of thought inspired by the West had penetrated Ottoman society long before Kemal's rendezvous with history in the 1920s. One observes this in the so-called Tanzimat (Turkish: "reorganization") reforms promulgated and effected between 1839 and 1876 that chipped away at theocratic elements of the old regime under the influence of European ideas about equality before the law and the desirability of neutral, nonreligious courts and institutions of education.[74] Third, one sees it in the well-known Young Turk movement—crucial for understanding Kemal's own intellectual development and the ideology of the early republic—that sought Ottoman rejuvenation, spiked with pungent Turkish nationalism, under the influence of Western Europe's democratic and secular institutions and a stadial understanding of historical progress traceable to the Enlightenment and the French Revolution.[75] Illustrative in this regard is the Young Turk intellectual Yusuf Akçura, who studied in Paris and there adopted influential ideas pertaining to Turkish nationalism, secularism, and historical progress.[76] The ideas of Young Turks triumphed in the constitutional revolution of 1908, when their Committee of Union and Progress forced Sultan Abdul Hamid II to reinstate the constitution of 1876, itself the fruit of the aforementioned Tanzimat movement but scuttled by the sultan two years later to restore power to himself. Finally, and crucially, secularism manifested itself in Young Turks' criticisms of Islam and Islamic institutions. While most Young Turks, whether from conviction or expedience, gravitated toward defining Islam as a "rational religion" in a vague, quasi-deistic manner, they generally abhorred the actually existing Islam in early twentieth-century Ottoman society. "Surviving in the world of modern civilization," as Kemal once remarked, entailed dispensing with "age-old rotten mentalities," "tradition-worshipping," "superstitions," and "nonsense."[77] In a particularly candid moment, he derided Islam as the "absurd theology of an immoral Bedouin, [a] rotting corpse which poisons our lives."[78] Discretion counseled against public utterances of this sort, but the underpinning sentiment reflected not-insignificant swaths of Young Turk opinion. At the very least, Young Turk opinion converged on a largely *instrumental* conception of religion, smiling on it so long as it shored up "Turkish" nationalist identity while, paradoxically, regarding traditional piety and practice as a retardant of civilizational advance in need of curtailment and control through secularism, laiklik, and a powerful state.

The Great War's outcome gave Kemal and his ideology an opportunity. Due to his courageous efforts to repel British forces at the Battle of Gallipoli (1915–16), saving Istanbul from occupation, he had become a national hero, recognizable across the Ottoman Empire. His refusal to concede immediately to the humiliations of the war's loss after 1918 and his daring conduct during the Greco-Turkish War (1919–22) added to his luster, even as the prior decision of the Sublime Porte (as the Ottoman government in Istanbul was called) to side with the Central Powers during the war had, fortuitously for Kemal, significantly discredited the imperial system. Once border reconfigurations from the fighting came into focus at the Treaty of Lausanne (1923), in the context of a massive Turk-Greek population exchange, the landmass of a new polity was constricted mainly to the Anatolian Peninsula, populated (due to the brutal actions against the Armenians) largely by ethnic Turks. Appeals to nationalism thus seemed all the more salient and plausible. Fusing nationalism with secularism and applying them aggressively to the incipient Turkish state constituted the key ingredients of Kemal's genius and the ideological basis of his authoritarian overreach.

Working with a Grand National Assembly (established in 1920) in Ankara that more often than not bent to his will, Kemal oversaw the dismantling of the sultanate, the drafting of a new constitution, and concomitantly, on 29 October 1923, the official founding of the modern Turkish nation. Abolishing the sultanate, still based in Istanbul at war's end, required a deft touch, but most people of consequence recognized that its time had passed. In lengthy, learned speeches before the assembly, Kemal made the crucial distinction between the (political) *Ottoman* sultanate (going back to 1299) and the (spiritual) *Muslim* caliphate (going back to Abu Bakr in the sixth century), arguing for their separation and for the elimination of the former. This formally took place on 17 November 1922, when the last sultan, the pitiable Mehmed VI, boarded HMS *Malaya* and left Istanbul through the Golden Horn, bound for Malta. The next day, Mehmed's brother, the mild and scholarly Abdülmecid II, was appointed as "spiritual" caliph, preserving (for the time being) a hallowed religious office widely esteemed across the Muslim world.[79]

But the caliphate's day, too, would pass, because Kemal felt that so long as the caliphate existed, it would serve as a rallying point for reactionary forces unwilling to countenance his secularizing aims. International pressures also came to bear on the situation, particularly from India in the form of a so-called Caliphate Movement that ascribed world-historical, pan-Islamic significance to Abdülmecid as the God-ordained leader to rescue Islam from the ignominy of European colonialism and lead it into new glory days. These Indians and Kemal's internal opponents both saw the office of caliph as a crucial link between Islam's future and its glorious past.[80] "Mustafa Kemal," as the historian Bernard Lewis once wryly observed, "agreed with his opponents in seeing in the Caliphate the link with the past and with Islam. It was precisely for that reason that he was determined to break it."[81] That fateful day came on 3 March 1924 when a bill abrogating the caliphate, championed by Kemal and calling for the expulsion of all members of the Ottoman dynasty, passed in the Grand National Assembly. Not wanting to cause controversy by drawing a crowd, the retiring Abdülmecid with his family secretly left the Dolmabahçe Palace along the Bosporus for the Çatalca train station the next morning, departing Turkey—forever. Few events in modern history rival the religious significance of this one, for Muslims, who were stunned by this action, and for the world at large.[82]

The abolition of the caliphate came in the context of a host of other modernizing, Westernizing legal measures intended to break the power of Islam in favor of secularism within a duality of Islamic and secular institutions going back to the Tanzimat period. On the same day as the caliphate's abrogation, a new parliament passed a Unification of Education Law, which closed hundreds of *mektebs* and *madrasas* and made possible a system of state schools at all levels, modeled on the French example and placed under a Ministry of Education. At the same time, Parliament established the Directorate of Religious Affairs (Diyanet) and the Directorate of Pious Foundations, state bureaucracies wresting power and wealth away from previous religious institutions dedicated to service and philanthropy, placing them directly under the office of the prime minister. Between 1924 and 1926, the entire legal and court system underwent restructuring, removing it from anchorage in Şeriat (Sharia), traditional Islamic jurisprudence, and basing it instead on the Swiss Legal Code, superintended by a Ministry of Justice. Although Turkey's new constitution (20 April 1924) paid lip service to Islam as the religion of the people, the relevant clause was removed in 1928, permitting the assertion of the principle of secularism (laiklik) in the revised constitution of 1937.

The sweeping nature of the changes reflected the dominance of the Republican People's Party, successor to the Committee of Union and Progress. Founded by Kemal in 1923, it ran the country with scant opposition for twenty-seven years, with Kemal serving as president. All the changes wrought in this period fundamentally disempowered the *ulama,* the traditional Muslim theological and legal authorities, centralizing oversight of society's religious sphere in the various state bureaucracies—a clear example of what chapter 1 called *conflictual integration.* In a very short period, as the social anthropologist Paul Stirling has summarized, "the religious authorities lost their power over justice and education, their right to nominate their own officials, and their control over the property on which their institutions depended."[83]

Sudden, large-scale changes tend to invite opposition. In Turkey the most serious took the form of an armed rebellion among Kurds in the eastern provinces. Condemning the "godless" republic and calling for the restoration of the caliphate, Şeyh Said of Palu, the hereditary leader of the Nakşbendi Sufi order, led a sizable revolt, beginning in February 1925. Roughly five thousand perished in the uprising, as Turkish forces destroyed lands, pillaged whole villages, and deported people throughout Kurdish areas. The government, moreover, acted swiftly on the legal front, passing the Law for the Maintenance of Order in March 1925, effectively handing itself dictatorial power for the next four years to suppress religious dissent and political rivals with impunity. So-called independence tribunals sprang up, administering swift justice to rebel leaders and attempting to deter those inclined to follow their example. Şeyh Said and forty-six others were tried by these tribunals in April 1925, receiving death penalties that were carried out the day following their sentencing.[84] Altogether, 7,500 people were arrested and 660 executed under this law, which also enabled a crackdown on the press, resulting in the termination of eight of the most important urban newspapers and periodicals and several provincial papers as well.[85]

Beyond helping to suppress the rebellion, the Law for the Maintenance of Order served as the basis for the further repression of traditional religious life and the assertion of combative secularism in the late 1920s and 1930s, with the government often reverting to what one biographer of Kemal has called "measured terror" to effect its will.[86] In November 1925, in a crushing blow to popular piety and cherished mystical traditions, Sufi orders (*tarikats*) and lodges (*tekkes, zawiyas*), judged as retrograde and potential nests of obstruction and dissent, were forcibly shut down and their assets confiscated by the state—an action perhaps comparable to the proscription of Christian religious orders during the French Revolution. This affected not only the Nakşbendi order but also the Bektashi, the Mevlevi, better known as whirling dervishes, and several smaller orders. Practically all *türbes* (tombs of Muslim saints), sites of popular pilgrimage and veneration, were closed at this time—at least officially. Concurrently, traditional Muslim titles marking status—*şeyh, derviş, mürit, dede, seyit, çelebi, baba, emir, nakip,* and *halife*—became illegal. Justifying these measures, Kemal blasted those "that today, in the luminous presence of science, knowledge, and civilization in all aspects," turn to people with such titles for guidance. "Gentlemen," he continued in the same speech, "the Republic of Turkey cannot be the land of şeyhs, dervishes, disciples, and lay brothers."[87] To be sure, much Sufi activity continued underground, and some orders simply relocated to other countries. The Bektashis moved their international headquarters to Albania, for example, even as government officials confiscated material from their lodges for display at a new Ethnographic Museum in Ankara as "relics of a bygone age."[88] Many other Sufi leaders protested silently or by refusing to take posts in the new religious bureaucracy. Compounding the tragedy of the Sufi orders, by the middle decades of the twentieth century the state permitted the enactment of Sufi rituals for the purpose of promoting tourism even as the actual orders remained legally banned.[89]

The same year as Sufism's interdiction, Parliament imposed a "hat law," a major instance of social engineering and intrusion into social custom. The law forbade traditional turbans and the fez (a brimless cap worn by Turkish men since the 1820s that had become associated with the Islamic faith), mandating instead that men wear Western-style brimmed top hats or else face one year in prison. Clothing of course carries enormous symbolic meaning, and, practically speaking, the new top hats impeded the Muslim prayer ritual, which required touching of the forehead. Vehement protests against the new law broke out across Turkey, especially in rural central Anatolia and along the Black Sea coast. Government forces ruthlessly quashed these dissenters, arresting hundreds and executing fifty-seven recalcitrant resisters. In one instance, local gendarmes fired into an angry crowd, killing twenty people. Many Turkish citizens, moreover, preferred exile to wearing an article of clothing associated in their minds with religious infidelity. "The number of rebellions, arrests, imprisonments, and executions in the aftermath of the Hat Law," the historian Camilla T. Nereid observes, leads one "to conclude that the rationale behind the hat legislation was to oppress and discipline Turkish society by forcing it to make resistance visible and thus possible to localize and crush."[90]

Reeducating society away from traditional norms and toward modern, secular ones presented a steep challenge to the new republic, but one it undertook on principle. Toward these ends, the government attempted to standardize all education and place it under the Ministry of Education, allowing at first but then abolishing religious instruction in 1927. In place of the closed madrasas, twenty-six *imam-hatip* schools (preacher-training schools) were permitted, along with a limited number of theological faculties in several universities, although the mandate of the latter entailed approaching religion "scientifically" and not through traditional methods of Qur'anic exegesis and interpretation. The twenty-six imam-hatip schools at first served 1,442 students in 1924; but only two of the schools remained open in 1926, serving 278 students, and they ceased operating entirely in 1931. At that time, only one theological faculty in Istanbul remained open, but it closed down in 1933 in the context of a purge of two-thirds of the university's faculty for being insufficiently Kemalist in outlook. From then until 1949, no legal education in Islam existed except for a few Qur'an reading schools in rural areas.[91] Parents could still provide religious instruction in the home, but as a matter of law, even this required government approval and oversight.[92] "The reform most damaging to the daily religious life of the people was the cutting off of almost all religious training," concludes Paul Stirling.[93] Finally, as the state subsumed and constricted Islamic education, it actively supported translations of irreligious Western Enlightenment texts such as Baron d'Holbach's *Le bon sens* and the publication of anti-religious journals such as *Hür Fikr* (Free Thought).[94]

Language policy constituted another arena of secularist ideology. In traditional Islamic theology, Arabic is a unique and sacred language. A translated Qur'an does not have the same sacred stature of the Qur'an in Arabic. Nonetheless, the government undertook the extensive Turkification of Islam in the 1920s and 1930s. In 1925 the Grand National Assembly commissioned a Turkish translation of the Qur'an, a multivolume Turkish commentary on the text, and a compilation of *hadiths* (sayings of Muhammad) in Turkish translation. Beginning in 1928, laws required that the Latin alphabet replace the Arabic in written Turkish. Turkish replaced Arabic in the muezzin's five times daily call to prayer as well as in the Friday prayer and sermon in the mosque. Perhaps not surprisingly, the government faced stiff resistance from a population shocked by these changes, especially with respect to the call to prayer and activities at the mosque. But in education, the shift from Arabic to the Latin alphabet eventually took root. "The basic purpose of this was not so much practical and pedagogical," as Bernard Lewis has observed, "as social and cultural—and Mustafa Kemal, in forcing his people to accept it [the Latin alphabet] was slamming the door on the past," insofar as younger generations now faced pressures to associate things Arabic with obsolescence and obscurantism as they lost the capacity to understand an important script of the Ottoman past.[95] "Change in the alphabet was strategic," adds Nevzet Çelik, "as it brought traditional

Muslim scholars and many other intellectuals into ignorance and not only obstructed people's access to religious texts, but intentionally aimed to prevent new generations from assessing the past, and to create a link with the adoption of secular values."[96] In addition, the state funded such nationalist enterprises as the Turkish Historical Society (1925) and the Turkish Language Society (1926) to promote Turkish identity and nationalism. Official histories received a facelift to foster Kemal's pet theories that Central Asia, where the Turks originated, was the cradle of all human society and that Turkish was the mother of all human languages.[97] These developments, too, emphasized discontinuity with the Ottoman and pan-Islamic past, even as the realities they reflected exacerbated regional tensions with Arabs, Kurds, Armenians, and Greeks.

Turkey's extensive Westernization program possessed additional aspects. These included jettisoning the traditional Muslim calendar and embracing the Western one; adopting European systems of measurements; encouraging the wearing of Western clothing across the board, not just headgear; and adopting the five-day workweek with a "weekend"—a change that directly impacted Friday as the traditional day of visiting the mosque and public prayer. Not least, the government encouraged women to participate in society alongside men, and to ditch traditional roles and religiously prescribed clothing, such as the veil. Later in the republic's history, as is generally known, bans against women wearing headscarves in public places and institutions of higher learning became a major flashpoint of secularist-religious conflict.[98]

And in all of this, mention has not been made of the cult of personality that developed around Kemal himself, nor of the fact that criticizing his reforms became officially impermissible. Policies even intensified under his successor, Mustafa İsmet İnönü (r. 1938–50). "Any questioning or criticism of or dissent from Kemalist reforms," as Abdullahi Ahmed An-Na'im has noted, "was . . . considered treason to the country. . . . Fear that political opposition or critical thinking could derail these new reforms meant that anyone who disagreed with or questioned them from any ideological or other perspective had to be silenced or forced into exile."[99] The ubiquitous presence of Atatürk's picture on posters and governmental documents, moreover, reinforced the pervasive and heavy-handed nature of Turkish nationalism and secularism, not to mention intentionally flouting Islam's long-standing reluctance to depict images of human beings.

In some respects, the dizzying changes brought to Turkish society in the 1920s and 1930s succeeded, insofar as cultural norms began to reflect political and legal changes. But this should not obscure the illiberal, top-down nature of the procedures that effected the changes, nor the Leviathan state required in the process, nor the dissent and enduring disapproval from large sectors of society, nor, finally, the violence often needed to maintain the changes. "There was dissent and opposition in the 1920s and 1930s," as the political scientist Sumantra Bose has observed, "all of which was ruthlessly crushed by the Kemalists, sometimes with brutal violence."[100] The discourse of secularism [in Turkey]," as the anthropologist Yael Navaro bluntly puts it, "is coeval with violence, . . . a statist culture of violence."[101] The Turkish Revolution, as the scholars Angel Rabasa and F. Stephen Larrabee add, was "a state-instituted, top-down enterprise in social engineering carried out by a small military-bureaucratic elite that imposed its secularist vision on a reluctant traditional society."[102]

The subsequent history of the Republic of Turkey, moreover, bears witness to how thin support for the revolution of the 1920s often was. Roughly a decade after Kemal's death in 1938, religious reaction set in and alongside it greater political pluralism to challenge what essentially had been a one-party nationalist-secularist state. But this reaction, and subsequent actions based on it, has never sat well with the diehard Kemalists, who frequently came up short electorally but who nonetheless dominated the ranks of the military, the judiciary, and other state bureaucracies. Thus, not once but on four separate occasions (1960, 1971, 1980, and 1996) military coups in Turkey aimed to overturn electoral outcomes by opposition parties and to restore Kemalism or updated variants of it. When pent-up frustration with the violence-inscribed system reached a saturation point in the 1980s and 1990s, and then with the surreptitious rise of the religious nationalist Recep Tayyip Erdoğan in 2001, anti-Kemalists have been able to turn the tables, ironically benefiting from Kemal's strong state and authoritarian modus operandi in doing so. To cite Bose again: "The political transformation of Turkey in the twenty-first century has meant that Atatürk's secularist legacy has proved to be not so eternal after all, while his legacy of snarling, vicious authoritarianism pervades the state—now [ironically] decisively taken over by anti-secularist forces. That has turned out to be Mustafa Kemal's legacy to the Turkish Republic and its people."[103] Recent religiopolitical shifts in Turkey, adds the scholar of religion Karen Armstrong, are in part the offspring of historical memory among Turkish Muslims who have experienced "[imposed] Western secularism and nationalism . . . [with] the violent destruction of previous Islamic institutions."[104]

The totalizing overreach inherent in Kemalism arguably has engendered violence in other ways, beyond Turkey's borders. As is well established, the Kemalist recipe of heavy-handed secularism and nationalism has proved influential for many other modern leaders throughout the Middle East and the rest of the Muslim world. Kemal's "authoritarian secularism," as An-Na'im writes, "has been a hallmark of several countries in the region, from the Ba'ath Party, dictatorship in Iraq and Syria and Arab nationalism in Egypt under Nasser to the French model of Tunisia under Bourguiba and Marxist Algeria under the FLN [National Liberation Front]."[105] Despite diverse antecedent conditions and degrees of variation, "Kemalist secularism has constituted a model for the entire Muslim world," echoes Pierre-Jean Luizard, a scholar of secularism in the Middle East.[106] For serious Muslims with a commitment to practice their faith, this has presented a twofold problem: it has led them to associate secularism with humiliating bans and constant harassment of their religious communities even as it has nourished extremist voices in their midst intent on rejecting secularism root and branch in favor of militant alternatives. Turkey's story thus "serves as a warning," according to the contemporary Muslim reformer Mustafa Akyol: "Secularization achieved by the wrong means may not give birth to a liberal state, but rather to a draconian one unchecked by all traditional constraints as well as modern ones." The main secular regimes in the Arab world—the republican dictatorships in Egypt, Syria, and pre-2003 Iraq—are examples of this huge problem. "The secularism of the young Turkish Republic was just too radical and illiberal," Akyol continues, "to be accepted by pious segments of the Turkish population. It did introduce some admirable reforms in a top-down fashion, such as advancing women's rights, but its authoritarianism created opposition—an opposition that manifested not just as resistance to authoritarianism but also to the secularism that came along with [it]. . . . It is unfortunate that this is the main model of secularism the Muslim world has been exposed to, whereas the more benign models of the secular state are largely unknown."[107]

Finally, and to spotlight one particular issue, one wonders, as a historical counterfactual, what might have happened if Kemalist overreach had not extended to abolishing the caliphate but had permitted it to exist in some nominal and largely spiritual form. Again, this hoary institution, permitting a type of Muslim "pope," commanded the loyalty of the faithful across the Muslim world. During its thirteen centuries, it had experienced many vicissitudes, to be sure, but it remained a potent symbol of Muslim unity and identity, and its abrupt abolition under Kemal appeared to many as an act of sacrilege and betrayal. It is no coincidence that the Muslim Brotherhood in Egypt (f. 1928), the model and spawning ground of numerous Islamist movements in the twentieth century, traces its origins directly to the caliphate's abolition as a "traumatic turning point."[108] Whether, absent its abolition, a more moderate, secular course in Turkey would have resulted in different historical outcomes is, of course, a speculative matter. Even so, one cannot help but wonder if we see here—as with the rise of the Cristeros in Mexico or Franco's Nationalists in Spain—an example of extremity begetting extremity, of embattled, violence-prone religiosity taking root and growing in the rich sediment provided by zealous secularist overreach.

CHAPTER THREE

Soviet Severities

Whoever is for Easter is against socialism.
—Slogan of the Soviet Union's League of the Militant Godless

IN OCTOBER 1917 (EARLY NOVEMBER BY THE GREGORIAN
calendar), the Bolsheviks, led by Lenin fresh from exile in Switzerland, seized
power in Petrograd—the founding act of what became known after 1922 as
the Soviet Union. The contours of its story are well known: not long after
prevailing in a brutal civil war, Lenin died unexpectedly in 1924, and the
mantle of leadership made its way to Stalin once he had triumphed over
his archrival, Leon Trotsky. Intensifying the violence and paranoia present
in the early regime, and adding to them massive, crash projects of industrialization and agricultural collectivization, Stalin exercised leadership
through World War II and into the early Cold War, eventually succeeded
after his death, in 1953, by Nikita Khrushchev. Khrushchev stood at the helm
for more than a decade, followed in 1964 by Leonid Brezhnev's long ten-
ure. After the deaths of Brezhnev's two aged successors in the mid-1980s,
Mikhail Gorbachev introduced reforms that contributed to the revolutions
in Soviet-dominated Eastern Europe in 1989 and then the collapse of the
Soviet Union in 1991.

From the outset, the one-party Soviet regime sought the demise of religious belief and institutions, using propaganda, reeducation efforts, and
more aggressive tactics as necessary. A post-religious civilization espousing
"scientific atheism" and the creation of a "new man" served as the final goal.
As the *ABC of Communism* (a popular explanation of party principles) put it
bluntly in 1919: "Religion and communism are incompatible, both theoretically and practically."[1] In various forms, these commitments impacted Soviet
client states, such as Mongolia in the 1930s and most of Eastern Europe
after World War II. They had grown from the soil of Marxist ideology and

the broader heritage of European and Russian radical thought in the nine-teenth century—what I have called *eliminationist secularism*. They bore fruit in the decades following the October Revolution of 1917, beginning with the regime's struggles against the Russian Orthodox Church, regarded as especially worrisome due to its size, wealth, and historical ties to tsarism. These struggles were never simple or straightforward but at times, especially in the 1930s, succeeded with appalling levels of violence and destruction. Incrementally, the onslaught against Orthodoxy spread to other religious communities within the vast multi-confessional, multiethnic empire that Soviet leaders inherited from the tsars and sought to hold together.

In each case, one sees eliminationist secularism at work, despite the fact that Bolsheviks did not have an agreed-upon "blueprint" for their religious policy. Marx and Engels had provided a theory about religion's decline but not a specific plan to eradicate it. To this point, permit a few additional cave-ats and qualifications. First, repression varied considerably with respect to time and place, and it was often shaped by local and regional factors. Some-times it was severe, sometimes moderate; sometimes operating through legal means, sometimes extralegal ones. Second, anti-religious motives mixed with others, including those based on class struggle, on worries about eth-nic separatism, and on fears of religious bodies encouraging "anti-Soviet" or "counterrevolutionary" mentalities. Third, although many religious elites complied with the new Caesar, sometimes to the point of sycophancy, believers did not simply keel over and accept their fate; they often put up resistance or coped by going underground, making tactical concessions, and/ or cultivating ties to coreligionists outside the Soviet Union.[2] Not infre-quently, zealous anti-religious measures produced ironic results, quickening the resolve among the pious to double down on their faith commitments. Fourth, state and party officials regularly adopted a strategy of involving the government in religious affairs by supporting factions, insisting on pliable people for vacant posts, and enlisting secret informants, among other means. Finally, although Soviet authorities had internal disagreements about how to implement eliminationist secularism, we might speak of two principal approaches: the passive and the proactive. The former believed that improv-ing the socioeconomic conditions of life should be the abiding policy goal. If this took place, religion would inexorably peter out, as classical Marxism forecast. By contrast, the latter approach—and the one more often in the driver's seat in the early regime—believed that religious actors constituted an especially dangerous and obstinate enemy and had to be aggressively countermanded. "We cannot be complacent and expect that religion...will die by itself without any struggle," wrote L. F. Ilychev, Khrushchev's chief ideologist, reflecting the latter position; "[rather,] it is imperative to oppose religion with militant, progressive, scientific-atheist propaganda."[3]

Caveats and qualifications notwithstanding, measures of eliminationist secularism in the twentieth century affected countless people throughout the Soviet Union and in states under its influence and authority after 1917. "Next to economic hardships," as the historian Richard Pipes has written, "no action of Lenin's government [and its successors] inflicted greater suffering on the population at large than the profanation of its religious beliefs, the closing of houses of worship, and the mistreatment of clergy."[4] A panoramic view of these actions, beginning with Orthodoxy then proceeding to other faith traditions in the Soviet Union, attests to a brutal legacy of repression, destruction, and death.

ORTHODOXY

From the October Revolution of 1917 until the outbreak of World War II, two major phases in the Soviet assault on religion took place. The first, early on called the "storm and push" phase by one of its leaders, Yemelyan Yaroslavsky, lasted from the outbreak of the Revolution until the late 1920s, with special intensity in the regime's early years and some relaxation later on—a time that corresponded to the economic policies of War Communism and Lenin's New Economic Policy (NEP). The legal dismemberment, financial ruin, and decimation of dissent within the Orthodox Church served as the initial goals, but repression affected several other faith communities as well. The 1929 law "on religious associations" after Stalin's accession to power inaugurated a second, more extreme phase, directed against practically all religious communities, spiking during 1929–32 and then again during the Great Terror of 1936–38. Only the outbreak of the Second World War led to the adoption of more moderate policies, motivated largely by Stalin's cynical desire to enlist religious sentiment in the war effort and placate ethnic minorities. A tenuous postwar modus vivendi prevailed between the state and (most if not all) religious communities, but after Khrushchev secured power, broad-based repression returned, especially between 1959 and 1964 but enduring with varying degrees of coercion and intimidation until the waning years of the regime in the 1980s.

Upon coming to power, Bolsheviks sought to build an atheistic Communist state on the ruins of "holy Russia." The liberal revolutions of 1905 and February 1917 had loosened ties between throne and altar and introduced some measure of pluralism. Still, as the historian Victoria Smolkin has summed up, "religion [on the eve of the October Revolution] remained at the core of politics, bureaucracy, culture, and education, and continued to be embedded in the places and practices of everyday life, ordering space and time, separating work and rest, shaping communal bonds around a shared history, and forming the foundation of individual and group identity."[5] Proudly borrowing from the playbook of the French Revolution, Bolsheviks issued decrees nationalizing ecclesiastical properties, establishing a secular civil service, and removing the registration of births, marriages, and deaths from religious authorities. Priests lost rights of ownership and means of support. A crowning "Decree on the Separation of Church and State and School from Church" (23 January 1918) deprived religious bodies of legal status and curtailed religious education, except in the privacy of the home. In addition, Bolsheviks seized church bank accounts, banned state subsidies to the church, and took away administrative control of parishes from the clergy, putting control in the hands of groups of lay parishioners (with a minimum of twenty), who were obliged to pay a special fee for the ongoing use of church buildings.[6]

The first Soviet constitution (10 July 1918) codified these measures. It permitted "freedom of conscience" and a narrowly defined right to private worship, banning all other forms of pastoral and social outreach. Atheism, by contrast, had no restrictions placed on it. In effect, the constitution and the prior decrees massively decentered religious bodies from mainstream society, forcing them to the margins of private life, whereas atheism became the normative ideological center of the new Soviet society.[7] These legal arrangements not only mark a turning point from the old regime to the new in Russia, they also possess a paradigmatic significance given their subsequent imitation by other Communist regimes in the twentieth century.[8] Importantly, throughout the entire existence of the Soviet Union, its leaders made public appeals to the freedom of worship in the 1918 constitution (and its successors) even if the same laws, combined with the party's anti-religious activities, decimated the public role of the church and served as a prelude to massive persecution. Many minority religious bodies existing in the shadow of the Orthodox Church—Protestants of various types, Old Believers and other Orthodox schismatic groups, Catholics, Jews, Buddhists, and Muslims—inclined at first to appreciate the new laws, and, with the exception of Catholics, some even enjoyed a tranquil period of the government's disinterest, not fully realizing that the changes afoot would ultimately deleteriously affect them as well.[9]

The reconfiguration of church-state relations set the stage for greater repression and anti-religious propaganda. Strong clerical expression of anti-Communist sentiment during the Russian Civil War (1917–22), not least that voiced by the newly elected patriarch, Tikhon of Moscow, contributed to the church's plight.[10] In retaliation, the new regime arrested and killed dozens of bishops and thousands of lower-level clergy, along with many monks and nuns and hundreds of activist laypeople. Numerous churches, monasteries, and convents were raided, desecrated, and shut down or turned into cinemas, schools, health centers, and the like. A department of the People's Commissariat of Justice, aptly nicknamed the "liquidation department," spearheaded these efforts, while a Commissariat of Enlightenment initiated anti-religious propaganda.[11] Streets, squares, and buildings named after church and imperial personages were rechristened to glorify heroes of socialism and enlightened thought. During the Civil War, the secret police, or Cheka, headed by Felix Dzerzhinsky, and/or Red Army forces sometimes arrived in a village and, with the support of local partisans, publicly humiliated the local priest, treating him as a symbol for all prerevolutionary ills.

The new regime especially had it in for monasteries and bishops. A tie exists between the two, because in the Orthodox tradition the higher clergy—the so-called "black" clergy—could come only from the line of celibate monks and not from the "white" line of married parish priests. The former tended to be more reactionary. By 1921, most Russian Orthodox monasteries were forced to close, the monks (and nuns) in them pauperized and sometimes slain if not aggregated into coerced work communes.[12] During Holy Week of 1918, Hermogenes, the bishop of Tobolsk and Siberia, was imprisoned and then drowned in a river. Joachim, the archbishop of Nizhny Novgorod, a notable scholar, was hanged upside down from the iconostasis of the Sebastopol Cathedral. Communist cadres tortured Bishop Makarii of Viaz'ma, placed him in a dungeon, and later shot him in a field with fourteen others. Drunken Red Army soldiers shot, mutilated, and castrated

Vladimir, the metropolitan archbishop of Kiev.[13] In the early 1920s, thousands of "black" clergymen began to populate the incipient Gulag system, soon mostly at the Solovetsky Island prison on the White Sea, appropriately enough a former monastery complex. Clergy not imprisoned were still considered *lishentsy*, disenfranchised people, who faced a host of penalties and deprivations.

As in the Spanish Civil War, violence extended to the dead. In 1919 Moscow launched a campaign of exhuming bodies of saints in an effort to expose veneration of relics as a sham imposed by the clergy on gullible believers. The opening of the sarcophagus of Sergius of Radonezh, among Russia's most revered national saints, on 11 April 1919 inaugurated this so-called exposure campaign, and it lasted roughly a decade, scandalizing and humiliating the faithful. "We . . . do not want this intrusion into our faith," one petition from believers in Tver protested; "we protest with all our soul and ask that you attend to our voice."[14] Newsreel footage from the era shows Bolsheviks, with approving doctors and scientists on hand, exultantly exhibiting decomposing skulls and bones as simple parishioners look on, saddened, dismayed.

While local Bolshevik thugs and sympathizers account for some of the early postrevolutionary violence, atrocities enjoyed sanction at the highest levels. This became especially clear during the so-called confiscation campaign following the civil war in 1922, when millions succumbed to starvation, cannibalism, and/or death, especially in the Volga region. With anti-religious efforts tasked to Trotsky, the new regime demanded that the church hand over all its valuables for famine relief with the intention of inventorying church wealth and calumniating church leaders if they refused.[15] Churches surrendered many valuable items voluntarily, but, heeding an appeal from Patriarch Tikhon, often retained consecrated items for sacramental purposes. Cunningly, Lenin espied in such resistance an "exceptionally beneficial" opportunity to gain a "crushing victory" over the clerical enemy. "[We can] ensure for ourselves for many decades the required positions," he wrote in a secret memo (19 March 1922) to his Politburo colleagues:

It is now and only now, when in the regions afflicted by the famine there is cannibalism and the roads are littered with hundreds if not thousands of corpses that we can (and therefore must) pursue the acquisition of [church] valuables with the most ferocious and merciless energy, stopping at nothing in suppressing resistance. . . . I have come to the unequivocal conclusion that we must now give the decisive and merciless battle to the Black Hundreds clergy and subdue resistance with such brutality that they will not forget it for decades to come. . . . [T]he trial of the Shuia rebels who oppose help to the starving should be conducted with maximum swiftness and end with the execution of a very large number of the most influential and dangerous Black Hundreds of Shuia, and insofar as possible, not only of that city but also of Moscow and several other church centers. . . . The greater the number of the representatives of the reactionary bourgeoisie and reactionary clergy that we will manage to execute in this affair, the better.[16]

The referred-to opposition in Shuia represented one among the eventually 1,414 documented cases of "bloody excesses" in 1922 as priests and parishioners tried to guard churches, monasteries, and other holy sites against despoliation. Numerous clergy were brought to "justice" in crude anticlerical trials, rehearsals for Stalin's spectacular show trials of the 1930s. In all, from the spring of 1922 until the spring of 1923, when confiscation efforts were in full force, fifty-five tribunals tried 231 cases involving 732 people accused of obstructing confiscations, of whom 44 were executed and 346 received prison terms.[17] This excludes thousands of summary executions, for which no reliable data exists, although estimates range as high as eight thousand. According to church records, 2,691 priests, 1,962 monks, and 3,447 nuns perished by violent means during this period.[18] Notably, the high-ranking metropolitan Benjamin of Petrograd was tried in the summer of 1922 for resisting confiscations, defrocked, and then secretly shot in the back of the skull on 11 August 1922, along with several others. By the end of 1923, twenty-eight bishops had been slain altogether. In retrospect, the confiscation campaign was clearly a ruse; as the famine played out, the government exported nearly a million tons of grain to help fund the Revolution, and church valuables yielded far less than the Bolsheviks had anticipated.[19]

The confiscation campaign facilitated another Bolshevik ploy: exacerbating divisions within the church. For some time prior to the Revolution, a split between traditionalists and modernizers (known as the Renovationist or Living Church) had developed. The modernizers by and large went along with the confiscation campaign, while the traditionalists, led by Patriarch Tikhon (placed under house arrest in May 1922) did not. Regarding the Renovationist Church as a tactical but dispensable ally, the Bolsheviks offered it public support, integrating it even into the party-state bureaucracy. Trotsky advocated assassinating Tikhon, a harsh critic of the Renovationists, but Lenin demurred, fearing a backlash. As things turned out, Tikhon, likely tortured and worried that the Bolsheviks were around to stay, coughed up a statement of support for the regime in July 1923.[20] The government consequently dropped its case against him, allowing many Renovationist churches to return to the Orthodox fold under Tikhon's leadership. When Tikhon died in April 1925, several potential non-Renovationist successors had either been slain, were languishing in prison, or were seen as tainted by the regime. The government successfully promoted the candidacy of Sergius, a former Renovationist, who in 1927 declared sycophantic support of the regime to the consternation of many coreligionists critical of both Tikhon and Sergius, whom posterity has judged harshly for his collaborationist stance.[21] Several bishops and many priests inside Russia in fact refused to cast their lot with Sergius (who was not installed as patriarch but served until 1943 only in a *locum tenens* capacity), preferring either the Gulag or the honest precarity of operating underground in what became a sizable, diverse Catacomb Church, also known as the "True Orthodox Church." For its part, the Renovationist movement did not subside until the 1940s.

Following the confiscation campaign and the church split, direct assaults on the church slackened in the mid-1920s, granting a reprieve and a partial return to normalcy. But this was never entirely the case, for anti-religious propaganda kicked into high gear at this time. Lenin himself had called for "untiring atheist propaganda and [an] untiring atheist fight."[22] Already by 1920 the fledgling government had set up official organs that, among other functions, helped promote atheism and combat religiosity; these included the Department of Cults within the People's Commissariat of Justice, headed by the fanatically anti-religious Piotr Krasikov; the secret security apparatus, or Cheka; and the Agitation and Propaganda Department of the Central Communist Party Committee (Agitprop). These organizations operated under the guidance of article 13 of the Eighth Party Congress (1919), which enjoined the party "to destroy the ties between the exploiting classes and the organizations of religious propaganda, [while] at the same time helping the toiling masses . . . to liberate their minds from religious superstition."[23] This mandate gave rise to a sizable propaganda campaign in the 1920s aimed to portray religion as a backward, counterrevolutionary force, inimical to modernity. Journals, newspapers, and magazines appeared with such titles as *Revolution and the Church, Village Godless, Militant Atheism, Atheists at the Workbench,* and *Godless.* These, along with the two leading Soviet dailies, *Pravda* and *Izvestia,* delighted in running pieces depicting clergy as hidebound, often lecherous ne'er-do-wells craftily misleading people.[24] Orthodoxy received the brunt of the ridicule, but other faiths got their share too.

The year 1925 witnessed the birth of the League of the Godless, a quasi-governmental organization, renamed the League of the *Militant* Godless in 1929. Led by Yemelyan Yaroslavsky, editor of *Godless,* it aggregated under its aegis several earlier anti-religious initiatives. With "the struggle against religion is a struggle for socialism" as its motto, it aimed to replace religious commitment with an atheistic, progressive, scientific mind-set among Soviet citizens. In addition to publishing, the league sponsored public lectures and debates, sent out anti-religious crusaders (*bezbozhniki*) to the countryside, established atheist cells in villages, waged a war of ideas in posters and cartoons, staged mock religious events, and worked alongside the comparably anti-religious Komsomol (the Communist Youth League) to ensure that young people got the message.[25] Capturing the hearts and minds of children and pitting them against older generations emerged as an especially vital goal for Bolsheviks in the 1920s. The league also supported the establishment of anti-religious museums (figure 5), usually setting them up in former churches and monasteries, in which religious belief was depicted in the most lurid and unflattering light possible. Petrograd's Kazan Cathedral and Moscow's Strastnoy Monastery (demolished by Stalin in the 1930s) housed two of the more famous museums. By the 1930s, around one hundred had cropped up in Russia and other Soviet republics, occupying synagogues and mosques as well.[26]

With the Komsomol, the league contributed to a boom of counter-rituals in the 1920s, meant to mock religion and heap scorn on traditional feast days. One so-called Anti-Christmas from the period, coordinated to take place in Moscow and hundreds of other cities, featured clowns mocking God, a figure of the deity embracing a nude woman, and mock priests and rabbis chanting an obscene liturgy—all culminating in images of Christ, the Buddha, Mohammad, Osiris, and other deities thrown into a raging bonfire, making clear that ultimately the struggle aimed at all faiths, not just Orthodoxy. Bolsheviks also promoted ersatz rites of passage, substituting "Red" secularist for religious meanings. Party members' babies were thus

Figure 5. Saint Volodymyr's Cathedral in Kiev during the Soviet era. The sign above the door reads: "Anti-religious Museum." Photographer unknown. Courtesy of Wikimedia Commons.

christened—or "Octobered," as the expression went—into the Revolution. "Red" weddings and funerals took place, the latter invariably taking the form of cremation—frowned upon by the church—with the first national crematorium provocatively installed in Moscow's desecrated Donskoy monastery.[27] Although often ineffective, these counter-rituals sadly often resulted in "the tragic polarization of village life."[28]

The years 1928–30 mark a major turning point in Soviet history, sometimes called the Second Revolution or the Great Turn. It included an even
more vicious campaign against the Russian Orthodox Church, and against
other religious communities too.[29] At this time, Stalin had secured absolute
power over rivals, ended Lenin's New Economic Policy, and begun the first
five-year plan of breakneck industrialization, collectivization of agriculture, and de-kulakization, the brutal repression of wealthy and uncooperative peasants. Already at the Fifteenth Party Congress in 1927, the former
Georgian seminarian insisted: "[The Party] cannot be neutral toward religion, and [must] conduct anti-religious propaganda against all religious
prejudices because it stands for science."[30] Stalin worried that measures
against ecclesiastical higher-ups had in numerous instances actually
empowered local parishes and the more well-to-do peasants (*kulaks*) who
patronized them and served on their councils.[31] A secret party memorandum entitled "On Measures for the Intensification of Anti-Religious
Work" (January 1929) noted, "Religious organizations are the only legally
existing counterrevolutionary organizations" and therefore a "merciless
war" must be waged against them.[32] Decrees and new legislation came
in 1929 that sought to cripple the church at the parish level; bureaucrats
spoke of a "kulak-clergy front" in need of countering and eliminating.[33] At
this time, there "was in effect," as the historian Gregory L. Freeze has written, "an attempt to disestablish the church at its grassroots, to eradicate
the parish as a center of religious activists and presumed opposition."[34]
Most crucially, a law on "religious associations" (8 April 1929) made the
registration of all religious groups compulsory and forbade any religious
activity apart from private worship as an illegal, anti-Soviet activity, thus
setting up waves of summary arrests and deportations to the Gulag. The
new measures forbade priests to join collective farms, deprived them of
social-security rights and housing opportunities, banned them from edu-
cating the young, made them subject to various fees, and saddled them
with onerous taxes.[35]

Meanwhile, an uninterrupted workweek was introduced that abolished
Sunday and other religious holidays in an effort to remake the Soviet experience of time and maximize efforts toward industrialization.[36] A 1929 memorandum from the League of the Militant Godless bluntly declared, "Whoever
is for Easter is against socialism. Religion is the enemy of industrialization
in the country."[37] Christmas holidays became "Days of Industrialization."

Adding to these measures, party officials encouraged greater anti-religious propaganda in a concerted effort to stamp out "superstition" once and for all and the reactionary mind-set enabling it. The anti-religious press in 1929 and 1930 brimmed with captions such as "Let us deal a crushing blow to

Figure 6. Cover of the Soviet-era magazine *Godless* (*Bezbozhnik*) from 1929, showing Stalin's five-year plan crushing figures representing Judaism, Christianity, and Islam. Artwork by staff of *Bezbozhnik*. Courtesy of Wikimedia Commons.

religion!" and "We must achieve liquidation of the church and complete liquidation of religious superstition." Priests and the pious, along with kulaks, were portrayed as rats, vermin, contemptible enemies of the people.[38] A 1929 cover of *Godless* revealingly showed a symbol of Stalin's five-year plan crushing figures representing Judaism, Christianity, and Islam (figure 6). Additional aspects of the "godless" five-year plan included the intensification of anti-religious efforts in education; the closing, repurposing, and destruction of churches; and stepped-up persecution of the clergy at all levels.

Practically all institutions of higher teaching and research set up special anti-religious departments. Theological seminaries, for the most part already closed in the early 1920s, completely ceased to function, except underground. A faculty committed exclusively to promoting "scientific atheism"—the so-called Institute of Red Professors (f. 1921)—received fresh purpose and funding, while many two-year evening "workers' antireligious universities" cropped up in major cities.[39] Overtly religious citizens faced obstruction in admission to schools and denial of promotion in the workplace. Beginning in 1928, anti-religious education became mandatory, starting in first grade. Children's literature, textbooks, field trips, and science experiments were enlisted in the struggle to win children over to atheism. Propaganda material from the time regularly features hopeful young people eager to participate in Soviet modernity impeded by an aged, hunched *babushka* (grandmother) intent on poisoning their minds with religion. "The attempt to pull children away from ideologically harmful influences and push them toward secularism and, ultimately, atheism, set up a conflict between public and private worlds, between state institutions and family that lasted for the entire Soviet period," as the historian Julie deGraffenried has remarked.[40]

While the 1929 law technically permitted one to practice one's faith within the confines of a church, Soviet authorities shut down thousands of churches during the late 1920s and 1930s. Although precise figures are elusive, compelling estimations suggest that in 1928 roughly thirty thousand churches remained open from a pre-1917 number of more than fifty thousand. Due to the Great Turn and collectivization measures, around 64 percent of these thirty thousand were closed by 1936. A final concentrated period of closures took place between 1936 and 1938, so that by the eve of World War II only about two hundred churches, 1–2 percent of the prerevolutionary total, were functioning in the entire Soviet Union.[41] Of the roughly one thousand plus monasteries and convents functioning in 1917, not a single one remained openly operating in 1939. The indignities visited on Orthodox churches at this time began to be extended to other faith communities and their architecture.

But numbers alone do not tell the full story. Beginning in 1929, prior to many church closures, Soviet officials had begun a campaign of silencing and seizing church bells—"aural icons" in the Orthodox tradition—to melt down for industrializing purposes. Their ringing recalled the traditional past. Taking them away thus purged the landscape of a potent religious symbol while feeding the exigencies of economic progress. Visual icons were targeted too, as icon painting, a hallmark of Orthodox worship, was rendered an illegal activity, punishable by up to four years in prison. Thousands upon thousands of icons were hauled out of churches, then smashed, burned, sold, or sent to museums.[42] Once shuttered, many churches were repurposed to serve as warehouses, prisons, clinics, factories, and the like, suggesting a tight link between processes of collectivization and industrialization and the church closures.[43] Not infrequently, and symbolically blunt, many former churches became cinemas regularly featuring anti-religious films, a still relatively new medium regarded by Soviet propagandists as a formidable weapon in their ideological arsenal.[44]

Yet many churches and monasteries were simply destroyed, their building materials used for various mundane purposes. This of course, too, made a powerful symbolic statement. The demolition of Moscow's imposing Cathedral of Christ the Savior, the city's largest church, serves as a case in point. Dating from the early 1800s, it witnessed in 1882 the premiere of Tchaikovsky's *1812 Overture*. In 1931, Stalin ordered it dynamited to create a palatial seat for the legislature, the Supreme Soviet (figure 7). Construction, however, came to a halt due to funding issues, the outbreak of war, and problems with flooding. Eventually, the space became a massive brutalist-style open-air swimming pool. Other destroyed churches include Saint Petersburg's Old Trinity Cathedral, the multi-domed Trinity Church in Novocherkassk, the Church of the Wisdom of God in Nakhichevan-on-Don, the Simonov Monastery complex in Moscow, and Saint Michael's Golden-Domed Monastery in Kiev. In point of fact, Kiev's skyline of holy sites witnessed almost complete obliteration by the late 1930s.[45] Sadly, these demolitions only scratch the surface of a vast, almost incomprehensible ruin of sacred architecture in both urban and rural areas—measures imitated by several

Figure 7. Destruction of Moscow's Cathedral of Christ the Savior in 1931.
Photographer unknown. Courtesy of Wikimedia Commons.

subsequent Communist regimes. "On the road from Moscow to Yaroslavl," Alexander N. Yakovlev, head of the Commission for Rehabilitating Victims of Political Repression in the 1990s, ruefully remembered, "dozens of shattered monuments of the past stood like silent witnesses to the crimes of the regime."[46]

Of course, Stalin's accession to power and the Great Turn also came with a tragic human cost. The imprisonment and execution of priests, religious, and hierarchs increased significantly under Stalin, spiking in 1929–32 and again in 1936–38—the years corresponding to the Great Terror, a country-wide, paranoid sweep against "enemies of the state," replete with high-profile show trials and executions, coming on the heels of some relaxation of militancy between 1933 and 1936. Article 58 in the Soviet Criminal Code against "counter-revolutionary activity" regularly served as the pretext for countless arrests during this time. In 1937, a census—officially suppressed because of the high number of citizens who still classified themselves as religious—made clear that religion remained a powerful force. The late 1930s therefore witnessed even greater intentional targeting of priests, as the notorious, top-secret "NKVD order 00447" (30 July 1937)—a directive against "anti-Soviet elements" first discovered in 1992—makes clear. (NKVD is the Russian acronym for the People's Commissariat of Internal Affairs, a secret police agency that was the forerunner of the KGB.) Twice this document singles out "church officials and sectarians" as desirable for elimination.[47] Data on the executions of priests in the city of Ulyanovsk shows that most of them took place in 1937 (53 killings) and 1938 (192 killings) with fewer executions earlier; the execution of 55 priests there on 17 February 1938 represents one of the largest of these events. On the eve of the Second World War, only a few thousand clergy were still active in the Orthodox Church across the country, down from about sixty-six thousand before the Revolution. The hierarchy had dwindled to two metropolitans and two bishops. Overall, across the Soviet Union, about thirty-five thousand priests were executed or imprisoned in the 1930s, with a large spike in numbers in 1937 and 1938. Some estimates are even higher.[48]

When one does all the math with respect to mortality from the Revolution to the outbreak of World War II, evidence suggests that sixty-eight bishops were slain, and tens upon tens of thousands of parish priests and religious, men and women.[49] Many of their fates have never been accounted for, and this does not include thousands of lay activists and representatives of other faiths that perished as well or wound up in Soviet labor camps, often disappearing forever.

All the while, Soviet authorities with the help of gullible Western sympathizers claimed to international audiences that religious freedom prevailed in the country and that no one was targeted for religious reasons, only for posing a threat to national security. The indictment of one Father Mikhail Yedlinsky, a priest serving in Kiev, is thus fairly typical: "He is charged with being an active participant in counter-revolutionary [activity]. . . . He made use of the church for slanderous sermons directed at Soviet power." A firing squad executed Yedlinsky on 13 November 1937; he was joined in death by the bishop of Zhitomir and some 200 priests under him, all shot in the early winter of 1937—the same year that witnessed the death of 122 priests and monks in Rostov-on-Don.[50] Such was the nature of this era, the brutality of which affected not only priests but parishioners too. "To be associated with the church," as the historian Dimitry V. Pospielovsky has helpfully

Figure 8. Soviet anti-religious propaganda at the entrance to the Dormition Cathedral at Kiev's Cave Monastery. The sign reads: "Monks—bloody enemies of the working class." Photographer unknown. Courtesy of Wikimedia Commons.

summarized the general situation of the Orthodox Church in the late 1930s, "was like being infected with the plague. It was dangerous to be seen having any contacts with her, as even a fleeting visit to a functioning church could mean the loss of employment and irreparable damage to a career. . . . In the 1930s people were arrested for such things as having an icon in the home, inviting a priest to perform a private religious rite. . . . Priests who were caught performing such functions were inevitably incarcerated, often disappearing forever in NKVD [successor to the Cheka] dungeons."[51]

The outbreak of World War II brought about a jolting reversal of fortune for the Orthodox Church as Stalin cynically recognized that he needed its support to whip up nationalist sentiment for the war effort. He also did not want to antagonize Orthodox communities in areas of Eastern Europe annexed to the USSR after the Nazi-Soviet pact of 1939. Metropolitan Sergius's own appeal to defend the homeland against fascist invaders played a key role as well, bringing him and Stalin into direct conversation in 1943 that resulted in a détente. Stalin blessed the holding of a bishop's assembly (*sobor*) to officially elect Sergius as patriarch of Moscow and reestablish a Holy

Synod. What is more, Stalin presided over the creation of a new body—the Council for the Russian Orthodox Church Affairs—to mediate church-state relations and, quite frankly, to limit the church's independence by means of what has previously been called conflictual integration.[52] During the war, churches held services again, and many surviving clergy returned to diocesan and parochial duties. In 1944 the Orthodox theological seminary in Moscow, closed after the Revolution, reopened along with several others, and by this time several monasteries trickled back to life. The seven-day week with Sunday as a day of rest returned as well, and organs of anti-religious propaganda found themselves somewhat if not completely muzzled; the League of the Militant Godless disbanded in 1943.[53]

After the war, Soviet officialdom duly noted the patriotic role played by the church, and greater concord between state and church prevailed. But not entirely. Numerous bishops and priests tied to the True Orthodox Church, who refused to recognize Sergius's leadership, remained in their places of exile or imprisonment unless they renounced their views. Non-Orthodox religious leaders in territories that had been under German occupation were dispatched to labor camps in high numbers for the slightest hint of having aided the enemy. The reality of so many Catholics and Protestants in these areas, moreover, led Moscow to rethink its strategies toward these groups and others that had thick ties to the West, while a bitter smear-and-hate campaign against the Vatican got off the ground. The Greek or Byzantine Rite Catholics in Soviet areas, moreover, faced extreme trials after the war (more about this later), caught between the contempt of Bolsheviks, on one hand, and long-standing rivalry with the Orthodox, on the other. The laws and decrees that had enabled the repressions of the 1930s, moreover, remained on the books and could be reactivated at the government's whim. Finally, producing independent samizdat literature and/or actively propagating one's faith could be met with stiff penalties.

Nevertheless, the wartime modus vivendi between the Russian Orthodox Church and the state generally prevailed after the war, continuing after the death of Stalin, in 1953, into Khrushchev's era. By 1957, about twenty-two thousand churches had become active again, up from a prewar low of only several hundred. Internationally, Russian Orthodox leaders were permitted to became involved in the Ecumenical Movement, later even joining the World Council of Churches (f. 1948); for this, they received pats on the back at home, especially when criticizing capitalism and showing support for Soviet foreign policy in such forums, as they were obliged to do. This, combined with government-produced booklets for Western consumption—notably *The Truth about Religion in Russia* (1942), issued by the Moscow Patriarchate—and the inclination of many Westerners to see Khrushchev as a liberal reformer, went a long way to persuade external audiences that a friendlier climate for believers had arrived.[54]

But the situation of the Orthodox Church, as well as other religious communities, actually worsened in the late 1950s and early 1960s as churches (and other religious communities) confronted a paradox presented by Khrushchev. On the one hand, after his Secret Speech of 1956, Khrushchev called for de-Stalinization, a remembrance of and reckoning with the regime's bloody excesses in the 1930s. On the other hand, Khrushchev made it clear that the Marxist-Leninist case against religion remained official ideology and should receive new life. Evidence of this stance in fact appeared as early as 1954 in a burst of anti-religious activity known as the "Hundred Days Campaign" and was underscored in several party reports and decrees from the mid-1950s.[55] Religious "survivals," as Khrushchev himself stressed at the Twenty-Second Party Congress in 1961, are "like a nightmare that prevail over the minds of living creatures."[56] Beginning two years beforehand, both anti-religious propaganda and the persecution of churches revived—not as brutally as during the 1930s, but intentionally, extensively, and violently nonetheless. A Central Committee Party resolution of 9 January 1960 left little room for doubt: "The Party has never reconciled itself, and never will, with ideological reaction. The struggle against religion must not only be continued, but it ought to be enhanced by all possible means."[57]

The successful launching of the first artificial satellite, Sputnik, in 1957 and the cosmonaut Yuri Gagarin's historic manned spaceflight into orbit in 1961 added a "cosmic" dimension to the promotion of scientific atheism, suggesting the almost limitless potential that Marxism-Leninism promised to Soviet citizens. "The voyages," as the historian Victoria Smolkin has noted, "were put forth as a counterexample and an antidote to the fear and weakness that atheists claimed were cultivated by religion."[58] To Khrushchev's simplistic way of thinking, the fact that Soviet cosmonauts did not encounter God in space undercut the credibility of religious belief. Propaganda posters from this time with titles such as "Heaven is Empty!" expressed this theme, practically equating the experience of spaceflight with irrefutable proof of a godless universe.[59] The All-Union Society for the Dissemination of Scientific and Political Knowledge, successor to the League of the Militant Godless, established a journal, *Science and Religion,* promoting atheism, the contents of which were echoed in major newspapers, lectures, films, and, not least, television, a new medium to reach the people. Around seventy propaganda films—led by one entitled *The Road from Darkness*—circulated in the early 1960s, a time when several high-profile "apostasies" from religion received considerable airtime in the Soviet media.[60] Secularist ideologues also staged "evenings of miracles without miracles"—workshops that aimed to show people that many things deemed miraculous in the natural world could be given a wholly materialist explanation. What is more, "scientific atheism" in the classroom received fresh emphasis for all grades, and university-level scholarship critical of religion became a major academic industry. Repeatedly, scholars, in a genre that has been aptly called "denunciatory ethnography," identified religion as a rural problem, the eradication of which could be hastened by exposure, analysis, and criticism.[61] Both cruder forms of propaganda and more refined scholarship depicted priests and monks as drunks, lechers, and worse. The veneration of holy sites, pilgrimages, and other forms of popular piety received ridicule and scorn as well.[62]

Still more forcible measures were brought against believers, beginning in the late 1950s, as the role of the Council for the Russian Orthodox Church Affairs (the Council for Religious Affairs after 1963) transmuted from a mediating body between church and state to a dictatorial administrator over the churches, replete with KGB agents and informants. The harsh anti-religious laws passed in the late 1920s served again as the basis for harassment of the Orthodox Church and other communities of faith. Priests were categorically denied the right to give religious instruction to children, engage in charity work, or do much of anything outside the four walls of a church.[63] The purging of the overtly devout from party organizations, employment, and educational institutions became widely practiced again, as did their reduction in pay and denial of promotion enjoyed by other coworkers. In several cases, authorities took children away from visibly pious families and placed them in state boarding schools. On charges both large and small, priests, monks, and religious activists found themselves arrested, beaten, exiled, and/or sent to prison. Soviet authorities even judged some forms of belief, especially among sectarian groups and political dissenters, as mental illness, with some believers winding up in psychiatric hospitals.[64] Not least, many churches and other buildings devoted to worship or religious instruction were shut down or denied registration in the first place. Five of the eight Orthodox theological seminaries that had opened in the 1940s closed their doors in the early 1960s. The number of active religious houses plummeted from seventy in 1959 to seventeen by the mid-1960s, while functioning churches and chapels declined from around twenty-two thousand in 1960 to around seven thousand five years later.[65] Non-Orthodox faith communities experienced comparable declines.

Noncompliance with Soviet authorities meant trouble. Priests and bishops who resisted measures against their flocks often found themselves forced into retirement, arrested, or subject to harassment. Defiant, pious young people were almost certain to receive summonses for obligatory military service. To turn our discussion from Orthodoxy for a moment, when a major Baptist body—the Union of Evangelical Christian Baptists—sought to heed the Soviet demand that its sermons be less proselytizing and that it rein in its youth outreach, a major split occurred, resulting in the creation of an independent branch known as the Council of Churches of the Evangelical Christians and Baptists, led by the gutsy Georgi Vins. Defiant of Moscow on numerous fronts, well connected to evangelical groups outside the Soviet Union, and a vocal advocate of freedom of speech and belief, this small Baptist denomination became one of the most persecuted religious bodies in the final decades of the Soviet Union.

But it was not alone. With the ouster of Khrushchev in 1964 and the coming to power of Brezhnev, and lasting until the days of Gorbachev, anti-religious repression in word and deed remained an enduring feature of the Soviet Union, even if it was more circumspect in nature and attuned to international perception surrounding human-rights issues, especially after the Helsinki Accords of 1975. Anti-religious propaganda persisted, if at lower decibels, and censorship of religious materials remained a reality of late Soviet society.[66] Until the 1980s, only a few churches and no monasteries were reopened, and several instances of church demolition took place. In the mid-1970s the Council of Religious Affairs acquired additional regulatory powers over all kinds of religious matters. It tended to smile on officially recognized religious bodies, especially those with an international profile willing to pay lip service to the regime, while making life legally and bureaucratically miserable for all others, especially the True Orthodox Church and groups such as the Jehovah's Witnesses, Latter-day Saints, and Seventh-day

Adventists—the latter three considered to be deviant Western-imported cults richly deserving harassment and extinction.[67]

All the while, the harsh 1929 law on religious associations remained on the books, even if enforcement of it never reached Stalinist or Khrushchevian levels. Still, in practice, this meant that all the Orthodox and other religious bodies had to register with the government and provide local authorities with a list of members—effectively giving authorities a tool for discrimination in their places of work, the allocation of housing, and the like, while also making surveillance and infiltration easier. The law forbade the religious education of children, except in the home, and made it extremely difficult for seminaries to operate. Anything that smacked of proselytism was strictly forbidden, as article 142 of the penal code forbade "the performance of deceitful acts with the aim of arousing religious superstitions among the public."[68] This extended to printing and circulating religious literature, including Bibles, or being complicit in smuggling them into the country. What is more, all charity and welfare remained off-limits to Orthodox and other churches—robbing them of something that historically had been central to their sense of mission. Finally, denial of ownership of church property by religious communities continued as the law of the land. This confronted churches with one of their most serious legal difficulties, making it easy to shut them down if any type of dissident activity was suspected. Political dissent among educated religious believers was considered a grave threat, with thousands who fitted this profile arrested and imprisoned or sent to psychiatric hospitals in the late Soviet era; less vocal and uneducated believers tended to be left alone.

Finally, archival evidence has made clear that from the 1960s until the collapse of the Soviet Union there was widespread infiltration of religious bodies by security-force personnel and their informants, aiding the government in exercising control over key appointments and decisions as well as providing general surveillance. A secret document—the "Furov Report"—of the Council of Religious Affairs (prepared for the party's Central Committee), which reached the West in the 1970s, indicated that sermons in particular were highly monitored and actively nudged toward certain ends. "If a priest gives a sermon, they . . . must contain no political or social issues or examples," the report states.[69] Sadly, the complicity of the Russian Orthodox Church in its own subjugation has also come into greater focus since the "archival revolution" of the 1990s. Servility at the patriarchal level, first practiced by Patriarch Sergius under Stalin, continued in various forms into the patriarchates of his successors: Alexius I (r. 1945–70) and Pimen (r. 1971–90). Especially docile clergy who voiced support for the regime even received honorary rank in the KGB![70] In the post-Soviet era, such revelations about the widespread control and co-option of churches by a Caesar philosophically committed to the eventual demise of religion ranks among the most difficult and vexing chapters of the Soviet story.[71]

ISLAM

The Soviet Union inherited imperial Russia's vast, ethnically diverse Muslim populations, concentrated largely in Central Asia, the Caucasus, Crimea, and the Volga region. Sunni Muslims made up the vast majority, some 90 percent, but there were also some Shia, especially in the areas of present-day Azerbaijan and Tajikistan. Sufism, the mystical strain in Islam, permeated practically all areas, influencing both mainstream jurisprudence and expressions of popular piety. A modernizing Muslim reformist movement (Jadidism) had arisen in Central Asia in the late nineteenth century, frequently butting heads with more traditionalist jurists and theologians, the ulama.[72] Under the tsars, Muslims of all stripes had experienced policies of pragmatic flexibility punctuated by periods of harsh repression, especially to stanch separatist movements. Directly after the October Revolution, Bolsheviks dealt gingerly with Muslims under a general policy of *korenizatsiya* (indigenization or nativization) that sought to instill Bolshevik principles and raise up native cadres, while permitting cultural and regional difference.[73] Accordingly, the party-state played down its own anti-religious tenets in Muslim areas, regarding their populations as colonized peoples freshly liberated from tsarist oppression. But all of this changed in the mid-1920s as the antithesis between Marxism-Leninism and Islam became pronounced, and later as Stalinist policies affected Muslim regions.

But in 1917 things looked different. After seizing power, the new Soviet government published an appeal, "To All Toiling Muslims of Russia and the East," proclaiming deliverance from colonialism to Muslims and promising that various national identities and religious beliefs would be respected.[74] Although the 1918 law of church-state separation applied in principle to all areas under Soviet control, it primarily targeted Orthodox communities, as we have seen. A special People's Commissariat for Muslim Affairs came into being under Stalin's Commissariat of Nationalities. In an appeal to the people of Dagestan, the future dictator promised that "the Soviet government ha[d] no thought of declaring war on the Shariah," in an effort to quell rumors to the contrary. Lenin, too, counseled a moderate course. Decrees and laws in the early 1920s went so far as to establish Friday, the Muslim day of prayer, in place of Sunday as a day of rest in predominantly Muslim regions.[75] Many reform-minded Muslims, or Jadids, felt that their hour had come and that dialogue and common purpose might be expected from the new regime.

Yet an uptick of countervailing utterances and actions in the mid-1920s indicated a coming showdown between Islam and Bolshevism, the worst of it taking place under Stalin. In the nineteenth century, Engels had already formulated the basic Marxist stance toward Islam: "The religious revolution of Mohammad was, like every other religious movement, reactionary," deserving obsolescence at some future point.[76] Soviet authorities bristled at the tenacity of Muslims' everyday piety, the obstructive spiritual and legal authority of local imams and mullahs, and a long-standing penchant for separatist movements in Muslim-majority regions. It might be well and good for Muslims to rebel against the tsars, but better not try this under the Soviets. The so-called Basmachi Uprising in fact repeatedly met stiff resistance, with the Red Army massacring twenty-five thousand rebels in 1918 in Kokand in the Fergana Valley in what became Uzbekistan.[77] As the 1920s progressed, Soviet sentiment about Islam grew more vocal and critical, typified in anti-Muslim propaganda and expressed later in the century by the Soviet Islamologist Liutsian Klimovich's contention that "Islam is an anti-scientific reactionary world concept, alien and inimical to the scientific Marxist-Leninist world concept."[78] As Soviet scholars researched the history of Islam, furthermore, they increasingly tagged it as a "feudal" phenomenon, riddled with oppressive class interests.[79]

The ending of the Civil War in 1922 and the Soviets' consolidation of power allowed for the new regime to construct its new vision for society in Muslim regions, Central Asia being among the most crucial given the large size of the Muslim population there and its arable land. It quickly became clear that a thriving Islam had no place in this vision. A resolution at the Twelfth Party Congress in April 1923 conveyed the writing on the wall: "Taking into account that the 30-million Muslim population of the Union of Republics has preserved almost untouched to this day numerous medieval prejudices, linked with religion and used for counter-revolutionary purposes, it is essential to work out forms of and methods of liquidating these prejudices, taking into account the peculiarities of the different nationalities."[80] This last line gives voice to korenizatsiya, which within limits allowed for the expression of ethnic-regional identities. Toward these ends, Moscow established several Muslim-majority administrative units (oblasts) in the early 1920s. In 1924 Soviet Uzbekistan and Turkmenistan were born from regions previously under the dominion of Turkistan, the Emirate of Bukhara, and the Khanate of Khiva. The nascence of Kyrgyzstan, Tajikistan, and Kazakhstan followed. While never solving the problem of ethnic tensions entirely, the creation of these and other "union republics" helped nurture a new political class, the members of which occupied Soviet party organs, ranging from a Central Asian Bureau of the Communist Party, the topmost plenipotentiary organ of the party in the region, down to regional and local bodies staffed by local apparatchiks, the foot soldiers who carried out the assault on traditional Islamic society.[81]

The assault began through the incremental legal strangulation of Muslim institutions. Stalin's promises to the contrary notwithstanding, all traditional courts administering Islamic or Sharia law soon came under siege, making way for the unimpeded reach of Soviet law in 1927, when a decree essentially outlawed Muslim courts and forbade the opening of new ones. In 1925, in Uzbekistan alone, eighty-seven Islamic courts existed; by 1928 not one remained in the entire Soviet Union.[82] A similar fate befell Muslim *waqfs* (endowed charitable foundations); these were gradually bureaucratized and subsumed by the state and regulated out of legal existence by 1930. The abundant Sufi brotherhoods under Soviet rule also found themselves headed for public extinction, even if they carved out a sizable unofficial life for themselves in the coming decades. Finally, Bolsheviks came after the *maktabs* and *madrasas*, which had provided traditional Muslim education under the tsars. Regarded as seedbeds of obscurantism and fanaticism, these schools had no place in the Soviet future, in which compulsory atheistic education was mandated with a remit of scrubbing young people clean of inherited religious prejudices.[83]

In the late 1920s, Stalin's consolidation of power and the beginning of large-scale processes of collectivization, de-kulakization, and industrialization dovetailed with extensive offensives against traditional Muslim society—what the scholar Walter Kolarz once described as the attempted "annihilation of Islam."[84] At this time, propaganda efforts accelerated, led by the League of the Militant Godless, the Komsomol, and other party organs, even if their implementation often proved blundering and ineffective.[85] Through movies, radio, theater, and lectures, Islam was portrayed as a stultifying, deceptive belief system, shackling young minds and working at counter purposes to socialism.[86] In this context, Soviet "Islamology" came into its own, an academic discipline freely combining the study, ridicule, and contempt of its subject matter.[87] Characteristic of other Soviet anti-religious efforts, a stark choice between science and religion, progress and backwardness, confronted Muslims. Muslims' holy days and prayer five times per day came under fire as time-wasting practices, injurious to the Soviet economy. Alcohol and pork were enjoined on entire populations. Muslim reformers, Jadids, who saw eye to eye with the Bolsheviks in some matters, found themselves shoved aside and repressed, accused of proffering cunning religious half-measures, a telltale trait of a "bourgeois" mentality. Muslims faced a policy of "no prayers, no Koran, no feasts" at this time, as one escapee from the Soviet Union summed up his experience.[88]

In Central Asia, Bolsheviks adroitly focused attention on the place of women in traditional Muslim society, arguing that the modern world had no place for the veil or body coverings, and that the emancipation of women meant harnessing their potential for labor. The attempted cultural revolution of women's roles in Muslim societies—usually described as *hujum*, the Uzbek word for "assault"—was one of the Communists' cleverest acts, because in a highly calculated fashion it elicited reprisals from traditional Muslim men and families against women who opted to modernize. Calling out and punishing these (often violent) reprisals in turn permitted greater Soviet intervention in Muslim societies as agents of liberation. The hujum campaign, as the scholar of Central Asia Shoshana Keller has written, "was closely bound to the effort to destroy Islam, and indeed for many Muslims the veil came to symbolize one's loyalty to or disloyalty to the community of believers, with all the weighty ramifications that came with such symbolism." Soviets of course could appreciate symbolism too, staging public burnings of veils and having partisan women dramatically unveil themselves during religious events. Enthusiastic local cadres sometimes even ran through the streets, forcibly ripping veils off women's faces. Such experiences, foisted suddenly and relentlessly on traditional societies, were at once "electrifying, enraging, terrifying."[89] Imams and other holy men unsupportive of the campaign faced exile, imprisonment, and sometimes death. Some went so far as to commit suicide, with one man explaining beforehand that he "did not wish to live through the shame of Muslim women going unveiled."[90]

The late 1920s and 1930s witnessed extensive mosque destructions and closures and additional forms of coercion and violence, not just in Central Asia but in the Caucasus, Crimea, and elsewhere too. Although Soviets left several showcase mosques open in major cities for diplomatic purposes, thousands of others under Stalin were either closed down, destroyed, or converted to serve nonreligious uses, including as anti-religious museums, cinemas, and public lavatories. Whereas in 1917 an estimated twenty thousand mosques existed in the greater Russian Empire, by 1929 fewer than four thousand remained functioning, and by 1935 only sixty registered mosques remained in Uzbekistan, four in Turkmenistan, and twenty in Kazakhstan, with a smattering elsewhere.[91] The mullahs and imams associated with particular mosques often found themselves arrested, exiled, or slain, although some managed to eke out a precarious covert existence, performing religious rites for people in secret. Usually the handiwork of revolutionary troikas (three-member teams) made up of hardcore Communist Party cadres, the closing of mosques and the forbidding of public religious expression affected thousands of Muslim villages in the 1930s.[92] One Central Asian villager's remembrance of the era speaks for many others: "There were mosques in the village, but all of them were torn down. From here to Qarashi [a nearby village] there was not one mosque. . . . People were not allowed to recite *namoz* [the five daily prayers]. For example, during Ruza [Ramadan], six or seven militia would come and find the place where people were praying and would not let them pray. . . . All of the mullahs were cut off, sent away, not allowed."[93] Thousands wound up in the Gulag prison camp system, where they received mistreatment not only by Soviet security forces but often by non-Muslim inmates.[94]

The Soviet assault on Islam in Central Asia and elsewhere took place in the context of Stalin's collectivization and de-kulakization campaigns.[95] The turmoil and trauma created by these actions are almost impossible to exaggerate. In the long run, collectivization rendered Soviet agriculture in Central Asia a cotton monoculture, dangerously dependent on goods from other areas to sustain life. In the short run, it was simply a nightmare. Rather than hand over livestock to the state, Muslim peasants, like those countrywide, regularly slaughtered their herds to enjoy one last feast.

Forced sedentarization of nomadic people in some areas proved equally catastrophic. Similar to the better-known case in Ukraine, collectivization in Kazakhstan led to a demographic implosion of genocidal proportions. Between 1929 and 1933, the quantity of livestock plummeted, precipitating famine and the deaths of an estimated 1.5 million people, nearly a third of the Kazakh population. Throughout it all, mosques fell victim to forcible closure and destruction, and the ulama were silenced and repressed. The general turmoil reached another high point in the Great Terror of 1936–38, resulting in the arrest, death, and/or exile of about fourteen thousand Muslim clergy in Central Asia alone and thousands of others elsewhere.[96] The remaining Jadids along with any public figure charged as a "counterrevolutionary" wound up persecuted or driven into hiding. As is well known, the revolution at this time began to devour its own; many party members who had carried out the mosque and madrasa closures earlier now found themselves liquidated in the paranoid atmosphere of the purges.[97]

The sudden shift in Soviet policy toward Orthodoxy occasioned by World War II had an analogue in Soviet-Muslim relations, at least with respect to relaxing the harsher elements of religious persecution.[98] Many mosques not destroyed flickered to life again in the 1940s along with various forms of public religious observation. In 1944, in addition to a state council for Orthodoxy, a general Council for Religious Affairs came into existence and within it a department to serve as a liaison between the Soviet state and Muslim peoples.

But the war also brought new burdens to Muslims in the form of conscription for military service. Moreover, forced deportations eastward whisked away more than a million Crimean Tatar Muslims, along with Chechens, Ingush, Karachay, and Balkars in the North Caucasus, between 1941 and 1944, on the grounds that they collaborated with German invading forces and sought independence; conveniently, this also facilitated the Russification of these areas, while it destabilized the regions in which the deportees landed by fomenting ethnic tensions.[99] In 1944, Crimean Tatars sometimes had only a few hours to pack their bags and leave their homes— often forever. Soviet agents loaded men, women, and children into cattle cars, in which they endured weeks-long journeys to Central Asian and Siberian locations, where they were essentially dumped, often without any prospect of housing. Short on food, water, and basic sanitation, thousands perished on these journeys or shortly thereafter, with overall mortality figures as high as half a million in what are now recognized as genocidal actions.[100] To add insult to injury, Soviet officials reconfigured and/or dissolved previous political units in areas where deportations had taken place, even deleting their histories in official documents and publications. "Not only was each nation's present obliterated, but its past [was] as well," as the historian Robert Conquest summarized in a groundbreaking study of these coerced resettlements.[101]

In the wartime context, so-called official Islam came into being. In 1943, Moscow allowed for the establishment of a state agency called the Spiritual Administration of the Muslims of Central Asia and Kazakhstan. In addition, three regional spiritual directories or "Muftiates" were established in the 1940s. Moscow hoped that by allowing limited religious activity under bureaucratic oversight, it could better monitor and control Muslims' religious activity. To head these directories, candidates had to show unswerving political loyalty. These so-called Red Muftis, who enjoyed scant support from the Muslim rank and file, willingly declared jihad against the Nazis, oversaw "registered" mosques, and sanctioned public events even on Muslim holidays. They regularly issued fatwas to accommodate Soviet needs, such as relaxing Ramadan fasts to encourage workers to stay on the job. After the war, they did the government's bidding by attempting to persuade Muslim leaders in the Middle East and North Africa that the Soviet Union stood on the right side of history and esteemed its religious minorities. Any practice of Islam not under their auspices that was sizable in scope was considered illegal and repressed.

The postwar era witnessed the prolongation of an approach based on such oversight and control, not on the aggressive violence of the 1920s and 1930s, although Khrushchev's anti-religious campaign between 1959 and 1964 applied to Muslims as well. In the late 1940s, the pilgrimage to Mecca, or the hajj, enjoined as a religious duty on all Muslims, became permissible again to a limited number of applicants. Several madrasas came back to life, allowing for theological education, although in constrained, surveilled Soviet terms. At the same time, anti-Islamic propaganda proceeded apace. The Soviet state remained committed to the triumph of atheism in the long term. Numerous strictures and regulations pinched religious practice, and Muslim dissidents faced harsh treatment. The publication of the Qur'an and other religious texts was tightly controlled, while stories about apostasies from Islam appeared frequently in the Soviet press. Remnants of the

Stalinist-era assault on Islam remained visually ever present, such as streets in the holy city of Bukhara renamed after the Paris Commune, Lenin, Stalin, Marx, and Engels.[102] Promoting pig farms in traditionally Muslim areas was a relished Soviet ploy, the success of which permitted one party newspaper to crow, "The pigs have triumphed over Islam."[103]

Seemingly incongruously, given the Marxist critique of nationalism, much governmental energy in the postwar period went into creating and stabilizing ethno-nationalities in Central Asia on the basis of the "istan" republics that had been created earlier. Soviet leaders reasoned that an expression of regional ethnic identity diluted explicitly religious Islam as a marker of identity and could even promote pan-Soviet loyalty to Moscow, ritualistically cast as a benevolent overseer of multiple nationalities spanning thirteen time zones. But this represented a highly controlled form of nationalism, the regional expressions of which were always understood as a "transitory" phenomenon in classical Marxist-Leninist terms.[104] Within this framework of interpretation, Islam might be countenanced as *heritage* but not as active *faith*.

Although the later Brezhnev and Gorbachev eras witnessed moderately better times for Soviet Muslims, the scars of past assaults did not vanish. Today, the sheer scale of these assaults, including the forced deportations of Muslim populations in the 1940s, is lost on most Westerners, the regions and people affected being simply too remote in time and place. But for Islam, as the historian Adeeb Khalid helpfully spells out, "the consequences [of these assaults] were devastating. In the history of Central Asia, the fury of the [Soviet] regime's attack on Islam and its institutions is comparable perhaps only to that of Genghis Khan, whose conquest of the region seven centuries earlier had caused massive destruction and long-term transformations in religious culture."[105] What were the nature of these transformations? To answer, permit several concluding observations.

Robbed of its historic learned presence and leadership, Islam was rendered more local and rural, synonymous with custom and tradition, with backwardness and the past. By virtually eliminating many structures of traditional Muslim education and high culture, by prohibiting the printing of new texts, and by breaking up age-old chains of oral transmission, the Soviets essentially turned Islam into the satirical caricature that they had of it. The carriers of the Islamic learned traditions, at least those who survived, fell silent in the face of Soviet pressure, leaving the transmission of the faith and discussion of Islamic theology to the less knowledgeable as well as to the politically compromised Red Muftis and their followers.

At the same time, Islam did not vanish. During the late Soviet period, a plucky "unofficial" Islam eked out an existence, sometimes right under the noses of Soviet security forces and propagators of anti-Islamic propaganda. Party higher-ups not infrequently reprimanded their underlings for participating in traditional Muslim activities. Closing mosques, moreover, sometimes seemed like a whack-a-mole affair; when one closed, a clandestine, "unregistered" one might pop up elsewhere. People also continued to seek out Muslim rites to solemnize births, circumcisions, weddings, burials, and the like. Itinerant mullahs often performed these ceremonies, traveling from village to village, living off gifts and handouts. Sufi shrines and brotherhoods also proved resilient in trying circumstances, playing a major role in unofficial Islam. Since making the hajj was almost impossible for the average Soviet Muslim, pilgrimages to the graves of Sufi holy men functioned as a substitute. While officials discouraged these and other Sufi-centered acts of piety, they nonetheless often turned a blind eye, requiring perhaps a bribe or some other favor in return. Since "the Soviet experience caused erosion in Islamic values and nearly annihilated the material Islamic culture," as the scholar of Soviet Islam Muhammet Kocak has summarized, "the transmission of Islamic culture . . . could only be possible through the activities of tariqahs [the Sufi brotherhoods]."[106] Tales of miracles associated with Sufis sent to the Gulags became a staple feature of popular piety.[107]

While popular Sufi practices were largely benign, the same could not be said about the well-documented rise of militant Islam in Central Asia (and across the border in Pakistan and Afghanistan) in the late Soviet period. In part, this development owes its genesis to the spread of the Salafist and Wahhabist strains of Islam from the Middle East. But newly fervent belief was not entirely an import, because it also represents a response to Soviet repression and Muslim militants' imitation of Soviet tactics. Muslim militancy, in other words, ought not to be seen simply as an atavistic throwback to a "medieval" mind-set, as it is sometimes characterized. More accurately, it was born from the combustible mixture of extremist interpretations of certain Muslim teachings, anti-colonialism, and the *modern* lessons learned from the secularizing Soviet experience. These lessons were not simply negative ones, because Islamic militants, inside and outside the Soviet Union, actually learned positive things from the Soviets. Put differently, Soviet-era secularism and persecution, ironically, played a constitutive role in the gen-esis of contemporary Islamic extremism. "The political goals of Islamist movements," as Adeeb Khalid helpfully explains, "owe a great deal, in their formulation, to modern revolutionary ideologies, and to Marxism-Leninism in particular. During the Cold War, Islamists tended to be rabidly anti-Communist in their stance because Communism was a rival ideology, one that rested on universal principles, and was hostile to all religions besides." But that stance, he continues, "should not blind us . . . to the fascination that Marxism-Leninism had for Islamists and the model it provided for success-ful political action." The success of the Bolshevik Revolution "trumpeted its anti-colonial credentials loudly," Khalid concludes; this and the efficacy of the tight-knit party and Communist cell structure enabling it were not lost on Islamists, even if "the revolution for which the Islamists worked was, of course, to be an Islamic one."[108]

Finally, the deracination of ancient structures of Muslim learning and years of pent-up resentment arguably made young minds all the more sus-ceptible to the darker, distinctly modern forms of Islamism wafting into the Soviet Union around the time of its collapse. This and the religio-political tinderbox created by the misbegotten Communist coup in 1978 and Moscow's invasion of Afghanistan in the 1980s—in which Soviet Muslims were humiliatingly drafted to fight against their coreligionists across the border—set in motion unhappy, violent historical forces, enduring, sadly, unto the present. While many other factors were certainly involved, "the direct and indirect role played by Communism in the growth of extremist Islam . . . is undeniable," as the historian of Communism Sylvain Boulouque has summed up.[109]

JUDAISM

The Soviet Union's interaction with Judaism is a complex topic, due in part to the fact that Bolshevism's leadership ranks included numerous Jews, each having forsaken Judaism qua faith to varying degrees, whether from conviction or from expediency. Of course, Marx himself was of Jew-ish background and had set the template of scorning religiously observant Jews in the expectation that they would exchange the God of Abraham, Isaac, and Jacob for the proletarian revolution.[110] Toward this end, Russian Bolsheviks set up a Jewish section (Yevsektsiya) within the party in 1918, composed of irreligious Jews with a mandate to bring about "the destruction of traditional Jewish life, the Zionist movement, and Hebrew culture"—all regarded as particularistic impediments to the universalist, internationalist Soviet vision.[111] Jews assumed these tasks in order to avoid the charge of anti-Semitism, which the Bolsheviks publicly stood against. But if Jewish faith posed a problem to the new state, the question of Jewish *nationality* was a somewhat separate matter, even if the two are not entirely detachable. As the Soviet Union took shape and made concessions to other national identities, the Jewish population was recognized as a legitimate nationality deserving of treatment like other non-Russian groups. In the late 1920s, Moscow even concocted a woolly-headed scheme to provide Jews with their own geographical enclave—the Jewish Autonomous Province of Birobidzhan—in Russia's far east, so long as its settlers agreed to live "without God and Torah" and labor for the socialist commonweal. Ultimately this project amounted to little more than an aspiration, fizzling due to the sheer remoteness of the land and because promoters of Zionism (an ideology despised by Bolsheviks) deemed it a poor substitute for a possible Jewish homeland in Palestine.[112] Once the actual state of Israel came into being in 1948, and even though the Soviet Union recognized it, things soon became more difficult for Soviet Jewry as Soviet leaders began to regard them, whether they were religiously observant or not, as a potential fifth column, harboring subversive loyalties to international Zionism and to the Western states that were more zealous in their support of Jewish nationhood.

Prior to 1917, the Russian Empire's circa five million Jews lived preponderantly in western areas within the so-called Pale of Settlement, from which they were largely forbidden to move. Clustered in urban ghettos and rural shtetls, they faced a host of discriminations and not-infrequent eruptions of anti-Semitic violence, although tsarist governments generally did not meddle with Jews' internal affairs.[113] The 1905 Revolution and the 1917 February Revolution legally emancipated the Jews, and even many non-Communist Jews initially welcomed the revolutionary events of October 1917, seeing in them further relief from discrimination and better educational and employment opportunities. To a degree, this became a reality for Jews willing to secularize and assimilate. Yet any sense of expectation was short-lived from the perspective of more religiously observant Jews once Marxist-Leninist teachings on religion became apparent and upon realizing that the laws and decrees crippling Orthodoxy carried implications for Jews as well. Since anti-religious Jewish Communists all too willingly carried out these measures, the Soviet assault on traditional Judaism can appear in part as an internecine Jewish conflict, a quarrel over the basic meaning of Judaism and the place of religious observance within it. But it was more than that.

From 1917 until the outbreak of World War II, and especially under Stalin, observant Jews and clergy faced hardships similar to those faced by other religious communities: legal discrimination, anti-religious propaganda campaigns, school and synagogue closings, surveillance, imprisonment, and acts of physical violence. These persecutions are regularly, and understandably, overshadowed by the genocidal assault on all Jews perpetrated by Nazi Germany in the 1930s and 1940s. Unlike the Nazi case, based on social Darwinism applied to ethnicity, Soviet persecutions were less lethal and part of the broader ideological sweep against all religious beliefs and practices. Yet as in the Nazi case, Soviet authorities could rely on deeper historical currents of anti-Semitism in carrying out their plans. But, again, the fact that it was largely irreligious Jewish Bolsheviks who took the lead in assailing traditional Judaism (preponderantly Yiddish in culture) made the struggle appear as an internal Jewish affair when in fact Marxist-Leninist ideology set the fundamental parameters of the conflict. As the historian Joshua Rothenberg once observed, "If the *Yevsektsiya* [the Jewish section in the party] had not existed, its acts [of repression against observant Jews] would have been executed by some other agency of the regime."[114]

According to Marxist-Leninist anti-religious theory, Hebraic monotheism numbered among the wiliest delusions ever concocted in human history. It conferred on Jews a stubborn religious exclusivism, while the threat of divine wrath served as a tool for keeping the lower classes meek and tractable. It had also engendered offshoot historical delusions: Christianity and Islam. The Hebrew prophets' appeal to a coming Messiah, moreover, served as a massive deterrent against exploited lower classes agitating for political revolution in the here-and-now. Devout Jews, moreover, had a track record of opposing their own enlightened thinkers, such as Baruch Spinoza, a hallowed figure in the Soviet intellectual pantheon. Religious Judaism, in short, preserved everything wrongheaded and backward in Jewish life and had thus made itself incompatible with the revolutionary movement. The evisceration of *religion* from Jewish consciousness emerged, therefore, as an important Soviet goal, while Jewish *nationality* within the Soviet Union was (at least partially) countenanced, not least because it might co-opt Zionism and, if effectively handled, could even serve as a stepping stone toward secularization and Sovietization.

Shortly after the Revolution, Soviets rendered illegal traditional Jewish structures of self-governance (*kehilot*) and came after educational institutions. The campaign against Jewish education began in earnest in 1921, and it focused on two types of school: the *hedarim*, religious elementary schools that taught the rudiments of religion and the Hebrew language, and *yeshivot*, more advanced Jewish schools where one studied Torah but could also train to become a ritual slaughterer (*shochet*) or ritual circumciser (*mohel*)— practices anathema to the Soviet mind. Between 1921 and 1923 more than one thousand hedarim were forced to close their doors, along with hundreds of yeshivot. Some religious education successfully went underground, to be sure, but Soviet authorities proved vigilant in ferreting out noncompliant teachers. Former instructors in fact were often compelled to sign pledges stating that they would not participate in illegal schools. The Soviet press in the 1920s reported numerous trials of teachers maintaining hedarim clandestinely or attempting to defend the pre-Soviet schools. Komsomol members were charged to expose illegal Hebrew schools and report them to the authorities.[115] Yevsektsiya officials condemned the Hebrew language as incurably reactionary and had it outlawed—the only language simply banned in the Soviet Union, in what one scholar has called an act of "spiritual extermination."[116] Instruction in Yiddish in a new secular, Soviet public-school system aimed to replace traditional institutions. "Our younger generation is being torn away from us by force," as Rabbi Moshe Eisenstadt of Petrograd sized up the school closures and other measures.[117]

The closing of synagogues and harassment of religious leaders followed closely on the heels of the campaign against Jewish education. The law of 23 January 1918 on the separation of church and state and the nationalization of religious properties applied to Jewish houses of worship as well. An estimated 650 synagogues were shut down in the early 1920s, with many retooled to serve nonreligious purposes. These ranged from small, rural houses of prayer to the large choral synagogues of Minsk, Kiev, Kharkov, and Odesa. The synagogue in Kiev became a social club, on the outside of which hung a red poster proclaiming, "Down with religion! Long live Soviet power and proletarian cultures!" In many instances, vandalism of Torah scrolls and liturgical items accompanied closings, and in the late 1920s a campaign to confiscate Jewish menorahs and other valuables paralleled the extraction of bells from churches. (The closing in a village of both church and synagogue in some instances took place together—the principle of equality applied to repression.) With the onset of Stalin's collectivization and industrialization campaigns and the 1929 law of religious associations, the scale of synagogue closures expanded before partial relaxation in the mid-1930s, only to peak again during the Great Terror, a time, incidentally, which also saw the purge of practically all Jewish Bolsheviks prominent in the Revolution's earlier phase. By the outbreak of World War II, no officially functioning synagogues existed in the Soviet Union.[118] Even if the Jewish faith hobbled on in a degraded and often underground fashion, a visitor to the Soviet Union in the 1930s nonetheless tellingly lamented that "religious Jews in socialist Russia [appeared] bereft of the means of self-expression they had been free to use under the tsars."[119]

Those Jewish religious leaders who did not choose emigration (which many did choose) but stayed to defend schools, synagogues, and other elements of traditional Jewish life met stiff resistance from Sovietized Jews and local authorities. For instance, Rabbi Mordechai Barishanski of Gomel, who made the case for hederim during a mock "community trial," received a sentence of multiple years of hard labor for counterrevolutionary activity. The widely respected leader of Lubavitcher Hasidism Rebbe Yosef Yitzchak Schneersohn received a death sentence for promoting underground education and networking Soviet rabbis.[120] Shmarya Yehuda Leib Medalia, chief rabbi of the choral synagogue in Moscow, received a death sentence (executed by shooting) for supporting illegal Jewish education and, improbably, colluding with German fascists![121] Like Orthodox clergymen, rabbis who did not abandon their vocations were considered disenfranchised people (lishentsy), scorned and stripped of their civil rights. The state often confiscated their homes, and finding legal housing elsewhere proved nearly impossible. Not infrequently rabbis resigned under pressure or were cajoled to sign statements such as "Our eyes have opened and we see now the stupidity and harm of religious superstition."[122] They also faced exorbitant taxes, forcing them to sell their personal belongings or endure arrest and deportation, although many went into hiding. As one anonymous writer described the scene in Vitebsk: "In the Vitebsk region, not a single rabbi is to be found in this city. They have all left for places where they are not recognized, less they be destroyed or prosecuted on account of the taxes."[123]

Soviet authorities and local party cadres conducted an offensive against the Sabbath and other Jewish holy days. So-called work on the Sabbath initiatives were staged, deliberately calculated to shock and dismay traditional Jews. These featured young Communist Jews sweeping streets or doing other menial jobs on the holy days. Similarly, they prepared hearty communal meals on Yom Kippur, when observant Jews normally fasted. Anti-Passover and Anti-Rosh Hashanah events took place, adapting the script from the Bolshevik campaigns against Christmas and Easter. For Anti-Passovers, so-called Red Haggadahs were invented, modeled on the traditional Haggadah. According to one version: "Wash off the bourgeois mud, wash off the mold of generations, and do not say a blessing, say a curse, devastation must come upon all the old religious laws and customs." "Instead of the story of how the sea was divided," according to one Anti-Passover directive, "we speak about the brave heroes of the Red Army. . . . Instead of the groaning of the Jews in Egypt and God's miracles, we speak about the real sufferings of the proletariat."[124] Prosecuted mainly in urban areas, the campaign against Jewish sacred time eventually came to rural shtetls as well, the effects of which have been aptly described by the historian Walter Kolarz: "One can well imagine what dismay the first desecrations of the Sabbath caused among the simple religious Jews of Soviet Russia's Western border areas. They regarded in great bewilderment this blasphemy which meant the collapse of the world of their ancestors. . . . People crowded around . . . to see with their own eyes the new communist monstrosity—work on the Day, which for thousands of years pious Jews of all lands had sanctified."[125]

The battle against Jewish holy days occurred in the context of broader campaigns of anti-religious propaganda, in which Jews were linked to the evils of capitalism and anti-Communist conspiracies. Soviet depictions of Jews drew on typical stereotypes, portraying rabbis with crooked noses, thick lips, oversized ears, and scraggly beards. The journal *Godless* published a weekly column entitled "Down with Rabbis," inventorying the latest rabbinical outrages against socialist progress. Sometimes the Jewish Yahweh was represented alongside other deities as, for example, in an issue of *Godless at the Workbench* from 1924, which depicts Jewish, Muslim, Buddhist, and Christian deities together. Behind each stands a wealthy capitalist holding tethers attached to the respective god's followers with text at the bottom of the page asking, "Which god is real? Answer: all gods are real so long as their master supports them." An additional panel elaborates that "religion is, always and everywhere, a weapon of class rule. . . . If religion grows out of date, they change it. But the change in religion only means that a worn-out, decrepit bridle is replaced with a new, up-to-date one."[126]

Soviet anti-Judaism came bundled with anti-Zionism.[127] Since the 1890s, under the leadership of the Austrian journalist Theodor Herzl, Zionism had expanded as a powerful force across Europe, attracting many Jews within the Russian Empire long weighed down by tsarist-era discrimination and persecution. Several Jews with Zionist leanings even gained victories in local elections after the February Revolution of 1917. But ultimately Zionism ran afoul of the long-term assimilationist goals of Marxism-Leninism. That some concessions were made to establishing a Jewish national identity *within* the Soviet Union in the 1920s should not be mistaken as an endorsement of the idea of Jewish nationality per se, much less of Zionist Jewish nationalism, but more as a stopgap measure. From the upper echelons of Soviet power, this measure represented the lesser of several evils, meant to co-opt international Zionism and countermand overtly religious forms of Jewish identity. "The [Soviet] idea was to create a new Jewish culture and a Soviet Jewish nationality, one which would be secular, socialist, and Yiddish. This nationality would have nothing in common with the religious, Hebraist, Zionist, bourgeois Jews in capitalist countries," as the political scientist Zvi Gitelman has summarized the Soviet stance.[128] Accordingly, not only people of significant religious stature faced persecution during the prewar Stalinist years; so did outspoken Zionists from all walks of life. "Especially harsh," as the historian Heinz-Dietrich Löwe has written, "was the persecution of Zionist organizations, clubs, sports associations, and the like, which, in spite of that, sprang up again and again until they finally had to succumb to unrelenting political pressure by the authorities." Even the Yevsektsiya was dissolved under Stalin's rule in 1929 because it had served its purpose in degrading traditional Jewish religious culture, and also due to fears that its continued existence might abet Zionist desires and thwart assimilation. "The attempted integration of Jews in the Soviet Union, therefore, has to be called 'negative integration,'" Löwe adds, "because it was to a considerable degree based on destruction and persecution."[129]

The impact of the Nazi-Soviet Pact and World War II slightly ameliorated the position of Soviet Jews—especially in comparison to those Jews who found themselves in German-occupied territories after 1941, where Nazi leaders stoked local anti-Semitic feelings and set in motion the machinery of the Holocaust. Half a million Jews fought in the Soviet Army, many receiving decorations. During the war, the relaxation of anti-religious policies redounded positively to Jewish communities. Some synagogues and schools were tolerated and many religious properties restored—work overseen after 1943 by a Jewish section within the newly created Council of Religious Affairs. During the war, the Soviet Union formed the Jewish Anti-Fascist Committee in Moscow, including a rabbi among its members, for the purpose of winning over Jewish public opinion in Western countries and procuring material assistance from Allied powers.[130] In 1943, the committee sent its chairman, Solomon Mikhoels, a luminary in the Moscow Yiddish theater, on a successful fundraising and publicity tour to various Western countries. The trip suggested that the story of Soviet Jewish life seemed poised for a better chapter after the war. But by the end of the war, the tide had turned again, as many Soviet authorities worried that the committee had become a rallying point for Jewish cultural and national aspirations. In the Soviet press, charges of "bourgeois nationalism" appeared often, taking aim at prominent Jewish intellectuals deemed too friendly with Zionism. Their international connections to other Jews, helpful to Stalin during the war, suddenly became a liability afterward. Then on 13 January 1948, in what was made to appear as a driving accident, Soviet security forces murdered Mikhoels as he traveled to receive a literary award in Minsk.

This kicked off massive repression of Jewish life in the Soviet Union known as the Black Years, lasting from 1948 until Stalin's death in 1953. The Jewish Anti-Fascist Committee was forcibly shut down in 1948, with some of its members arrested and falsely convicted of espionage and treason. Thirteen Jews were killed on 12 August 1952 in an event known as the Night of the Murdered Poets, since several victims were major Yiddish literary figures. Waxing Zionism after 1948 only aggravated the situation. Yiddish, once exalted over Hebrew as an acceptable Soviet language, now too came under attack from Soviet authorities, who closed Yiddish printing presses, theaters, schools, and other cultural institutions.

Following Stalin's lead, party and government organs railed against "rootless cosmopolitanism" in an effort to target all Jews who harbored Zionist sentiments. It became politically impermissible at this time to speak of Jews as victims of the Holocaust, for in the Soviet mind, many of those who perished during World War II were to be remembered first as *Soviet* citizens. In January 1953, several prominent Jewish physicians charged in the so-called Doctors' Plot found themselves arrested for allegedly trying to poison Stalin and other Kremlin leaders. Although Soviet officials clumsily attempted to portray this as a hoax after Stalin's death, subsequent evidence has suggested that the scheme might have borne witness to a larger campaign promoting countrywide harassment and mass deportations of Jews to Siberia.[131]

The repressive milieu carried implications for Jewish religious life. Authorities regularly denied Jews permits to reestablish synagogues, seeing them as potential nests of Zionism in addition to being spigots of religious obscurantism. Rabbis and Jewish activists were regularly monitored, arrested, and deported. Security forces broke up unauthorized prayer gatherings, while legal Jewish entities found themselves subjected to mountains of paperwork and onerous taxation. Fearful of reprisal, many parents refused to speak Yiddish to their children or instruct them in the basics of religion, lest officials deny them employment and educational opportunities. Soviet authorities regularly demanded that heads of offices and industrial enterprises engage in "prophylactic work" aimed at intimidating observant Jews and preventing them from practicing their faith in the first place.[132]

Although Khrushchev abstained from the more outrageous forms of Stalinist anti-Semitism, he carefully avoided criticizing Stalin for his anti-Jewish antics and permitted only a symbolic revival of Yiddish culture during his time in office. Jews also experienced repression in Khrushchev's anti-religious campaign after 1959, when hundreds of synagogues were closed again and many Jewish institutions were identified with economic crimes and espionage on behalf of Israel. Jewish anti-religious propaganda—typified most scurrilously in a book, *Judaism without Embellishment* (1963), produced by the Ukrainian Academy of Sciences—became more intensive and vitriolic, with the usual anti-Semitic tropes depicting Jews as money-grubbing, obscurantist, and disloyal. As Cold War political intrigue intensified, Soviets increasingly portrayed Israel as a pariah state and Zionism as an American and Jewish tool to promote "racist imperialism." It also drew Moscow closer to Israel's Arab adversaries. More controversially, the Soviet press began to apply the term "fascism" to Israel and its supporters, forging subtle associations between anti-Zionism and anti-Semitism that have enjoyed a long life not only in the Soviet Union but within the discourse of the political Left in Western countries until the present.

The Six-Day War in 1967 made a bad situation worse. The Soviet Union broke off diplomatic ties with Israel and vociferously took the side of the Arab states, which were prepared to assault a large segment of world Jewry only twenty years after the Holocaust. Even for the Russian Jews most inclined to full assimilation, the Soviet stance on this conflict proved to be the straw that broke the camel's back, as they realized that they might forever be viewed as second-class citizens in the Soviet Union. To be sure, for some even this did not matter, and they accepted acculturation, if not full assimilation, their Jewish religious roots largely deracinated. But thousands of others, both religiously observant and not, "voted with their feet," forming queues at emigration offices to depart for Israel, once emigration laws were liberalized in the early 1970s. By the late 1970s, roughly a quarter of a million Jews had left the Soviet Union for their ancestral home in Palestine, constricting further an already weakened religious life in the land they left behind while adding to Jewish-Arab tensions in the Middle East. Thousands more followed in their footsteps in the 1980s.[133] In 1978 the historian Joshua Rothenberg could describe Soviet Jewish life thus: "Of the thousands and thousands of synagogues and prayer houses, only several dozen remain after the ravages of fifty years. Of the many thousands of religious schools, both elementary and advanced, practically none has survived. The thousands of rabbis have been reduced to a mere handful who still function in a religious capacity."[134] The widow of the political dissident Anatoly Marchenko poignantly expressed the liminal position of religiously deracinated Jews in the late Soviet period: "Who am I? . . . Unfortunately I do not feel like a Jew. . . . [A] general common bond is lacking . . . community of language, culture, history, tradition. . . . By all of these I am Russian . . . and nevertheless, no, I am not Russian. *I am a stranger today in this land.*"[135] Finally, reflecting on Soviet efforts to degrade Jewish religious life and promote assimilation, the Jewish poet Menakhem Bereish once observed: "We Jews, who have no desire for national suicide, cannot fail to recall that throughout history we have reacted to those who have suppressed our soul in the same way as those who have murdered our people. And inevitably we ask whether in this [Soviet] case we have not encountered merely a new form of anti-Semitism, which does not declare itself as such. . . . Antioch wanted nothing but good for the Jews when it attempted to convert them back to God. The Roman emperors also wanted nothing less. And did not the Catholic Inquisition merely wish to save

Jewish souls? At first glance the parallels [with the Soviet Union] may appear somewhat strange, but perhaps they are not."[136]

BUDDHISM

Given the small size of the Buddhist population in the tsarist Russian Empire and its distance from major centers of power, the Bolsheviks at first paid Buddhists little heed, regarding them mainly as backward, colonized peoples who should be grateful for their emancipation from tsarism. Buddhist monasteries and traditional ways of life continued functioning after 1917 as they had before. In 1926, a Congress of Soviet Buddhists took place in Moscow, at which Buddhists and Communists appeared to see eye to eye on many issues, especially with respect to the "nationality" question. Delegates to the gathering sent a telegram to the Dalai Lama, telling him that the new administration boded well for Buddhists in the Soviet Union.[137] By the late 1920s, however, the tide had turned; ideological differences became more apparent, and harsh propaganda efforts and political repression ensued. Soviet campaigns against Buddhists became so scorched-earth in fact that they merit being seen as anticipations of subsequent Communist attempts to eradicate Buddhism in Mongolia, China, and Tibet—all profiled in chapter 5.

When Marxist-Leninist theorists considered "religion," they generally had in mind the Abrahamic faiths. Buddhism thus presented something of a quandary. At first glance, Buddhism appeared intriguing from a Soviet point of view; it possessed an egalitarian ethic and possibly a revolutionary attitude, insofar as it had been born in part as a revolt against the Hindu caste system. In certain respects, Buddhism could even claim to be atheistic. Yet the Buddha's revolt against caste, or so leading Soviet theorists ultimately argued, was overwhelmingly spiritual in nature and thus failed to recognize, as Marx would have it, the material basis of existence. What is more, the idea of reincarnation appeared to serve the interests of ruling classes, promising the downtrodden rewards in another life for passive, pious behavior in the present one; Buddhism encourages "social passivity and . . . aloofness from the concrete historical situation," as the *Great Soviet Encyclopedia*'s entry on Buddhism chides.[138] Buddhism's categorical rejection of violence, furthermore, stood in stark contrast to the Bolshevik willingness to employ it as a political tool. Finally, as was the case with other faiths, Buddhists possessed thick ties to coreligionists in nearby countries and thus presented the abiding problem of fraternizing with Soviet enemies. Japan, which had humiliated Russia in the Russo-Japanese War of 1904-5, was of particular concern to Soviet leaders prior to the Second World War as the island nation sought to stoke "Pan-Buddhist" and "Pan-Mongol" sentiments to destabilize the governments of China and the USSR.

Comprising roughly half a million people, Buddhists in Russia existed in three distinct ethnic groups at the beginning of Soviet rule: among the Buryat-Mongols living near Lake Baikal in Eastern Siberia (Buryatia); among the Tuvans, who occupied a border region with China (Tuva), annexed to the Russian Empire only in 1914; and among the Kalmyks north of the Caspian Sea (Kalmykia), who had earlier migrated there from farther east. Tibetan Buddhism—sometimes called "Lamaism" in the West due to the importance attributed to spiritual leaders known as lamas—represented the dominant form of the faith. Famously syncretistic in its ability to absorb elements of pre-Buddhist faiths, especially species of shamanism in areas that fell under the Soviet Union, this branch of Buddhism established itself in Mongolia in the sixteenth and seventeenth centuries and spread from there among the Buryats, Tuvans, and Kalmyks toward the end of the seventeenth century.[139]

The monastic brotherhood (sangha) and monastery-temple complexes (datsans) made up key elements of Soviet Tibetan-Mongolian Buddhism. As spiritual guides and political magnates, chief lamas oversaw vast estates relying on the work of younger monks and Buddhist laypeople. When the Bolsheviks assumed power, roughly thirty-seven monasteries with fifteen thousand lamas existed in Buryatia. Seventy monasteries and sixteen hundred lamas could be found among the Kalmyks, while Tuvans boasted around twenty-two monasteries and two thousand lamas. All Buddhist activity took place under the titular head of the Khambo Lama, an office established under Empress Elizabeth in 1741, which functioned not unlike that of the Dalai Lama in Tibet.[140]

The commonalities between Communism and Buddhism expressed at the 1926 Congress of Soviet Buddhists owed much to a reform movement spreading through monastic institutions in the early twentieth century, sometimes called Neo-Buddhism or Buddhist modernism. It owed its genesis in large part to the Khambo Lama Agvan Dorzhiev (1853-1938), once a tutor for the Dalai Lama and an emissary for Tibetan Buddhism, who in 1909 obtained permission from the tsar to establish a Buddhist temple in

Saint Petersburg, Europe's first Buddhist structure.[141] Worried about Buddhism's survival under the new Soviet regime, Dorzhiev shrewdly pointed out similarities between the two ideologies, claiming that Buddhism, rightly understood, was more a philosophy than a religion and was actually compatible with Marxist atheism. Some of Dorzhiev's disciples audaciously claimed Lenin to be a manifestation of the Buddha, who in turn should be reckoned as Soviet Communism's true founder!

Flattered by the comparisons, some Soviet scholars reciprocated with their own positive responses, but most were simply nonplussed, and ultimately little came of the comparisons. As Stalin consolidated power and began collectivization and de-kulakization efforts in the late 1920s, ideological rapprochement receded, and stark antagonism and repression arose. Around this time, the League of the Militant Godless gained a voice in Buddhist areas, criticizing Buddhist modernism as yet another example of a deceptive bourgeois half measure. "Buddhist atheism has nothing to do with militant atheism based on the Marxist appraisal of the laws of nature and society," the journal *Godless* pointedly asserted in September 1930.[142] The role of traditional Tibetan healing practices proved to be a wedge issue that Communists used to accuse of Buddhists of enmity toward modern science. Lamas in particular faced severe scrutiny, criticized as "feudal lords," inherently reactionary, inimical to socialist progress, and prone to collude with foreign powers. Already in 1928, onerous taxes hit monasteries, and many lamas were arrested, imprisoned, and deported. During Stalin's reign, Dorzhiev was exiled to Leningrad, arrested there in 1937 for treason, and later died in prison in Ulan-Ude, likely tortured beforehand. Around the same time, Soviet authorities arrested and shot lamas associated with the Buddhist temple in Leningrad before ransacking and closing it.[143]

As the tiny Buddhist community in Leningrad was liquidated, matters went from bad to worse in all three Soviet Buddhist regions as anti-religious campaigns ramped up and as collectivization, de-kulakization, and industrialization processes were imposed in mercilessly top-down fashion on mostly nomadic peoples, generally judged by Soviets as inherently unproductive and regressive in outlook.

In Buryatia, harsh taxation policies against monasteries gave way to more direct attacks after 1929. Beginning in that year, Buddhist holidays were banned. Authorities then closed one monastery after another, with the majority of closures coming during the second five-year plan, from 1933 to 1937. The great Tsongol Datsan monastery, a major seat of Buddhist learning for two hundred years, was shuttered in 1931. In some cases, monasteries were burned to the ground, while others became dwelling places on collective farms or served other purposes. Although some artistic treasures made their way to an anti-religious museum established in Ulan-Ude, many were lost, melted down for ammunition, or completely destroyed.[144] A similar fate befell monastery libraries. During the process, religious elites—lamas but also some shaman priests—found themselves arrested, deported, or forced into hiding. The harshest single attack on lamas came in November 1938, when 1,864 were arrested; 968 were convicted, the majority never heard from again. But this was true for practically all of the some fifteen thousand lamas deported in the 1930s.[145] "The Buddhist clergy as well as Buddhist laity had to endure incredible suffering, humiliation, and persecution [at this time]," as one eyewitness recorded.[146] "The physical violence against Buddhism at this time was . . . far-reaching," echoes the scholar Melissa Chakars.[147] General unrest from the repression and collectivization measures elicited harsh Soviet reprisals, resulting in the deaths of thousands of innocent Buryat citizens. To add insult to injury, Stalin redrew the political map, separating some lands from the Buryat-Mongol Autonomous Soviet Socialist Republic, in an effort to disperse the population.

Before it was formally annexed to the Soviet Union in 1944, Tuva existed as a Soviet satellite state under the watchful eye and interventionist hand of Moscow, which saw Buddhism behind the pan-Mongolian anti-Soviet movement and a general mentality of opposition. Consequently, by the late 1930s Tuva, too, witnessed the virtual eradication of Buddhism, with all its monasteries liquidated and lamas killed or deported. Local Soviet partisans were in fact so vicious in their attacks that Moscow even had to intervene at points to counsel moderation. Still, repression proceeded apace, with the harshest measures coming in 1937. Collectivization mandates came later to Tuva, from 1949 to 1954, at which time further resistance from the population brought harsh reprisals.[148] As the historian James Forsyth has nicely summarized: "Moscow . . . unleashed a cultural revolution [in Tuva] aimed at the 'liquidation of feudal chiefs [lamas] as a class' and the abolition of religion aimed at the wholesale destruction of Buddhist monasteries and the victimization of lamas and shamans." To weaken Tuva's age-old connection with Mongolia, Tuvan, a Turkic language written in a Latin script, was introduced to replace official Mongolian.[149] "The repression affected almost all people," as one eyewitness lama remembered; "I know, I saw it."[150]

Kalmyk Buddhists in the North Caucasus region arguably had it even worse. Historically loyal to the tsars, who had granted them land "for all eternity" for fighting against Napoleon in the early nineteenth century, they experienced considerable violence during the Russian Civil War for not siding with the Red Army. At this time, many monasteries came under siege; statues of the Buddha and Buddhist saints were used for Soviet rifle practice. This precedent, and a combination of anti-religious and collectivization measures in the late 1920s, sealed the fate of the Kalmyks, who revolted against the Soviet yoke on several occasions only to encounter brutal repression. The last two Kalmyk monasteries—the Yandyk-Mochazhnensk and the Zagan-Amansky—were forcibly closed in 1936, after which not a single monastery remained in all of Kalmykia. About seventy temples (khuruls) were closed or destroyed as well. Collectively charged with treason, Kalmyk monks were arrested, hastily tried in NKVD tribunals, and deported or slain shortly thereafter. Roughly five thousand people were affected. By the outbreak of World War II, public Buddhism in Kalmykia had massively declined. Accusing the Kalmyks of continued intransigence during the war, Stalin decided in 1943 to deport the entire population by cattle car to Siberia and Central Asia, precipitating the deaths of about 28,000 people and possibly more (of a population around 134,000) in the process.[151] "Early one frosty December morning," as one remorseful Soviet observer described the deportations, "the Kalmyks had to leave their homes forever. They silently submitted to their fate in accordance with the religion, Buddhism, but all my ideas were overthrown. . . . Never before in my life have I seen such a tragic expression on the faces of the men carrying out the orders of the Communist state." Thereafter, authorities scrubbed the word "Kalmyk" from the *Soviet Encyclopedia,* and Kalmykia vanished from the map—its lands absorbed into other provinces and all its towns given new socialist-inspired names.[152]

During the more relaxed atmosphere of the early Cold War, some measure of restoration took place in Buddhist areas. Soviet authorities allowed, for instance, the opening of two monasteries in Buryatia: Ivolginsky, an entirely new monastery, and Aginsky, the resurrection of a former monastery in the Aginsk region.[153] But these were mainly showpieces to give the impression that religious freedom prevailed and an effort to garner support from neighboring Buddhist countries and the international community.

Monasteries also necessarily stood under the direct control of a new, highly Sovietized organization, the Central Spiritual Board of Buddhists of the USSR, which made it imperative that Buddhists honor the workers' state as much as their faith. As part of the de-Stalinization process, Khrushchev publicly acknowledged the genocidal measures against the Kalmyks and permitted many who had not perished to return to their former lands by the Caspian Sea.

Despite these measures, the party line remained that Buddhism represented a reactionary mind-set, meriting ongoing skepticism and state oversight lest it fan itself to life again. In a typical case, one Tuvan lama received a five-year sentence in 1965 simply for possessing contraband Buddhist literature.[154] A *Handbook of Atheism*, published in Moscow in 1971, glossed the previous assault on Buddhism favorably, noting that "as a result of the victory of the great October Revolution, the building of socialism and the creation of a new culture, the influence of Lamaism on the Buryats, Kalmyks, and Tuvians has steadily declined." The author then rued the fact that Buddhism was not yet "completely eradicated"; ongoing vigilance was necessary because "Buddhism perpetuates an unjust social order in the world and promotes a bourgeois attitude to society."[155] Furthermore, in 1972, in a case widely covered in Western media, the monk and citizen of Buryatia Bidia Dandaron, who had criticized past Soviet actions and vocally advocated for the rights of Buddhists, was arrested and sent to a labor camp, dying two years into his sentence. Four of his colleagues and former students wound up in a psychiatric hospital for exhibiting an unhealthy fondness for religious belief.[156] The Buddhism permitted to exist in the Soviet Union, in the final analysis, had no choice but to genuflect before official ideology and support Soviet foreign policy. As a case in point, the Khambo Lama Eshi-Dershi Sharapov was obliged in 1959 to issue a public statement expressing anger at "reactionaries" in Tibet for resisting the Chinese Red Army's invasion there, which resulted in the destruction of nearly all of Tibet's monasteries and the deaths of thousands of monks.[157]

While a noteworthy revival of interest in and practice of Buddhism took place during the waning years of the Soviet Union, this should not diminish recognition of the comprehensive and brutal assault against Buddhism that took place decades earlier, the legacy of which endures today among younger generations, in what constitutes general amnesia about Russia's Buddhist past. Hardly a "single memorial remains" of Buddhism, as one scholar and visitor to several Soviet Buddhist areas sized up the situation in 1958: "In Asia Minor and Greece the ruins of ancient temples have been preserved, making it possible to study the ancient culture of Hellas. Nothing remains of Buddhist temples in Buryatia and Kalmykia. The fate of Lamaism in the USSR deserves attention as an example of the complete destruction of a religion and the destruction of a religious group as a group."[158] "Temples, spiritual literature, priceless treasures of the datsans were destroyed, plundered," observed the Khambo Lama Munko Tsybikov in 1991, surveying the earlier Soviet damage: "Religious figures were persecuted; thousands of lamas went through the torments of the Gulag."[159]

CATHOLICISM

Before 1917, around eleven million Catholics lived in the Russian Empire, most of them ethnic Poles, Ukrainians, Belarusians, Lithuanians, Latvians, Armenians, and Germans, with smaller numbers among other national groups. Predominantly located in sensitive western and southwestern border regions, they represented three principal worship rites: Latin, Armenian, and Greek (or Byzantine), all recognized by the Vatican.[160] Shifting western border configurations between 1917 and 1945 resulted in sometimes more, sometimes fewer Catholics under Soviet authority. The Soviet republics of Lithuania and Ukraine (the former politically independent between 1918 and 1940) stood out for having populations with especially high percentages of Catholics. Lithuanians observed mostly the Latin Rite; Ukrainians, the Greek or Byzantine Rite, although they had been in communion with Rome and under the authority of the Pope since the Union of Brest (1595–96). Their existence had long vexed the Russian Orthodox clergy, who tended to regard things Catholic as worrisomely Westernizing.

For their own reasons, Bolsheviks regarded the Catholic Church as an especially obdurate enemy. Not only was it a time-tested manufacturer of religious "opium," early Soviet leaders saw it as a major obstacle to the global spread of Communism and the attainment of more immediate foreign-policy goals, while it also impeded the internal consolidation of their regime by challenging its monopoly on truth and power. These concerns were built on the fact that Marxists and other nineteenth-century radicals despised "Rome" as the symbolic center of postrevolutionary reaction. The Vatican's global reach and its own claims to universality, to say nothing of its ties to many non-Russian ethnic identities, presented additional reasons for Bolshevik anti-Catholicism.

Under the tsars, Catholics did not enjoy the status of the Orthodox, to be sure, but they possessed limited rights and enjoyed a considerable social presence; the imperial government even maintained a permanent Legation to the Holy See in Rome. With other religious minorities, many Catholics welcomed the 1905 Revolution and the February Revolution of 1917 and the measures of religious pluralism that they brought. But the Bolshevik Revolution brought darker tidings and harsher realities. The Soviet government's various anti-religious actions between 1917 and 1920—most receiving Catholic bishops' strong rebukes—nationalized Catholic property and wealth and deprived priests of basic civil rights, including the right to vote and receive a ration card for food, while taxing them exorbitantly. Prohibitions against religious education resulted in the closure of most Catholic parochial schools in Soviet territory, including Saint Catherine's in Petrograd, which boasted some twenty thousand elementary and fifteen hundred gymnasium students. Most Polish-language Catholic schools in western regions were shut down shortly after the Revolution. A similar fate befell most diocesan seminaries as well as a major Catholic theological academy in Petrograd. When added up, the Bolsheviks' decrees in education largely severed the connection between the Catholic Church and its youth, while constraining its ability to train future priests and teachers.[161] For those with historical memory, it appeared as if the Jacobin assault against the church during the French Revolution had returned.

Eduard von der Ropp, metropolitan archbishop of Mohilev (in present-day Belarus), at first tried to seek out a modus vivendi with the new regime, convinced that it would not last long. Things turned out differently. Along with several Polish clergy, he was arrested in Petrograd in April 1918 and charged as a counterrevolutionary, eventually winding up in Moscow's notorious Lubyanka prison. Large-scale Catholic demonstrations for his release failed to change the Bolsheviks' minds and only led to the arrests and deportations of other priests, several of whom died in captivity. Ropp himself faced execution before the Vatican intervened at the eleventh hour and arranged for a prisoner swap with a jailed Polish Communist, Karl Radek, later a victim of Stalin's purges.

The Russian Civil War added to the woes of the Catholic Church. The Treaty of Brest-Litovsk (3 March 1918) that ended the Great War between

Russia and Germany encouraged Poles, Latvians, Lithuanians, Belarusians, and Ukrainians—all with sizable Catholic populations—to agitate for national independence, thus incurring retaliation from the nascent Soviet regime, which often blamed Catholic clergy for stoking nationalist passions. Soviet atrocities against Poles in disputed border areas during the Polish-Soviet War (1918–21), an often forgotten theater of the larger Russian Civil War, were especially brutal, including mass shootings, torture, and burial of opponents alive.[162] Poles often responded in kind. The Treaty of Riga (1921) ended the war and stabilized (at least for a period) the Soviet-Poland border regions, even if it could not reverse the dislocation, famine, and other miseries stemming from the conflict.

Lenin's campaign to confiscate church valuables for poor relief in 1922 applied to Catholics as well as to Orthodox. When the Catholic Church protested, the Soviet attack on Archbishop Ropp developed into a more comprehensive assault on the entire Catholic hierarchy. Ropp's successor, Archbishop John Cieplak, and his assistant Monsignor Constantine Budkiewicz emerged as especially critical voices of Soviet policy. They and fifteen other defendants, mostly Poles, were arrested on the night of 2 March 1923, among them Leonid Feodorov, exarch to Russian Catholics of the Greek Rite. Sent to the revolutionary high court in Moscow, all faced treason charges in a high-profile trial lasting from 21 to 23 March, an event covered by the *New York Times* reporter Francis McCullagh. According to his reportage, defendants appealed to "the law of God and conscience" as higher than Soviet law. Their arguments did not fly, as the prosecutor, worked into an anti-religious fury, responded: "Your religion, I spit on it, as I do on all religions—Orthodox, Jewish, Mohammedan, and the rest. . . . There is no law but Soviet law and by that law you must die."[163] Not surprisingly, all were found guilty, but only Cieplak and Budkiewicz received death sentences. Vatican intervention through another prisoner exchange spared Cieplak, but Budkiewicz met his end with a bullet to the back of the head. Others received harsh labor sentences. The trial marked the beginning of an assault on other Catholic prelates in the coming years. By 1926, not a single Catholic bishop presided in the entire Soviet Union.[164] Rome tried to reorganize the hierarchy clandestinely through secret appointments administered by the Jesuit Michel-Joseph Bourguignon d'Herbigny, who was sent to Moscow under the pretext of an Easter pastoral visit to Catholics resident in the Soviet capital. But his efforts largely came to naught. Within several years, all those whom he had appointed were imprisoned, exiled, or executed—and the Vatican abandoned its efforts.[165]

The fate of bishops extended to parish priests and church buildings, as indicated by the vitriol of the magazine *Godless* in 1923: "A more bitter struggle is in progress against the Catholic clergy than against the Russian church, because the Catholic organization is more powerful [in foreign affairs] than the Orthodox. . . . It is not surprising that Pius XI is so firmly defending [the Orthodox patriarch] Tikhon."[166] The struggle only intensified from the late 1920s through the Great Terror of the 1930s. According to diocesan recordkeeping, 1,195 Catholic churches and chapels presided over by 896 priests (of various nationalities) existed in Soviet territories in 1918. By the eve of World War II, virtually all of these churches had been closed, destroyed, or put to other uses, save two: Saint Louis des Français in Moscow and Notre Dame de France in Leningrad, both mainly serving foreign visitors and promoting the illusion of religious freedom. The inability to pay taxes or failure to pass an inspection constituted the most common reasons for the church closures, and often Soviet authorities disingenuously claimed that they acted only in response to the wishes of local working people. In many instances, altars were desecrated and relics destroyed or else moved to anti-religious museums. Explosives demolished entirely several historically significant Catholic churches in Belarus and Ukraine.[167]

Apart from priests serving foreigners in Moscow and Leningrad, and those operating underground, nearly all Catholic priests active at the time of the Revolution found themselves deported, imprisoned, or slain by 1939.[168] Sometimes they numbered among general deportations to efface or dilute regional Catholic and ethnic identities and/or to address security threats. The year 1937 was especially grim as the NKVD claimed to discover numerous "spy nests" in Catholic areas. "Under cover of cross and cassock," the charge went, Catholic priests had a hand in these and thus received just punishment. The devastation in the late 1920s and 1930s also extended to Armenian Rite Catholics in Armenia and Georgia, German Catholics in Crimea and the Volga region, and Catholics of diverse ethnicities elsewhere. As one source from the Volga region described the scene: "Priests were imprisoned for conducting services in secret, and frequently they ended up dying of starvation. Many were shot. With the passage of time the majority of the cathedrals were either closed or converted to Komsomol clubs. Letters from the laity all agree: 'our main wish is to escape this hell.'"[169] "The times of Diocletian begins for the Church," as the exarch Leonid Feodorov summed up the general Catholic experience in the 1930s to the Ukrainian Greek Catholic archbishop of Lviv, lamenting "God's abandoned and devastated churches. . . . I would never have thought that we would be asked to carry such a cross."[170]

Repression of people and property received support from the anti-Catholic dimension of Soviet propaganda generated in the 1920s and 1930s. Much of this propaganda mirrored motifs and tropes aimed at the Orthodox and other faiths. But anti-Catholic propaganda can be distinguished by its obsessive focus on the pope (marked by his papal tiara in posters and cartoons) as the alleged grandmaster of Western warmongering against the Soviet Union in cahoots with international capitalism and other bourgeois and reactionary forces. By implication, Catholics within Soviet territories amounted to untrustworthy minions of foreign powers, more loyal to Rome and to their respective ethnic identities than to achieving the "new man" of Soviet aspirations. Opportunistically, Soviet propagandists took full advantage of preexisting Orthodox-Catholic divisions, manipulating long-standing Eastern stereotypes about Catholics in an effort to portray them collectively as a repugnant cultural other, inherently foreign and averse to Soviet/Russian interests.

This emphasis intensified after the outbreak of World War II when Stalin, suddenly smitten with the political uses of Russian nationalism, moderated his stance toward the Orthodox Church. But a comparable moderation did not take place for Catholics. In many respects, the war worsened their situation, especially for Catholics in Belarus, western Ukraine, and the Baltic states, occupied by the Soviets in 1940 as a consequence of the Molotov-Ribbentrop Pact. At this time, the Marxist-Leninist critique of religion and an inflamed Russian nationalism, taking strategic advantage of long-standing Orthodox-Catholic enmity, entered into a dark alliance of convenience to the detriment of millions of Soviet Catholics. The devastation appears most clearly in the postwar fate of Catholics in Lithuania and Ukraine.

Between 1918 and 1940, Lithuania—like Latvia and Estonia—operated as a free and independent country, delivered by the course of World War I from the clutch of the tsars. A robust national identity with Catholicism as its centerpiece took shape in these years. The church boasted two archdioceses, with nine hundred churches and chapels and around fifteen hundred priests in addition to several monasteries, orphanages, hospitals, and four theological academies, the most significant among them in the city of Kaunas. Pope Pius XI referred to Lithuania as "the most loyal daughter of Rome in the north of Europe." The Soviet occupation and annexation of Lithuania in 1940 spelled doom for Catholic culture. Copying from the playbook of the October Revolution and imposing Soviet law, Communists nationalized church property, closed seminaries, forbade religious education while mandating education in Marxism-Leninism, pulped theological books in libraries, and shut down the religious press, as well as surveilling priests and hitting them with punitive taxation. In addition, Soviet security forces killed seventeen priests and expelled the papal nuncio, Luigi Centozo. In the so-called Black June of 1941, around seventeen thousand Lithuanians considered to be "anti-Soviet elements" were taken from their homes at night and deported in cattle cars to Siberia to facilitate the Sovietization/ Russification of the country. Thousands of others fled the country or simply disappeared, the ultimate whereabouts of some still unknown today.[171]

Of course, the German invasion and occupation of Lithuania between 1941 and 1944 came with its own cruelties (and, sadly, some Lithuanian participation). But Soviet persecution of Catholics resumed once the republic was wrested back under Soviet control near the end of war, where it remained until the collapse of the Soviet Union in 1991. Lithuania stood out as the only Catholic-majority republic in the Soviet Union. The postwar years were especially brutal. "The decade of 1944–1954," the scholar Pranas Dauknys has written, "must be considered the most horrifying [for Catholics] in the entire 1,000 years of Lithuanian history."[172] Hundreds of churches were closed; sacred art was destroyed and looted. No fewer than 142 NKVD agents, archival evidence has revealed, were assigned to repress the Lithuanian priesthood.[173] Practically every priest remaining in the country had to present himself for interrogation at centers set up in the country, where they were asked to sign an oath of loyalty to the state and endorse the existence of a Soviet-manufactured progressive new "national" church severed from Rome. While a few capitulated, the majority did not, and this pseudo-church never became viable. For his intransigence, Bishop Teofilius Matulionis experienced arrest multiple times before being sent to Siberia, as was his fellow bishop, Pranciŝkus Ramanauskas. Bishop Vincentas Borisevičius was shot by a firing squad, his body later discovered in a mass grave. Hundreds of parish priests were imprisoned, and many of them were also sent to the Gulag. The

"Lithuanian priest" is practically a stock character in some Gulag literature. Only one bishop remained in Lithuania by 1947, the same year that Soviets outlawed monastic life and disbanded monasteries. All of this took place in the context of a protracted Lithuanian resistance movement, amid more general deportations of people, resulting in the removal of thousands of additional Lithuanians to labor camps and resettlement communities in eastern locations, especially to Irkutsk Oblast and Krasnoyarsk Krai.[174] Altogether, at least one hundred and thirty thousand people were forcibly transported in the deportations of 1941 and 1945–52, and this does not account for thousands of political prisoners who met a similar fate. Today, Lithuania observes the annual Mourning and Hope Day on June 14 in memory of these outrages.

The Khrushchev and Brezhnev years witnessed continued Soviet hostility to Lithuanian Catholicism, if in less direct, brutally oppressive ways. In 1961, Vilnius's Saint Casimir's Church, closed in 1949, was turned into a museum of atheism. (Casimir is Lithuania's patron saint.) Authorities made sure that a chronic shortage of seminarians and priests beset the church. In addition to the considerable church life that functioned underground, a public church managed to revive itself, even if it was plagued by bribed informants and KGB (previously NKVD) agents, who went so far as to train people to pose as Catholic priests, providing special classes for them to learn how to go through the motions of the Mass and discharge other priestly duties![175] Parish life thus took place under the constant fear that one's fellow parishioners or even family members might snitch. But popular piety sometimes managed to show signs of life. Nowhere is this more evident than at the "Hill of Crosses," a pilgrimage destination in Šiauliai in rural central Lithuania, where people since the 1830s had traveled for prayer and erected wooden crosses. Worried that it served as a powerful symbol of Lithuania's religiopolitical identity, the KGB bulldozed the site three times from the late 1950s to the 1970s, but people kept coming back, often at night, to put up crosses. Eventually, the KGB gave up, but not before adding the phrase "bulldozer atheism" to the Lithuanian lexicon.[176]

In the late Soviet era, church leaders who promoted or even countenanced dissent were harshly and sometimes lethally reminded of who was in charge. The priest Antanas Šeškevičius, for instance, was tried and convicted for catechizing children in 1970. For attempting to expose religious repression, the priests Leonas Šapoka and Leonas Mažeika were slain in the early

1980s, a time when many priests were threatened, beaten, attacked, and left for dead. KGB forces arrested and roughed up Father Ricardas Cerniauskas in the summer of 1981 for having led a religious retreat for young people. A highly suspect "accident" claimed the life of Father Bronius Laurinavičius on 24 November 1981 shortly after he had become a member of the Lithuanian Helsinki Group, a human-rights group dedicated to promoting political reform.[177]

This organization did not labor alone. Inspired by the papacy of John Paul II practically as much as Poles were, Lithuanian Catholics became a beacon of dissent in the late Soviet period, helping orchestrate numerous public protests and generating a large body of samizdat literature critical of the regime. In 1978, the Catholic Committee for the Defense of the Rights of Believers flickered to life, to Communists' disapprobation. Earlier, in 1972, the *Chronicle of the Catholic Church in Lithuania* began operation at the instigation of the intrepid Jesuit priest Sigitas Tamkevičius. Edited clandestinely by priests and nuns, it became one of the best-known samizdat periodicals in the late Soviet era and was regularly translated into several European languages. Despite harassment and threats looming over the heads of its writers and publishers, it appeared in eighty-one issues from 1972 to 1989, chronicling religious repression and other human-rights violations in Lithuania, the Soviet Union, and other parts of Eastern Europe.[178] It also inspired the *Chronicle of the Catholic Church in Ukraine,* another underground publication, issued in the 1980s by the suppressed Ukrainian Greek Catholic Church.

Which brings us, finally, to the Soviet Union's harsh measures against the Greek or Byzantine or "Uniate" Catholic churches in its territories, especially Ukraine.[179] In 1944 Soviet forces reoccupied Galicia in western Ukraine, home to around four million Greek Catholics (so-called because they used the Eastern Greek liturgy), aggregated into four dioceses under one metropolitan, ten bishops, and some three thousand priests, in addition to boasting 127 monasteries and five seminaries.[180] In a series of cunning policy maneuvers that would bedazzle Machiavelli, Stalin instrumentalized the Moscow Patriarchate (revived from the dead to foster wartime Russian nationalism) to do his bidding by urging and ultimately coercing all Ukrainian Greek Catholic churches to return to the Orthodox fold—something planned earlier in the war when Soviet forces first occupied Galicia—and assigned them to state-security organs charged with strict secrecy. Presumably, it was better in Stalin's eyes—and in those of his chief underling in Ukraine at the time, Nikita Khrushchev—to deal with one morally compromised church in a controlled framework than with two similar ones, even if there is something patently absurd about a political regime philosophically committed to atheism entering into complex theological issues of Christian ecclesiology and helping broker a "reunion." The additional fact that the Greek Catholic hierarchy did not rebut Ukrainian nationalism to his liking incensed Stalin, inclining him to adopt policies that mirrored those of past tsars, who similarly had pushed for reunion of Catholics and Orthodox in the nineteenth century. The Moscow Patriarchate ignominiously fell in line, intoxicated by theological predilection, political pusillanimity, and sudden opportunity.

When the Ukrainian Greek Catholic churches demurred, actions by the Kremlin and the Moscow Patriarchate—the former clearly running the show, as archival evidence has made clear—sought to bring them to heel. In fact, the pressure began beforehand, in the fall and winter of 1944, when many Greek Catholic priests discovered that they were summoned to mandatory regional meetings organized by NKVD agents to hear speakers disparage the papacy and Roman Catholicism. And then, on 11 April 1945, Soviet authorities acted aggressively, arresting the entire Greek Catholic hierarchy in their territories, including the metropolitan Josef Slipyi, who had recently replaced the respected former metropolitan, Andrey Sheptytsky (d. 1944). The arrest, torture, and deportation of hundreds of parish priests followed, while seminarians found themselves conscripted for military service. Police searches of the Cathedral and Episcopal Palace in Lviv and Stanislav took place in this context, resulting in the confiscation of religious valuables and archival material. The arrested bishops languished in prison for a year without trial before being convicted in 1946 of collaborating with German forces and given various sentences of forced labor. Among the bishops, only Metropolitan Slipyi survived. Some priests finished their sentences, but the majority perished or simply disappeared, while a similar fate befell many monks and nuns, reflecting a concurrent, brutal campaign against Ukraine's Greek Catholic monasteries.[181]

With the Greek Catholic Church in Soviet territories virtually leaderless and thrown into confusion, "patriotic" new leaders emerged, willing to work toward reunion with Moscow under the auspices of a Sponsoring Group for the Re-Union of the Greek Catholic Church with the Russian Orthodox Church. Led by the Lviv priest Havryil Kostelnyk, long browbeaten and compromised by Soviet security organs, the group proclaimed itself the only legitimate legal Catholic Church leadership and began preparing for a conference (*sobor*) of reunion. This conference took place in Lviv from 8 to 10 March 1946, after which the Ukrainian Greek Church merged with the Russian Orthodox Church. Recalcitrant priests not already in diaspora were either driven underground into a "catacomb church" or arrested by Soviet security forces. When the jurisdictionally separate Mukachiv-Uzhorod diocese in recently annexed Transcarpathia resisted the direction taken at the conference, its leadership faced sustained Soviet pressure—with its bishop, Theodore Romzha, dying under mysterious circumstances on 1 November 1947, later confirmed to have been killed by NKVD forces personally sanctioned by Khrushchev. A mop-up operation followed, in which all Greek Catholic monasteries in Transcarpathia were closed, with some later turned into Orthodox monasteries. For the remainder of the Soviet Union's existence, the Ukrainian Greek Catholic Church was officially forbidden—an example of "ethnic ecclesicide," to use a locution of the historian Bohdan R. Bociurkiw.[182] The repressed clergy shared the fate of nearly half a million western Ukrainians, forcibly resettled from Galicia and often dispersed into work camps. While a catacomb church managed to survive in the late Soviet period, its adherents were closely monitored, interrogated, and sometimes assaulted by security forces. Only at the height of Gorbachev's reforms in 1989 did Greek Catholics regain their legal existence.

One might plausibly wonder if the Soviet Union's strange and severe policy toward the Ukrainian Greek Catholic Church represents a turn away from Marxist-Leninist teaching on religion and a reversion to traditional Russian caesaropapism, as some have argued. In some respects, this was perhaps so, and certainly the forces of Ukrainian national separatism and Russian realpolitik figure into the mix. But a contrapuntal point by Bociurkiw is more apposite: "While it might be argued [in the case of the suppression of the Ukrainian Greek Catholic Church] that the Church-State partnership was the result of Stalin's deviation from the Marxist-Leninist line on religion, even in the choice of methods to effect the 'reunion,' one can detect a basically anti-religious tendency of displaying the practical superiority of force over belief, of politics over religion, of opportunism over martyrdom, not to mention the compromising of one Christian church by having it join with an avowedly atheist regime in destroying another Christian church."[183] Again, Machiavelli would have been impressed.

But, of course, Soviet power and Marxist-Leninist religious policies were felt not just within the Soviet Union but also across those parts of Eastern and Central Europe that came under Soviet control after World War II. This is the topic of the next chapter.

CHAPTER FOUR

Eastern Europe

Our life was brutally changed in 1950. The communists took over everything
and sent us to various localities to work in the factories.
—Sister Barbara Kovacova, Sisters of Charity (Slovakia)

Dissenters must be exterminated like a weasel in the chicken coop.
—Saying of the Albanian government about dissenting clerics

THE AGREEMENTS REACHED BY STALIN, CHURCHILL, AND
Roosevelt at Yalta in 1945 effectively meant that the Soviet Red Army's
advance would establish the USSR's control of vast stretches of Eastern
and Central Europe at the end of World War II. The next year in a speech
given in Fulton, Missouri, Churchill memorably described an "iron curtain"
having descended across the Continent, dividing Western Europe from the
"Soviet sphere"; those countries—Poland, Czechoslovakia, Hungary, Romania, Bulgaria, Yugoslavia, Albania, and the eastern parts of Germany—now
faced an "increasing measure of control from Moscow." Exhausted from the
war and Nazi occupation, with limited means of doing otherwise, people
in what came to be called "people's democracies" had little choice but to
endure the course of events, hoping that better days might nonetheless lie
ahead, somehow.

The Sovietization of these areas proceeded in fits and starts at first, but
by the late 1940s the political dynamics that shaped the "Eastern bloc" until
the annus mirabilis of 1989 were everywhere apparent. Effectively, this
meant at least five things. First, signs of fledgling political pluralism gave
way to Communist-dominated "fronts" in all countries, with party leaders
beholden to Moscow for financial, military, and diplomatic support. Josip
Broz Tito's Yugoslavia, which acrimoniously broke with Moscow in 1948,
was the exception that proved the rule—an act of autonomous Communist

assertation that heightened Soviet involvement in the remaining countries to stanch the spread of "Titoism." Second, "antifascism" dominated the political vocabulary; anyone deemed to have collaborated with Nazi forces faced harsh, often lethal reprisals. Third, the Soviet NKVD, in collaboration with local Communist parties, quickly set up secret-police operations in its own image, often using people whom it had trained in Moscow during the war, to scare and silence critics; thus originated the infamous secret security forces, such as the Stasi in East Germany, the Securitate in Romania, and the Sigurimi in Albania. Fourth, Moscow and local Communist partisans portrayed Stalin as a savior-like figure, benevolently rescuing the peoples of Eastern Europe from the clutches of German aggression and the looming menace of Western capitalism and imperialism. Finally, as the United States and its Western allies looked askance at developments in the east, the bipolar realities of the Cold War came into focus—epitomized by the Berlin Airlift of 1948-49—with Moscow pitted against Washington in a conflict with both European and global, tactical and ideological, dimensions.[1]

To make sense of it all, Marxist-Leninist intellectuals interpreted the outcome of the war in world-historical terms. Fortuitously for Eastern Europe, so some argued, the Red Army had transported humanity there beyond capitalism and "bourgeois democracy" to a new stage of reality, ripe with promise. What was real was right, as Hegel famously said. The war and its outcome, in other words, had accelerated the inevitable course of history, making full-blown Communism patterned on the Soviet model possible, perhaps within a generation's reach.[2] From a sense of both gratitude and duty, those living in Eastern Europe should consign the past to oblivion, spurn other options, and labor toward a Marxist-Leninist commonweal.

The postwar situation dramatically and severely impacted religious communities across Eastern Europe. From the earliest days of the Soviet occupation, as the historian Anne Applebaum has written, "communist leaders instinctively hated and feared church leaders, and not merely because of their own doctrinal atheism. Religious leaders were a source of alternate moral and spiritual authority."[3] Sooner or later after 1945, therefore, the Communist governments—despite overtures to freedom of conscience in most postwar constitutions—pressed for the nationalization of church property, the severance of church ties with the West, the censorship of religious writings, the removal of uncooperative clergymen, and the setting up of legal and bureaucratic mechanisms to control and degrade religious institutions.

The Communist bid to dominate education, along with the diffusion of anti-religious propaganda, in conquered areas, augured for enduring enmity between the devout and their new political masters. While these measures were not as gut-wrenchingly lethal as Soviet persecutions in the 1920s and 1930s, religious communities in most of the Eastern bloc nonetheless lived in an atmosphere of extraordinary repression and fear for most of the Cold War. Early on, this meant violent attacks against the clergy and efforts to dismantle religious institutions outright; later, it more often meant their co-option and control by state organs, party apparatchiks, and browbeaten or collaborationist clergy. Throughout, it meant the steady drip of atheist indoctrination. A *tour d'horizon* of the general situation after the war followed by profiles of three Soviet-bloc countries—Romania, Czechoslovakia, and Albania—supports these points.

POSTWAR

Immediately at the war's end in occupied areas, Soviet forces oscillated between a mentality of reprisal and caution with respect to religious authorities. On the one hand, in a situation of general mayhem and plunder, they targeted anyone deemed to have collaborated or sympathized with Nazi authorities, or even suspected of having done so, leaving nuanced judgment for another time. Polish Catholic priests had it particularly hard and, if not killed, wound up in Soviet labor camps in large numbers. Slander campaigns against the clergy soon began in practically all areas under Soviet control. An "example" was made of some individuals, such as the Hungarian Lutheran bishop Zoltán Túróczy, tried for "anti-Soviet" activities in 1945 by a "people's court" and sentenced to ten years of hard labor in an effort to scare and silence others.[4] In the Balkans, occupying forces sometimes shot the village priest to make a statement in a particular area.[5] On the other hand, Soviet authorities were capable of strategic restraint, permitting the function of some religious institutions and even reopening others, in an effort to distinguish the new occupiers from their Nazi predecessors. Dialogue between Communists and Christian intellectuals even took place in a few areas as everyone turned to the postwar rebuilding of society, with committed Marxist-Leninists hoping that religiosity would decline under suitable educational reforms and with the passing of an older generation.

By the end of 1947, however, even modest collaborative efforts began to break down, replaced by tension between incipient Communist regimes and the "reactionary" clergy, along with their religiously devout laity. An NKVD guideline of 2 June 1947 called for all cultural activity in the Soviet orbit "to generate antipathy for the churches."[6] The logic of totalitarianism, moreover, entailed a profound suspicion of "civil society" and an urge to bring all associations dedicated to social amelioration under centralized state control. Churches, monasteries, seminaries, youth organizations, and religiously affiliated schools and camps, in addition to being ideologically wrongheaded, loomed large as obstacles to the expansion of governments' powers. Because of its ties to the West and to the several Eastern European national identities, the Catholic Church in particular presented a formidable challenge. "The battle against the enemy activity of the [Catholic] clerics is without a doubt one of the most difficult tasks in front of us," as Julia Brystiger, a Polish Communist, sized up the matter in 1947. Or, as Stalin himself opined at a Cominform meeting in October 1949 about the situation in Czechoslovakia: "We have to fight a systematic war against the hierarchy," bringing churches there "under our full control."[7]

Although "full control" proved elusive, harsher measures—not only against Catholicism but against other faith communities too—became the norm in practically all Soviet-bloc countries in the late 1940s and early 1950s. While uneasy détente between most churches and states characterized the later Cold War period, repression never entirely abated. To be sure, the Soviet satellite countries did not all march in lockstep; in some (like Poland and East Germany) a gutsy religious sector exhibited noteworthy defiance, while in others (like Albania) something approaching complete state mastery was achieved. Docile Orthodox clergy arguably had it best if they did not buck the party line and genuflected to the Moscow Patriarchate, an ignominious spiritual shadow of Kremlin power in the postwar period. Nonetheless, across the Eastern bloc in the early Cold War, religious communities, large and small, faced repression from newly installed, often insecure Communist regimes.

Following the Soviet model, governments pursued the confiscatory "nationalization" of church properties as a means of achieving control, defunding religious activities, and realizing Marxist-Leninist socioeconomic principles. During land reforms in Hungary, the state deprived the Catholic Church of more than three-quarters of its land and the Protestant churches of nearly half of theirs, promising compensation that never came.[8] These policies seem mild in comparison to those in other countries, such as Czechoslovakia, Bulgaria, and Albania, where religious communities forcibly lost practically all their property. When faced with protests, officials often described the actions as necessary for economic reform rather than as an open attack on religion.

Putatively "democratic" constitutions drafted in Eastern Europe's new states included language about freedom of conscience, as agreed to at the Potsdam Conference, but that was generally interpreted to mean freedom of worship alone within the walls of churches, as had been the case in the Soviet Union, not a more general free exercise of expressions of faith. Similar language about freedom of speech and the press proved bogus when Moscow-backed authorities started to harass and shut down religious publications and presses along with those of dissident political voices. "Democratic 'freedom of speech' in this country means that any opinion that differs from the official one is silenced," thundered Hungary's Cardinal Mindszenty in 1950 in an impassioned pastoral letter.[9] Due to actions of the German Democratic Republic, "the Catholic Church has not a single periodical," complained the bishop of Berlin, Cardinal von Preysing.[10] Throwing up obstacles to and surveilling the religious press, practicing outright censorship, and trying to block access to religious literature printed outside the Iron Curtain bloc were practices maintained by most Communist governments throughout the Cold War.

Perhaps surprisingly, several Eastern-bloc states retained the Erastian relationship between church and state that had prevailed prior to the war—a phenomenon one might think of as "Stalinist caesaropapism." It extended to creating or reinstating variously named secretariats or ministries of ecclesiastical affairs and even providing clerical salaries. But since the governments were philosophically committed to Marxism-Leninism, these bureaus generally functioned as a keep-your-friends-close-and-your-enemies-closer instrument of political control. The bureaucratic involvement with religious bodies during the Soviet era was essentially "deceptive," as the scholar Zsuzsánna Magdó observed, "and should not be mistaken for an ideological reconciliation between Communism and religion."[11] The existence of religious entities—to use the Romanian Orthodox Church an example—allowed the government to exercise extensive sway over ecclesiastical appointments and devise other means of control, censorship, and infiltration, while also providing a theological fig leaf to justify the persecution of non-Orthodox religious communities, most notably Eastern Rite or Greek Catholics, who were forcibly suppressed in Romania as they were in the Soviet Union.[12] Over time, these ministries reduced the churches to quasi-appendages of the state, eliminating refractory clergymen and making possible extensive government involvement in church affairs. They also played major roles in restricting seminary education, manufacturing shortages of capable clerics, and enabling the religious vocations of potential collaborationists. Since the collapse of Communism, archival evidence has revealed extensive secret-police infiltration of major religious bodies.[13]

Among the wiliest tactics employed among Eastern-bloc governments was the grooming and promotion of "progressive" factions among the clergy—so-called peace priests or patriotic priests, as they were called— ordained leaders who felt that Marxism and Christianity were ultimately reconcilable and were willing to countenance, and even defend, legal strictures on religious expression. This tactic accomplished two aims at once: it sowed divisions within churches, between these factions and their more intransigent coreligionists, while cultivating an opportunistic, compliant clergy willing to do the government's bidding in both domestic and foreign policy.[14] In Catholic-majority countries, such as Czechoslovakia and Hungary, the government and its clerical quislings championed an exclusively "national church," cut off from the influence of Rome. In predominantly Orthodox countries, such as Bulgaria and Romania, the Moscow Patriarchate provided the template: pandering to Caesar, criticizing the West, and countenancing the constriction of religious activity to a purely "spiritual" plane. Often granted privileged freedoms to travel abroad to participate in organizations such as the World Council of Churches, these "progressive" priests gave the impression to international audiences that the religious sphere in their countries did not suffer as much as critics claimed. For their aversion to making waves, they were often regarded skeptically by their own flocks, seen as untrustworthy men on the make.[15] By contrast, governments plied them with plaudits and praise; in Hungary, for example, "a veritable proliferation of honorary titles, medals, sashes, orders, and decorations [were made available] for cooperative clergy," as the political scientist Pedro Ramet has noted.[16] "By selecting suitable personnel [politically docile clerics] to run the Church," as the Czech scholar Alexander Tomsky once observed, "the State has tried to use the Church structure to undermine the Church's own spiritual autonomy."[17]

Religious orders proved more intransigent, and they paid a price for it. In keeping with an Enlightenment-era critique that regarded cloistered monks and nuns as social parasites engaged in useless contemplation, Eastern-bloc Communists zealously targeted them. In the late 1940s and early 1950s, Hungary dissolved practically all orders, upending the vocations of around ten thousand people, men and women, whether cloistered or mendicant.[18] Transport trucks sometimes pulled up at religious houses in the middle of the night, removing people to other locations, where they had to find work in factories or in agriculture, although many fled abroad. Communists worried especially about the influence that female religious orders (often dedicated to teaching) wielded over the minds of young people. Throughout the Eastern bloc, therefore, authorities took actions aimed at crippling women's religious congregations. The first battle against nuns in Poland, for example, closed or secularized schools run by orders and banned nuns from teaching. In 1954, a Polish government operation with the code name "X-2" established eight labor camps—euphemistically called "centralized convents"—in the areas of Cracow and Poznan Voivodeship for deposed nuns transferred from Silesia.[19] This is part of a larger story, movingly told in "Sister Survivors of European Communism," a research project led by American nuns that tells the stories of women religious under Communism as they coped with states' efforts to suppress their work.[20] But male orders, sometimes involved in teaching too, also felt Caesar's wrath. Agencies dedicated to propaganda often portrayed religious houses in the most lurid and worrisome terms: nests of illicit sexual activity, hatcheries of political dissent, drains on the economy.

Such propaganda and the expulsion of religious orders from teaching reflected a broader Communist effort across Eastern Europe to control the formation of youth. "Those who own the youth, own the future," as a slogan for the Communist German Young Pioneers put it, reflecting Marxist-Leninist views on the mutability of human nature and the priority given to the ideological formation of children and teens. Children are "our cleanest and best human material," echoed the first East German prime minister, Otto Grotewohl, in 1949.[21] In June 1948, some sixty-five hundred schools in Hungary under coercion abandoned their previous religious identities and become state schools. Comparable actions took place in other countries in the late 1940s and 1950s, ending or greatly curtailing religious education. Children were sometimes asked to publicly renounce religious belief or face expulsion. Historical materialism displaced religious content in the classroom. Officials also expected teachers to focus on the harm historically perpetrated by "superstition": thus pedagogy emphasized witchcraft trials, the Crusades, the Inquisition, and churches' general complicity in oppression.[22] For many teachers, these requirements created a crisis of conscience, compelling them to teach against the grain of their convictions. Not a few left the teaching profession or, if shirking their duties in the eyes of authorities, found themselves purged or demoted. Teachers caught sneakily instructing in religious matters, when not relieved of their duties, received detention duties, forced to learn or relearn and parrot the leaden truths of Marxism-Leninism. When parents clamored for religious instruction, they were reminded that they risked damaging their child's prospects of future education and job placement.[23] The widespread nature of this threat, a pervasive reality in most Eastern-bloc countries, anguished religious families throughout the Cold War.

Besides focusing on schools, governments targeted youth organizations with religious content—such as the YMCA, deemed a "tool of bourgeois fascism" by the Polish government. In the German Democratic Republic (GDR), the Communist Young Pioneers and Free German Youth replaced Catholic and Protestant youth organizations.[24] In 1954, the GDR introduced the so-called *Jugendweihe* (dedication of the young), a secular alternative to the common religious confirmation ceremony for adolescents, intended by the recitation of a solemn oath to demonstrate that a particular young person had come of age and affirmed Marxism-Leninism. To the delight of GDR officialdom, the admissibility of permitting one's child to participate in these ceremonies created a huge rift within churches—some deeming it harmless and perfunctory, others as an unwarranted capitulation to Caesar.[25] In Poland, authorities targeted Caritas, the nation's largest Catholic charity, which operated thousands of orphanages; it was placed under state administration, its leadership summarily dismissed.[26]

As governments tightened their grip on society, some intrepid priests and prelates cried foul. State-security forces in turn frequently launched "whispering campaigns" against outspoken clergy to smear their character and undermine their authority. Across the Eastern bloc, priests were arrested in droves; by 1953, about a thousand languished in prison in Poland alone, with many others sent to labor camps or subjected to the indignity of regular interrogation and surveillance. A parish priest in Krotoszyn, Poland, was investigated as "a definite enemy of the current reality, which he reveal[ed] in sermons with double meanings, individual conversations, and confessions."[27] Bulgarian Communists confined the metropolitan of the Bulgarian Orthodox Church, Stefan I, to a monastery and classified all priests in Bulgaria as having either a positive or a negative attitude toward government. Those with a negative attitude experienced repressive actions, resulting in the incarceration of about 10 percent of all clergy.[28] Not least, in Albania the entire Catholic hierarchy, as well as many Muslim and Orthodox clergy, found themselves in the crosshairs of a vicious Communist regime, resulting in arrests, imprisonments, and executions.[29]

Due to their ties to the Vatican and their generally higher levels of education, upper echelons of the Catholic hierarchy became the focal point of intense Communist opposition. The cases of four prelates—Archbishop József Cardinal Mindszenty of Hungary, Archbishop Josef Beran of Czechoslovakia, Cardinal Stefan Wyszyński of Poland, and Archbishop Aloysius Stepinac of Yugoslavia—epitomized the nature of the ideological standoff. Among these, the case of Mindszenty best illustrates the extent to which a Communist regime was willing to go to silence and intimidate critics. Mindszenty served as the archbishop of Esztergom and hence the "Prince Primate" of Hungary after 1945—not an unimportant figure. In full agreement with the dim view of Communism held by Pope Pius XII, Mindszenty encouraged Catholic solidarity against the new regime by urging special devotion to the Virgin Mary and by refusing to give in to requested concessions. Not one to mince words, he counterattacked whenever he felt the regime encroached upon the church, and he refused to break ties with the Vatican, as the Hungarian government had requested. After weeks of harassment, police finally arrested him in December 1948, charging him with treason and espionage in addition to minor currency infractions. He was then taken to the Arrow Cross building in Budapest, the site of a notorious prison, where his confinement included sleep deprivation, beatings with a rubber truncheon, drug injections, and having to wear a clown suit. The show trial that took place concurrently, broadcast throughout the country, dragged on until the cardinal finally publicly "confessed" to various ludicrous crimes. Having provided security forces with language for a menacing new phenomenon, "Mindszentyism," the aged cardinal was convicted and put in prison, where he languished until 1956. The Hungarian Uprising of that year permitted him to escape to the American Embassy, where he remained for a period before eventually being able to travel to Vienna.[30]

The lessons from Mindszenty's persecution and those of other prelates sent a clear message: if *they* were not above ill-treatment, no one was. And the threat extended far beyond Catholicism to smaller religious communities, the leaders of which faced harassment and state violence in large numbers. Both the Reformed and Lutheran communities in Hungary experienced their share of arrests, imprisonments, show trials, and executions before assuming a more docile posture before the government.[31] As the Bulgarian government began to control and compromise its Orthodox community in 1949, fifteen Protestant pastors were sentenced to prison, four of them receiving life sentences and nine receiving fifteen years.[32] The Muslim minority (around 15 percent of the population) in Bulgaria encountered relentless repression—mosques and madrasas demolished, Qur'ans burned, the defiant removed to labor camps. Coercive measures of assimilation included bans on the Turkish and Arabic languages and a nationwide mandate for all Muslims to adopt Slavic names. By the 1980s, "Muslim culture in Bulgaria was shattered," as the scholar of Eastern Europe Pedro Ramet has summed up.[33]

Religious communities and movements originating in the United States such as Jehovah's Witnesses, the Seventh-day Adventists, and the Church of Jesus Christ of Latter-day Saints (the Mormons) faced particularly harsh scrutiny, especially if they engaged in missionary activity, a cardinal sin under most Communist regimes. During the forty years of its existence, the GDR imprisoned six thousand Jehovah's Witnesses, often in the wake of press campaigns against them and police disruptions of their services. Officials accused them of seeking to revive a fascist system under the pretense of religion, despite the fact that the Nazi government had persecuted them as well![34]

Tragically, Jews, the primary victims of the wartime Holocaust, experienced anti-religious and anti-Zionist prejudice throughout Eastern Europe as anti-Semitism also raged in the Soviet Union in the late 1940s and 1950s and with the same vague association of Jews with "capitalism," "America," "bourgeois mentalities," and "rootless cosmopolitanism." Lingering patterns of local, popular anti-Semitism made the situation still more difficult. Fusing long-standing currents of anti-Semitism and Marxist critiques of religion, Communists castigated Hebrew as the language of superstition and disloyal Zionists. "Good riddance" was the response of several regimes, as the children of Abraham left in droves for Palestine during the middle decades of the twentieth century. In the early 1980s, for instance, the Jewish population in Romania had dropped to 30,000 from a postwar total of around 420,000; in this same period Czechoslovakia's numbers dropped to around 2,000 from a postwar figure of 44,200. In Bulgaria, fewer than 5,000 Jews remained just before the Berlin Wall fell, compared to about 52,000 at the end of World War II.[35]

Although some of the worst anti-religious persecutions in the Eastern bloc took place in the late 1940s and 1950s, much repression took place later as well. Alongside high-profile cases of political imprisonment and torture, a catalog of recurring indignities suffered by religious believers— worse in some countries than in others and worse at some times than at others—included exclusion from party membership and its perks, from the officer corps in the military, and from upper-level jobs in government, industry, and education; coerced participation in atheistic youth organizations; persistent fear of surveillance and arrest; worry that one's neighbors and perhaps even fellow parishioners served as government informants; having to endure countless hours of Marxist-Leninist educational programming; having constrained ability to provide catechesis for one's own children; pervasive censorship; restricted access to religious literature; and extreme difficulty in being able to travel abroad. To be sure, many regimes struck deals with religious communities and worked out various forms of modus vivendi. Rarely did anti-religious repression neatly achieve its desired results. Not infrequently, in fact, the opposite took place, as vigorous underground religious communities sprang up. Even so, the official line on religion (whatever the policy results in individual countries) regarded it as a remnant of the past, a hulking obstacle to Marxist-Leninist civilizational renewal, a yawning sinkhole in the stadial path of progress. As the Czech Communist newspaper *Rudé právo* (Red Justice) put it in 1984: "All religions inhibit man's moral development, which molds his best characteristics. . . . [R]eligion necessarily causes dichotomy in moral consciousness and creates two rival authorities—the authority of God and the authority of society in which man lives. Morality that is derived . . . from God's demands inevitably clashes with the moral demands which flow out of the needs of societal life."[36] The implication is clear: the religiously devout and their clerical enablers amounted to second-class citizens, pinioned and put up with for the time being, perhaps, but ultimately inimical to the secularist common-weal, nasty flies in the ointment.

ROMANIA

Communist rule arrived quickly in postwar Romania with the ending of the monarchy and the proclamation of the People's Republic on 30 December 1947. Under heavy Soviet influence, led by Gheorghe Gheorghiu-Dej, the fledgling government merged the Communist and Social Democratic parties into one Workers' (later Communist) Party and essentially banned all others.[37] Although later distancing itself from Moscow in the name of "autochthonous socialism," this single party wielded exclusive power from 1947 until the collapse of the regime in December 1989. Committed to Marxist-Leninist atheism and willing to persecute all faith communities at first, the regime came to give preferential treatment to the Romanian Orthodox Church (which represented more than 80 percent of the population), reasoning that the dialectical exigencies of history might need a while to take hold in this pious, rural land and that Orthodoxy had served as a key element of national cohesion and could be instrumentalized as "heritage" in the short term. Fortunately for the Communists, they dealt with feckless and compliant bishops, who appealed to the Orthodox notion of "symphonia" to justify their docility. But this did not entirely spare the Orthodox from repression, even as it all but assured it for Catholics and Protestants, two groups concentrated in Transylvania among Hungarian- and German-speaking minorities, as well as for a handful of Muslims and a sizable Jewish community that had managed to survive the Shoah. Thus, religious persecution in Communist Romania had a distinctively xenophobic cast—hitched to philosophical atheism, on the one hand, but to the priority of "Romanian heritage," on the other.

But in the immediate postwar years, a more general anti-religious repression held sway, as part of a broader witch hunt against a vast array of political enemies. Recognizing the obstacle presented by religion in establishing dominance over civil society, Communists interrogated and arrested numerous religious leaders, exiling some while imprisoning, torturing, and killing others. Recent scholarship offers fairly reliable figures for the immediate postwar period. Seventeen Orthodox prelates were denied their seats, and fifteen were exiled; 1,888 Orthodox, 235 Greek Catholic, and 174 Roman Catholic priests were arrested, along with 102 Protestant pastors, 23 Muslim imams, and 13 Jewish rabbis. The early years of Communist rule, as the Romanian historian Lucian Turcescu has summed up, "were marked by numerous arrests and imprisonments, deportations, and extra-judicial killings perpetrated by the regime that was Stalinist in nature. Many bishops, priests, monks, nuns, and ordinary believers from all denominations, including the Orthodox Church, were tortured or died in the Communist prison system, the so-called Romanian Gulag."[38]

Despite a nod to liberty of conscience in the constitution (1948), decrees and legislation in the regime's early years sought to undermine religious bodies. Agrarian reforms during Soviet occupation right after the war permitted the extensive seizure of church properties. Decree 177 (On Religious Denominations) in 1948 made the legal existence of religious bodies—fourteen in all—wholly dependent on state recognition, while granting a newly established Ministry of Religious Affairs the right to verify, inventory, and control all church assets. The government refused to recognize the so-called Army of the Lord, an influential evangelical renewal movement within the Orthodox Church; for his defiance, its leader, the poet Traian Dorz, spent seventeen years in prison and under house arrest. Several Protestant bodies were forced to merge or lose recognition. Decrees on education abolished confessional schools and those operated by foreigners, paving the way for nationalized education at all levels that came to be anchored in Marxist-Leninist historical materialism. A handful of seminaries survived the onslaught, but appointments and curricula were always subject to state oversight and supervision.[39] Roughly concurrently, the party began to promote atheism nationwide, setting up a Society for the Popularization of Science and Culture, which was tasked "to fight obscurantism, superstition, mysticism, and all other influences of bourgeois ideologies."[40] Directed by a presidium of intellectuals, the society could boast of thirty-seven branches and three thousand propagandists by 1951.[41] Its activities laid the groundwork for successive atheist campaigns in the future.[42]

Romania's Greek and Roman Catholics experienced acute hardship during the regime's early years. Imitating Stalin's policies in Ukraine, the Romanian party-state summarily dissolved Romania's small Greek Catholic Church in December 1948, transferring its buildings and land to the Orthodox Church, while attacking Roman Catholics and smearing the Vatican. All seven Greek Catholic bishops refused the dissolution of their church and wound up in prison because of their stance. Five died in confinement—from cold, hunger, disease, or hard manual labor—and were buried in unmarked graves. Vasile Aftenie, the vicar-general of Bucharest, was cruelly tortured, his limbs dismembered. The sole survivor, Iuliu Hossu, spent twenty-two years in prison and forced domicile. Roughly six hundred additional priests wound up in prison, some carted off to Soviet labor camps, with only about half of them surviving. Confronted with these grim realities, and facing both penury and threats of harm, about a quarter of the Romanian Greek Catholic clergy finally capitulated, allowing the government to crow about "voluntary" conversions. Religious houses, both men's and women's, proved more recalcitrant, but they too could not resist the tide of events. In one case, at the Basilian monastery in Bixad, fifteen truckloads of Securitate agents showed up to dislodge the monks, keeping an angry local population at bay with machine guns. Seventy-six intrepid Orthodox priests—exceptions, not the rule—who protested the treatment of Greek Catholics found themselves in jail. The complicity of the Romanian Orthodox patriarch Justinian and other Orthodox clergy in this entire process—which culminated in coerced reunion at the Church Union Congress in Alba Iulia in December 1948—has remained a delicate topic in Catholic-Orthodox relations until the present.[43]

The Romanian Latin Rite Catholic community, located primarily in Transylvania and Moldavia, fared little better. Accused by the regime of being "submissive to a foreign ruler" and prone to fascism and "undemocratic" mentalities, bishops, priests, and the lay devout alike experienced vicious treatment in the 1940s and 1950s. Authorities suppressed dioceses and orders, closed down churches, and deposed intransigent bishops. No fewer than 106 parishes required military occupation to bring about the desired result; in several cases conflicts erupted that produced injuries and, in one case, death. In July 1949, all Catholic religious orders were suppressed, their members forbidden to teach or to hold public-service jobs.[44] Abrogating the Concordat of 1927, which had given Catholics in Romania considerable freedoms, the regime forbade all contact with Rome and threw out the papal nuncio, Monsignor Gerald Patrick O'Hara, an American by birth who was branded as a CIA agent, but not before he had consecrated several bishops and apostolic administrators in secret, sowing seeds for an underground church that managed to hobble along.

Some Catholic leaders and seminarians, along with several Orthodox and those from other denominations, wound up at the notorious Piteşti and Sighet prisons, where they experienced brutal interrogation, sleep deprivation, forced marches, exposure to the cold, and much worse. In addition, these prisons practiced extreme forms of "reeducation" and "brainwashing" techniques, usually called the "Piteşti experiment" or the "Piteşti system," carried out under the direction of Eugen Turcanu, who enjoyed the tacit approval of the Romanian Securitate (figure 9). To create the "new man" (*omul nou*) of Communist fantasy, prisoners were asked to confess crimes, renounce their faith, snitch on their friends, and embrace Marxism-Leninism. To produce these results, unspeakable tortures were devised, bringing inmates to the brink of death, as the method stipulated, without actually killing them. Having prisoners commit blasphemy against their religious beliefs was standard practice. Forcing them to torture one another was

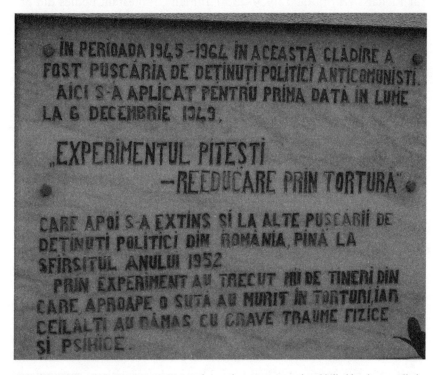

Figure 9. Plaque in Romania recognizing those who were tortured and killed by the so-called Piteşti prison experiment. Photographer unknown. Courtesy of Wikimedia Commons.

another. A sadistic experience for the devout involved guards plunging their heads into buckets of urine and fecal matter in a parody of the baptismal rite. One survivor later reflected, "There is no other mind than Lucifer's capable of imagining the Piteşti system that kept a man suspended between to be and not to be, at the limits of madness and reality."[45] No stranger to the Soviet Gulag, Aleksandr Solzhenitsyn, when he learned of what happened in Romania, recognized it as infinitely worse than his own experience and possibly "the most terrible act of barbarism in the modern world." While not all inmates received such cruel treatment, estimates of the deaths of political detainees in Romanian prisons or in forced labor camps, such those set up to build the Danube–Black Sea Canal, number more than a hundred thousand.[46] The report of a post-Communist Romanian presidential commission, published in 2006, gave the figure of six hundred thousand political-crime sentences during the Communist era.

A particularly well-known case of torture involved the Lutheran pastor Richard Wurmbrand (1909–2001). Initially, Protestant bodies did not appear to be as serious a threat to the state as Catholicism, but that gradually changed. The fact that most Lutherans were of German descent and Calvinists were of Hungarian descent did not help matters. For his part, in addition to giving rousing public sermons, Wurmbrand proclaimed the categorical incompatibility of Marxism and Christianity, thus incurring his arrest and imprisonment. Passing through multiple penal facilities, he experienced solitary confinement, torture, and brainwashing attempts. Released in 1956, he faced confinement again after refusing to quit preaching and was given a twenty-five-year sentence, during which he became eligible for a ransomed amnesty in 1964 negotiated by the Hebrew Christian Alliance and the Norwegian Mission to the Jews (Wurmbrand was born a Jew). Urged to accept the arrangement and become a voice for the persecuted in the West, Wurmbrand departed Romania in 1964 and emigrated to the United States, where he began a laborious odyssey of consciousness-raising, speaking in numerous countries, including testimony before the U.S. Senate, and writing numerous books, including *Tortured for Christ,* a volume that conveys his prison experience. In his testimony before the Senate, he memorably described "the times of brainwashing. Those who have not passed through brainwashing can't understand what torture it is. . . . From 5 in the morning until 10 in the evening we had to sit like this [erect without moving] and hear: 'Communism is good. Communism is good. Communism is good.

Communism is good. Communism is good. Christianity is stupid! Christianity is stupid! Christianity is stupid! . . . Nobody more believes in Christ. Give up! Give up! Give up!' For days, weeks, years, we had to listen to these things."[47]

Non-Orthodox Christians made up the lion's share of repressed believers, but Romanian Jews received harsh treatment too. Early nationalization measures resulted in the liquidation of 256 Jewish charities, including orphanages, children's homes, and hospitals, to say nothing of the closure of all Jewish schools. Communists forced the country's chief rabbi, Alexandru Şafran, from office, replacing him with a more pliable figure. Soviet-style anti-Zionism, especially after the founding of Israel in 1948, impacted Romania too, resulting in the purging of "rootless cosmopolitans" (Stalin's phrase for Jews) from the Communist Party and in the derision of the Hebrew language and Jewish cultic practices as superstitious holdovers from a bygone age. Those Jews perceived as recalcitrantly Zionist received harsh prison sentences in Sighet, Piteşti, and other sites, where they experienced the same torture and brainwashing tactics as Christians and other political prisoners. Not surprisingly, many Jews wanted to leave it all behind and head for Israel. The government soon saw fit to make exit visas obtainable in exchange for Israel supplying the country with needed drills and pipes to help the county's ailing oil industry. By 1951, roughly 115,000 Romanian Jews had departed for Israel. Breaking from the pattern of many other Communist states, the Romanian government under Nicolae Ceauşescu in the 1960s and 1970s sought closer ties with Israel. But this was largely a political calculus based on the desire for Israeli loans and an opportunistic scheme that allowed Romania to profit from the exit visas issued; state coffers gained a minimum of three thousand dollars per head and up to twenty-five thousand dollars for the release of Jewish scientists and engineers. The numbers alone tell a story. Around four hundred thousand Romanian Jews survived the Holocaust; only ten thousand remained in the country to witness the revolutionary events of 1989.[48]

While the worst anti-religious persecutions took place early in the Cold War, Romania remained a repressive surveillance state until the demise of Communism, with little toleration for dissent, religious or otherwise, and scant legal opportunity for disfavored believers to practice their faith except behind the closed doors of worship spaces. Orthodoxy's accommodating relationship with the regime came into its own in the 1960s and 1970s after a wave of persecution against Orthodox monasteries in the late 1950s, which closed many of them, greatly restricted the number of novices, and led Patriarch Justinian to reform monasticism away from contemplation and prayer to emphasize "useful trades." With Justinian's passing, Iustin Moisescu became patriarch in 1977 and promptly distinguished himself as the most accomplished toady of them all. Astoundingly, he praised Ceaușescu "for securing complete freedom of all religious cults in our country" and often seemed more eager to do the government's bidding than the government even desired.

General secretary of the Communist Party beginning in 1965 and Romania's president from 1974 until 1989, Ceaușescu worsened the repressive atmosphere, cracking down on the public celebration of religious holidays, destroying sacred architecture, and engaging in numerous skirmishes with religious communities in the twilight years of the regime. A telling case involved the Christian Committee for the Defense of Religious Freedom and Freedom of Conscience (1978), which arose among Baptists, a denomination whose growth in membership had long unnerved the regime. Organized by intrepid critics of the regime disillusioned with the subservient attitudes displayed by fellow Baptists, the committee drafted and published on 5 July 1978 "An Appeal to the Romanian Council of State" to air and seek redress of grievances. Selectively quoting this document offers insight into the repressive atmosphere of the time. On behalf of all believers, the writers asked for

2—the right to practice religion in church, private homes and in public without official approval.

3—the right to make church appointments: to appoint leaders, hierarchs, priests, pastors, and theological professors . . . [without] interference by the Department of Cults.

5—the right to express religious opinions in public as does atheist propaganda at present.

7—the right to give religious instruction to children and young people.

11—the right for Christians to have higher posts in the economy, education, university life, the diplomatic service, etc.

16—the right of Romanian Christians to refuse to sign an oath of loyalty to the Communist Party, or an opportunity for those who do sign, not to accept atheist indoctrination.[49]

Shortly after publication, this document's drafters were all either arrested or driven into exile, ushering in a particularly bleak time for believers during the 1980s—a decade when, according to official figures, 15,087 Securitate agents, 507,002 official informants, and an unknown number of other collaborators contributed to the Stalinist environment. "Citizens survived," as the political scientist Lavinia Stan described the times, "by keeping silent, turning a blind eye to injustice inflicted on relatives, neighbors, and friends, downgrading their life expectations, [and] living parallel lives of solitude."[50]

Such a bleak reality was felt by all people, the devout and non-devout alike—and even by Orthodox Christians too, despite their preferential status. In fact, the 1980s witnessed the government revealing its true colors with respect to the Orthodox Church in matters having to do with church buildings. This had long been a vexing issue for minority faiths, as obtaining a license for a new construction or for the expansion of an existing building proved virtually impossible. Petitioning for the latter in fact led in several cases to the government's decision to tear down a church entirely.[51] In the 1980s, Ceaușescu launched a major construction project in and around Bucharest, the centerpiece being a sprawling, new presidential palace surrounded by other public office buildings. Under this pretext, the government destroyed or mutilated twenty-four churches, mostly Orthodox, and three monasteries, including the Văcărești monastery, among the most revered religious sites in the country. Three synagogues met their end as well. The government claimed the new construction necessitated the demolitions, but subsequent evidence has made clear that the actions also stemmed from a calculated decision to undermine the church's authority by depriving it of prominent locations in the nation's capital. Clergy's protests, and clever engineering to relocate some churches, staved off utter destruction, but the extensive damage done and the impotence of religious figures to halt it spoke volumes about the actual situation.[52]

Given the climate of religious repression in the late 1980s, it perhaps should not be a surprise that the cataclysmic changes that swept Communism from power in Romania erupted after László Tőkés, an outspoken Reformed pastor in the city of Timisoara, refused to vacate his parish when his supervisor, under government pressure, tried to relocate him. Although not without bloodshed, the mass protests that his intransigence inspired, coming on the heels of the fall of the Berlin Wall in November 1989, spread from Timisoara to Bucharest and other cities, toppling the Ceaușescu government in December 1989, allowing for the public celebration of Christmas for the first time in decades.

CZECHOSLOVAKIA

Created as an independent country only after World War I, Czechoslovakia was reestablished after World War II, minus Subcarpathian Ruthenia, which the Soviet Union incorporated into Ukraine. In the elections of 1946, the Communist Party did well in Czech lands, while the (non-Communist) Slovak Democratic Party prevailed in Slovakia. But in February 1948, the Soviet-backed Communists extended their power over the entire country in a determined coup d'état.[53]

In addition to a small Orthodox community, the few Jews who had survived the Holocaust, and several small Protestant bodies, the major religious communities in Czechoslovakia included Roman and Greek Catholicism, the Moravian Church, the Hussite or Czechoslovak Church, and Lutheranism, preponderantly in Slovakia. Members of all these communities clashed with the Communist regime at some point, although the Czech Communists tended to frown less on Protestant bodies and the Hussites, wishfully interpreting them as forerunners of their own enlightened outlook and a potential common foe against Catholicism. Roman and Greek Catholics (80 percent of the population) experienced the worst repression—by far. Harsh, Stalinist-style persecutions occurred in the late 1940s and early 1950s, ebbing considerably during the so-called Prague Spring that began in January 1968. The Soviet military's crushing of this movement in August 1968, however, returned the country to a climate of fear and repression, lasting in various forms of severity until the end of the regime.[54] Between 1948 and 1989, official records document 205,486 individuals imprisoned for political reasons and 248 sentenced to death; another 282 perished attempting to flee the country. Around forty-five hundred inmates, moreover, died in Communist prisons and labor camps.[55] Religious repression in Czechoslovakia evinced two aspects: undisguised brutality early on, combined later with attempts to co-opt and control religious communities through legal and bureaucratic means—all amid a steady din of officially sanctioned antireligious propaganda.

Although inclined to tread lightly in religious matters directly after the war, the general secretary of the Czechoslovak Communist Party and the country's first postwar president, Klement Gottwald, turned his back on piecemeal negotiations that had been taking place between the Catholic Church and the state, clearly stating in 1948: "Our populace has no choice. We must see the church as an enemy"—a sentiment that brought him into direct conflict with the Catholic primate and archbishop of Prague, Josef Beran, a staunch critic of Communism. The year 1948 also witnessed the passing of two laws designed to undermine Catholic power and influence. The Law Concerning Agrarian Reform resulted in the state's appropriation of virtually all the church's lands, while the Law Concerning Education suppressed Catholic and other religious schools, nationalizing education at all levels. In 1949, a state Office of Religious Affairs came into existence under the Ministry of Culture amid a flurry of other laws and decrees that, inter alia, forbade church marriages apart from civil ones, made state licensure necessary for all ministers, drastically limited seminary and other forms of theological education, and denied religious organizations the right to perform social work. Interestingly, continuing Central European Josephist traditions, the state agreed to provide clerical salaries, but clerical appointments had to be approved by the state, and all appointees had to swear an oath of loyalty to the state; thus, the paycheck should be seen not as government generosity but as a tool of Caesar's control. "The state has the supervisory authority over the possessions of the church and of religious communities," the new legislation sweepingly proclaimed.[56]

Beginning in 1950, the government targeted religious orders. Planned in 1949 under the direction of Communist Party General Secretary Rudolf Slánský, launched on the night of 13 April 1950, "Operation K" (for *kláštery,* the Czech word for monastery) designated a sudden, nationwide crackdown on Czechoslovakia's religious houses. A mix of state-security operatives and police and military units surrounded seventy-five Czech and sixty-two Slovak houses, focusing on the largest orders—Salesians, Jesuits, Redemptorists, Benedictines, Franciscans. Startled men awakened to learn that "due to the will of the people," their centuries-long "anti-state" activities had suddenly reached an end. Commanded to dress and pack essentials, they were unceremoniously loaded into trucks for deportation to predetermined concentration centers. Weeks later, a second phase of the operation brought the total to 219 religious houses and 2,376 religious. The suddenness and severity of the operation meant that little opposition occurred, except in several Slovak areas where local, pious populations made loud but ultimately ineffective protests. The party-state targeted male orders first, but 1950 also witnessed "Operation R" (rehol'níčka is a Slovak word for nun), in which female convents and religious houses were overtaken and disbanded too, upending the vocations of thousands of women.[57] These measures added up to an unprecedented event: the sudden liquidation of religious institutions, some of which had existed for more than a thousand years. In the process, artwork vanished, manuscripts and whole libraries were destroyed, and other ecclesiastical valuables were looted. Credible reports exist of nuns being raped. Many religious not tried or imprisoned or forced into secular vocations or the army wound up at so-called concentration monasteries, in which prisonlike conditions and coercive labor practices prevailed, including harsh work in linen factories and deadly uranium mines. "Our life was brutally changed in 1950. The Communists took over everything and sent us to various localities to work in the factories," one Slovakian Franciscan sister remembered.[58] Emptied religious houses became military barracks, hospitals, warehouses, and the like.[59] Prague's famous Břevnov monastery—the abbot of which, Anastáz Opasek (1913–99), was condemned for high treason and espionage in one of many show trials—became the Interior Ministry's Central State Archives.

The assault on monasteries coincided with harsh measures against the Catholic hierarchy more generally. A series of arrests and show trials resulted by 1956 in the incarceration of 384 Catholic priests, according to official figures. By the early 1960s, 450 priests, 375 monks, and 120 nuns languished in prison, in addition to hundreds detained in monastery concentration camps. Every Catholic bishop, except the auxiliary bishop of Prague, Antonín Eltschkner, was interred. Archbishop Beran wound up under house arrest until he was permitted to leave for Rome to be made a cardinal in 1965 on the condition that he never return. In addition, in 1951 the so-called Babice case took place in Babice, Moravia: a scenario of multiple show trials involving more than one hundred people charged with anti-state activities. Eleven received undeserved death sentences, including the Catholic priests Jan Bula, Václav Drbola, and František Pařil.[60] Not least, mention should be made of the priest Josef Toufar, who died in February 1950 after being interrogated and brutally tortured by security forces. His trial was sparked by the so-called Číhošť miracle, which took place in December 1949 in the remote village of Číhošť when a wooden cross in the Church of the Assumption allegedly moved spontaneously at a service in which Toufar had presided. The government's desire to discredit the church and Toufar's refusal to deny the miracle led to his torture and untimely end. The event became famous due to the Czech Communist documentary, *Alas for the One through Whom the Umbrage Comes,* which lampooned the occurrence as a hoax, and through a novel, *The Miracle Game,* by the Czech author Josef Skvorecky, who interpreted the event as an example of the government's gratuitous cruelty toward religious believers.[61]

The only major religious community that arguably had it worse than the Roman Catholic Church was the Greek Catholic Church, located predominantly in eastern Slovakia. Experiencing a fate similar to that of Greek Catholics in Ukraine and Romania, this church body was summarily dissolved in the postwar era and placed under the jurisdiction of the Orthodox Moscow Patriarchate in a plan known as "Action P," where "P" stood for *pravoslavizácia* (Orthodoxization). Roughing up Greek Catholic monasteries took place prior to the concerted attack against all monasteries in 1950, with the dissolution of Slovak Greek Catholicism formalized at the Sobor of Prešov on 28 April 1950. Cynical manipulation and police intimidation reminiscent of Lenin's tactics were seen as necessary all along, as a Communist Party report from February 1949 makes clear: "Preparation for the process of Orthodoxization must be very thorough and it could last for several weeks. Yet the attack on the Greek Catholic chapter and clergy must be carried out swiftly. Greek Catholic priests have large families. Facing a decision to reunite with Russian Orthodoxy or lose their livelihood, many will likely opt for transition." While many priests grudgingly, often only superficially, complied, a determined minority resisted, sowing seeds for a future clandestine church. Forcibly removed from their parishes, these priests were often relocated with their families away from Slovakia and then shunted into blue-collar jobs if not placed in monastery prisons or labor camps.[62] Happily, the events of the Prague Spring permitted the relegalization of Greek Catholicism in the late 1960s. Yet after the Soviet clampdown during the repressive 1970s and 1980s, the church stood under "constant surveillance" by state authorities, its priests often experiencing intimidation, harassment, and interrogation. "Only after the collapse of Communism in November 1989," as the Slovak scholar Jaroslav Coranič has summed up, "was the Greek Catholic Church's forty years of 'Babylonian captivity' finally brought to an end."[63]

From the earliest days of the regime, the party-state aimed to sow divisions and mistrust between Catholics and other religious bodies and *within* the Catholic Church itself. It accomplished the former by showing favoritism to Hussite and Protestant churches, as mentioned, invoking the legacy of Jan Hus qua reformer to indict Catholicism as obscurantist and backward-looking. It also made sure that socialism-friendly theologians, such as the Protestant theologian Josef Lukl Hromádka, enjoyed a broad platform to disseminate their views, especially if they were willing to pull punches in their criticism of the regime, fulminate against Western capitalism and imperialism, and advocate for the compatibility of Marxism and Christianity. Supporting such figures accomplished two aims at once: internally, it drew a contrast between permissible and impermissible forms of religiosity; externally, it gave the impression that the regime might not be as bad as its critics claimed. A well-meaning, largely innocent dupe, Hromádka was appropriately devastated by the Soviet invasion of Czechoslovakia in 1968 and honorably called into question many of his former views.[64]

With respect to fostering internal Catholic strife, President Gottwald noted as early as 1949 the desire "to provoke a political crisis among the clergy, and thus create hostility and conflict among them."[65] Toward this end, the party-state endorsed "progressive" Catholic organizations, such as Catholic Action in 1949 and, two years later, the National Committee of the Catholic Clergy, later called the Peace Committee of the Catholic Church. In 1971, the Association of Catholic Clergy *Pacem in Terris* came into existence, cleverly employing in its title the name of the famous 1963 encyclical by Pope John XXIII to bolster its legitimacy.[66] These organizations aimed to nurture leaders friendly to state policies and critical of the Vatican and the West more generally. To be sure, not all members were obsequious toward the regime, and some, such as Prague's Archbishop František Tomášek, exhibited a profound conflict of conscience. Many others joined out of fear or helplessness, while not a few were blackmailed into joining. Even so, these organizations encouraged and actively rewarded collaborationists, typified by the priest and theologian Josef Plojhar, who slavishly did the government's bidding, dying appropriately enough at the Soviet Embassy in Prague in 1981 at an event celebrating the Bolshevik Revolution. Numerous priests, subsequent archival evidence has corroborated, cooperated with or were themselves members of the secret police, who waged a constant war of surveillance and intimidation against a sizable clandestine church, which included bishops secretly appointed by the Vatican. This underground church gained steam in the final decades of the regime, contributing through samizdat literature to currents of thought leading to the Velvet Revolution (or Gentle Revolution) in 1989 and standing in stark contrast to the collaborationist wing of the church. Until 1989, incidentally, the state reserved for itself the right to approve all episcopal appointments, and it intentionally left many sees vacant or leaned on temporary replacements known as "capitular vicars" instead of appointing "reactionary" figures. In 1972, not counting underground leaders, only one of Czechoslovakia's thirteen dioceses had a resident bishop.[67]

Thus, the regime in Czechoslovakia, as in Romania, ultimately found it more expedient to control the church by internal infiltration and handpicking its leaders than to continue a direct confrontation. "The atheist regime is happy to reward such clergy for blurring the evangelical message," as one critic summed up the government's strategy, for "lukewarm priests provide justification for lukewarm or collaborationist attitudes among the parishioners." But these leaders represented little more to the state than a useful "relic of the past," an evil to be tolerated and manipulated for the time being.[68]

Whether Catholic or Protestant, conservative or progressive, all faith communities in Czechoslovakia faced a barrage of atheist propaganda, begun during the earliest years of the regime and continued with varying intensity until 1989. In 1953, the party newspaper *Rudé právo* clearly stated: "Every religion, with its faith in eternal life, with its preaching humility, resignation to fate, love even of the enemy, with its rejection of the workers for true happiness on earth, is in absolute and sharp contradiction to the communist world view." Books and other media treating religion favorably were practically impossible to publish, while those extolling "scientific atheism" were ever present. The incremental atheization of education in the early years of the regime was formalized and extended in 1959 with a new resolution to carry out a "cultural revolution" in education. Bratislava witnessed in 1971 the establishment of an Institute for Scientific Atheism, which published a bimonthly journal, *Atheism;* a similar institute arose within the Czechoslovak Academy of Science.[69] Finally, the party-state removed most religious symbols from public life—a reality typified by the excision of the double cross from the Slovak coat of arms in 1960 and the erasure of the word "saint" from town names.[70]

Curiously, the party-state permitted some theological education, allowing for six theological faculties and two Catholic seminaries. But these were in effect state institutions, and the state deliberately controlled and choked off enrollments for the ministry, resulting in an ever-declining number of priests per capita with respect to the population. Bratislava, for example, had 160 priests for a hundred and fifty thousand inhabitants in 1948, but only twenty priests for four hundred thousand inhabitants in 1987. Seminarians were forbidden to possess foreign religious literature, to listen to foreign broadcasts, or to contact clergy outside Czechoslovakia apart from government permission and oversight. Seminary coursework even included mandatory classes in Marxism-Leninism. To enforce these measures and create a climate of fear among young priests, state-security forces heavily and successfully recruited young informants from the ranks of seminarians and theology students.[71]

Although the Prague Spring brought brief amelioration, the situation worsened again in the post-1968 era with a nationwide crackdown. Politically vocal and activist clergy and laity found themselves susceptible to the confiscation of religious materials, harassment, arrests, and imprisonment. The election of the Polish Pope John Paul II in 1978 brought even harsher treatment, reflecting the government's anxiety that the anti-Communist dynamism of Polish Catholicism would trickle into Czechoslovakia. On 27 March 1983, to provide one example, the state-security apparatus carried out a large-scale operation against underground religious orders, resulting in the arrest and imprisonment of some 250 brothers. In another illustrative affair, in April 1982 a sixty-two-year-old Franciscan father, Jan Barta, was arrested and sentenced to eighteen months in prison simply for conducting Mass after his state-required license had been suspended.[72]

Anticipating changes to come, however, the 1980s also witnessed some emboldened voices for change, beginning with that of Archbishop Tomášek, who took inspiration from John Paul II's example and became increasingly critical of the government's anti-religious policies. Several intrepid priests and laity were signatories of Charter 77, a grassroots initiative criticizing the government for not respecting basic human rights.[73] In another, specifically religious instance of courage, a group of Moravian Catholics in 1987 drafted a thirty-one-point petition calling for religious freedom and redress of past mistreatment. Listing several of these points, in conclusion, gives an indication of the repressive nature of the regime before the watershed changes of the Velvet Revolution. Specifically, the petition demanded

1) that the state not interfere in church activities. . . .

7) that all religious orders be allowed to function openly and to admit new members. . . .

8) that believers be permitted to establish independent lay organizations. . . .

20) that the advocacy of Christian ideas enjoys equal legal status with the promotion of atheist ideas. . . .

23) that there be a cessation to arbitrary removal of crosses, statues, chapels, and other religious and cultural monuments.[74]

As such dissent intersected with larger geopolitical developments, most of these demands astoundingly became a reality after 1989, as we know from hindsight. Without hindsight, however, the situation for the devout in mid-1980s Czechoslovakia appeared gloomy and trying, as summarized in 1983 by a correspondent for London's *Times:* "The repression of religion in Czechoslovakia is now generally considered to be the worst in any communist country outside Albania, where religion is forbidden altogether."[75]

ALBANIA

As the Nazi bid for European mastery unraveled in 1944, the National Liberation Movement, led by the Communist Party secretary, Enver Hoxha, seized power in Albania, which had been occupied by Italian and German forces during the war. The son of an imam, smitten by eighteenth-century *philosophes* and historical materialism while studying in France as a young man, Hoxha became a diehard Marxist-Leninist and a rapt admirer of Joseph Stalin.[76] Dispatching rivals with aplomb and breaking with nearby Yugoslavia in 1948, Hoxha and his allies turned the People's Republic of Albania into one of the most isolated and ruthless one-party states in the Soviet bloc, imitating Stalin's efforts at rapid industrialization, collectivization, and de-kulakization. When Nikita Khrushchev distanced himself from Stalin's legacy in the 1950s, Hoxha demurred, breaking ties with the Soviet Union and acquiring a new patron in Mao Zedong's China. Then when Deng Xiaoping criticized Mao's legacy in the late 1970s, Hoxha proclaimed "national self-reliance," leading Albania down a rabbit hole of isolation, paranoia, and poverty.

Hoxha's brand of eliminationist secularism and the surveillance state enforcing it stand out for their severity: a vicious assault against the clergy amid a general effort to crush dissent in the early Cold War and the de jure criminalization of religion after 1967, making Albania, as the government then proudly crowed, "the first atheist state in the world." Indeed, the intensity of government-orchestrated anti-religious activity, yoked with Hoxha's xenophobic nationalism, which cast religion as inherently "foreign" and divisive, set Albania apart even from other Marxist-Leninist regimes during the Cold War. The persecutions experienced in the small country affected all major religious groups: Catholics, the Orthodox, Sunni Muslims, and Shia Muslims—the latter closely attached to the Bektashi Sufi order, which made its international headquarters in Tirana after leaving Turkey in 1925 in response to Kemalist authoritarian secularist reforms.[77]

Since 1967 stands out as a pivotal date for making sense of what happened in Albania, we might speak of persecutions before and after this watershed year.

In imitation of the Soviet model, the new Albanian government, on the basis of an Agrarian Reform Law (1945), nationalized religious properties throughout the country, making life miserable for anyone who resisted. Hoxha and his key deputy, Mehmet Shehu, previously a leftist brawler in the Spanish Civil War, targeted the well-educated Catholic clergy in particular, branding them as fascist collaborators and/or American or Vatican spies. In May 1945, the regime expelled the Apostolic delegate, Archbishop Leone Nigris, and summoned the archbishop of Shkodër, Gasper Thaçi, and the archbishop of Durrës, Vincent Prendushi, for talks. When both refused to cut ties with the Vatican and preside over an exclusively national church, as Hoxha demanded, retribution came quickly. Thaçi died at the hands of the state-security apparatus, or Sigurimi, while under house arrest in 1946; Prendushi received twenty years of hard labor but perished under mysterious circumstances and likely torture in 1949.[78]

The two archbishops' fates reflect a larger picture. In 1946, the government expelled all foreign priests, monks, and nuns, massacred twenty parish priests, and incarcerated many more. It also banned the Jesuit Order in 1946, after the show trials and executions of the Jesuit vice-provincial, Gjon Fausti, and the seminary director, Daniel Dajani.[79] The Franciscans, who had had a presence in Albania since the 1200s, faced even worse persecution and complete dissolution in 1947. Bodies of slain priests and brothers often wound up in unmarked mass graves, while the living faced indignities such as having to walk the streets wearing a placard that said,

"I have sinned against the people."[80] Catholic opposition to these outrages met a pitiless will to power, resulting in more arrests, imprisonment, torture, and bullets to the back of the skull. "Dissenters must be exterminated like a weasel in the chicken coop" tripped off the lips of the assailants.[81] In February 1948, the party-state executed four other bishops, wiping out the entire hierarchy except for the aged Bernardin Shllaku, bishop of Pulati, who managed to hang around until the 1970s. When the Catholic carnage is tallied, between 1945 and the early 1960s, the government violently eliminated ten members of the hierarchy, fifty-six parish priests, thirty Franciscans, thirteen Jesuits, ten seminarians, and eight nuns. With other political dissenters, those imprisoned at godforsaken places such as the notorious Spaç prison in northern Albania endured unspeakable cruelties, as cataloged by the Jesuit Giacomo Gardin, who spent twenty years in prison collecting stories from fellow inmates: "Most of them were beaten on their bare feet with wooden clubs; the fleshy part of the legs and buttocks cut open, rock salt inserted beneath their skin, and then sewn up again; their feet, placed in boiling water until the flesh fell off, were then rubbed with salt; their Achilles' tendons were pierced with hot wires. Some were hung by their arms for three days without food; put in ice and ice water until nearly frozen. . . . [Some were put] on a bed of nails and covered with heavy material; put in nail-studded cages which were then rotated rapidly."[82] By 1971, only sixteen priests remained in the country, twelve in prison and two in hiding. "Inhuman tortures" and "bitter historical realities" were the order of the day, as the Franciscan priest Zef Pllumi recounted in his memoirs of imprisonment.[83] Since 2016, the Catholic Church has officially recognized thirty-eight Communist-era Albanian martyrs, thirty-one of whom perished between 1945 and 1950. Several number among the circa six thousand bodies still not accounted for from Communist-era violence, according to a 2021 report by the International Commission on Missing Persons.[84]

But the regime had it in not just for Catholicism but for "religion" as a whole, although the Orthodox and Muslims experienced less severity at first than Catholics. Nonetheless, in January 1949, the government issued a far-reaching Decree on Religious Communities that required all faiths to profess absolute loyalty to the regime and to submit all appointments, publications, homilies, and bylaws for government approval. Additional postwar regulations and mandated "charters" in 1950 and 1951 forbade religious communities to educate the young, own real estate, run publishing houses, operate hospitals, or set up philanthropic or welfare organizations. Institutions that had existed for decades—such as a Catholic orphanage in Shkodër caring for a thousand children—were suddenly plunged into turmoil.

Sunni Muslims and the Bektashi Sufis too felt the government's iron fist. Several high-profile muftis, charged with fomenting dissent, received prison sentences, including Mustafa Efendi Varoshi (mufti of Durrës), Hafez Ibrahim Dibra (former great mufti of Albania) and Xhemal Pazari (a prominent sheikh from Tirana). By 1947, the regime had incarcerated forty-four Muslims clerics, executing twenty-eight of them in its first decade in power. Others simply went missing. Clergy unwilling to submit absolutely to the new Caesar found themselves, if not dead or incarcerated, replaced with obsequious alternatives. Sowing internecine divisions among Sunni and Bektashi Muslims was another favorite government tactic, which also worked *within* the Bektashi community, which split into pro- and anti-government factions, culminating in a macabre triple murder at the Bektashi global headquarters on 18 March 1947, the details of which remain shrouded in mystery. But this did not stop the government from using the event to shut down hundreds of their Bektashi lodges (*tekkes*).[85]

State-sponsored cruelty also impacted the Orthodox community, historically suspected of harboring sympathies for neighboring Greece. Communist officials infiltrated its churches and monasteries and shuttered the main Orthodox seminary in Korçë. Two outspoken critics of the regime, the metropolitan of Tirana, Kristofor Kisi, and Bishop Irene Banushi were deposed, the former imprisoned and dying from poison in 1958. A similar fate befell the metropolitan of Elbasan, who was sentenced to twenty years in prison, most spent at the infamous Burrel work camp in central Albania.[86] Not least, the Albanian Orthodox Church lost its autocephalous status (which had been fully granted only in 1937) and humiliatingly had to submit to the politically compromised Moscow Patriarchate. To replace Kisi, the government tapped Pais Vodica (a married priest and hence technically ineligible to serve as bishop from the standpoint of Orthodox theology) to head the pinioned Albanian church.[87] "[The] then powerful sought to assassinate God. . . . They re-crucified Christ, not just for the period of a few days . . . but for entire decades," as Archbishop Anastasios, the first post-Communist primate of Albania, once reflected on the Orthodox experience during the Cold War.[88]

The assault on religious leaders in the late 1940s and early 1950s did not end religious practice, to be sure. But it certainly curtailed it, instilling fear in laity and leaders alike, at a time when the Sigurimi's mandate against political enemies, the state's surveillance apparatus, legal strictures against religion, and a network of prison and labor camps expanded rapidly. The harassment, imprisonment, and execution of clergy persisted in the late 1950s and 1960s, if less feverishly than in the immediate postwar period. In many places, simply staffing religious services became a major issue, and scant funds were available to maintain houses of worship. What is more, the government ramped up anti-religious propaganda at this time, branding both Christianity and Islam as "foreign" impositions, inherently retrogressive, inimical to the true interests of the Albanian people and the dialectical progress of history. "The only religion of Albania is Albanianism," Hoxha liked to say, quoting a nineteenth-century poet, fusing the universal discourse of militant secularism with a visceral nationalism.

In the 1950s, the regime secularized education in a Marxist-Leninist direction.[89] Brochures appeared in the centralized school system with such titles as "Religion, Opium of the People" and "Is Religion against the People's Democracy?" Hoxha himself addressed the party and educational establishment in a speech entitled "On the Sources of Religious Beliefs and How They Should be Combatted."[90] Anti-religious films, books, radio transmissions, and periodicals proliferated. Feuerbach, Marx, Engels, and Lenin became classroom staples, fed, without competing views, to young people during an enormous demographic upswing and a general expansion of literacy in the postwar period. This point merits emphasizing because illiteracy had reigned in Albania's small population at the end of World War II; postwar Communist ideology, therefore, created a major split between the old and the young, the latter saturated in historical-materialist pedagogy and propaganda from their earliest days.

The situation in the country worsened in the mid-1960s as Hoxha, beholden to Mao Zedong after 1961, felt Albania should undergo a yet more radical Cultural and Ideological Revolution, not unlike that which took place in China. Hoxha made clear its anti-religious dimension on 6 February 1967, inciting young people to cast off religious "mysticism" as antithetical to Marxism-Leninism and modernization. In an open letter ("On the Struggle against Religion and Religious Conceptions and Customs") on 27 February, he argued: "We must direct our struggle against religion as much as against religious dogmas and the idealistic and mystical viewpoints of religious philosophy ... [and] against religious practices."[91] On 19 November, a notorious new decree (#4337) repealed previous laws that paid lip service to freedom of conscience, essentially criminalizing religious belief and practice in all forms.[92]

This measure coincided with a state-orchestrated campaign against sacred architecture, in which indoctrinated youth and party loyalists in conjunction with military and police forces set about demolishing the material culture of Albania's religious past. Astoundingly, in the span of a few years, all churches, chapels, seminaries, mosques, madrasas, monasteries, and Sufi shrines in the country, in addition to many Ottoman-era tombs (*turbe*), were either destroyed or repurposed for nonreligious purposes, such as gyms, granaries, cinemas, warehouses, or military barracks. Orthodox icons, wrenched from churches, became firewood; Qur'anic calligraphy in mosques, plastered over with concrete; sarcophagi of Bektashi saints, vandalized. Spectacular footage exists of whole churches being dynamited and of the Red Guards of the Albanian Youth (Albania's equivalent of Mao's Red Guards) hacking at their religious heritage with pickaxes. A remarkable

Figure 10. Interior of Saint Nicholas Church, Shkodër, Albania. The church was closed by the Communist government in 1967 and turned into a gymnasium. Later it was destroyed, using tanks and heavy artillery. Photograph by Angjelin Nenshati. Courtesy of the Site of Witness and Memory Archive, Shkodër, Albania.

photograph displayed at the Site of Witness and Memory (a current museum on religious persecution in the city of Shkodër) shows a female gymnast swinging on flying rings in the city's cathedral above where the altar once stood (figure 10). Partisans set fire to the Franciscan cloister in Shkodër, killing four elderly friars. An eyewitness in the village of Kastrati remembered a military truck suddenly pulling into town one day, stopping in front of the church, and then proceeding to destroy the bell tower, remove the crosses, and convert the church to an "other use," enlisting the coerced labor of the church's former priest in the process.[93]

In all, the late 1960s witnessed the destruction, vandalizing, or repurposing of 2,169 sacred sites, which the government, incredulously, attempted to portray as a spontaneous, popular uprising.[94] To be sure, some structures held to have extraordinary cultural significance survived as "national monuments," yet still others with a venerable history—such as the Saint George Orthodox Cathedral in Korçë, the Church of Vau i Dejes, and the Fushë Çela Mosque in Shkodër—were reduced to rubble, the stones used for mundane purposes such as lining riverbeds or paving city sidewalks. Not uncommonly, repurposed buildings underwent modifications to blunt their original religious intent lest they have "negative psychological influence on the younger generation," as one Marxist-Leninist theorist put it.[95] Finally, in 1968, an atheist exhibition, later a museum, opened in Shkodër to document the extirpated world of religious belief.

Amid the destruction, the regime denounced Muslim and Christian clergy as social parasites, minions of outside powers, and worse. Those who resisted found themselves, if not murdered, in prison or labor camps such as Burrel and Spaç in northern Albania alongside thousands of other religious dissenters and political prisoners (figure 11). Many underwent compulsory "reeducation" classes and were tasked to perform menial jobs such as cleaning toilets or sweeping streets. In several cases, ousted clergy lost ration cards (necessary to acquire food) and literally starved to death. Beards, seen as a religious symbol, were rendered illegal. In one sensational episode, in April 1967, forty Orthodox priests were rounded up and taken to the city center of Delvinë, where they were spat upon and had their vestments removed and beards shaved in an act of public humiliation.[96]

The frenzy against religion in the 1960s (technically extralegal) preceded constitutional changes in the 1970s. Article 37 of the revised constitution of 1976 made clear that "the state does not recognize any religion and supports

Figure 11. Spaç prison in northern Albania, where political and religious dissidents were held during the Communist era. Photograph by the author.

and develops atheistic propaganda in order to implant in mankind the scientific-materialistic world-view," while article 55 forbade "the creation of any type of organization of a fascist, anti-democratic, *religious,* or anti-socialist character." The revised penal code of 1977, in addition to prohibiting public religious expressions, set three- to ten-year prison sentences for producing, storing, or distributing religious materials.[97]

An additional decree (#5339) from the 1970s took issue with names. The party-state forbade parents to choose biblical or Qur'anic names for their children and enjoined them to change their own names if derived from these sources, selecting instead from three thousand suitably secular and "national" names listed in the *Dictionary of People's Names.* Altering place names did not lag far behind. In the mid-1970s, a campaign to abolish city and village names with religious meanings—particularly those with the word "saint"—was effectively carried out.

Finally, holidays such as Christmas and Easter and the Muslim Eid al-Adha wound up on the chopping block, as did periods of religious fasting.

Sigurimi spies cunningly tried to entrap practicing Christians and Muslims during religious fasts, such as Lent and Ramadan, by distributing forbidden foods in school and work, and then publicly denouncing those who refused to eat. "On religious holidays," as one survivor of the regime remembered, "the cinemas in Korçë [his hometown] would show attractive films for children and youth, at a price 5–10 times less than the usual price. . . . This was another way to prevent people, especially young people, from contact with institutions of faith."[98] Ersatz "holy days" were offered up instead, including ones to celebrate the establishment of the Communist Party, national independence, and even the country's acquisition of electricity.[99]

No doubt, true believers in the government's atheist system existed after 1967, but the devout and even moderately devout chafed under the anti-religious measures and resorted to clandestine practices when possible. Secret baptisms not infrequently took place; in one case, an Orthodox woman hid their child's baptism from her own husband, worried that he might expose her.[100] The faithful hid sacred books and objects in secret locations. In private, Muslims greeted one another with the traditional "mashallah" (as God wills) or "inshallah" (if God wills), a criminal act if caught. Ramadan and other fasting periods were observed with great circumspection.[101] Pilgrimage sites, which the regime shut down, sometimes received the faithful furtively and at night. Clandestine religious services also took place in homes or in remote areas among trusted family members and friends. But since the Sigurimi employed countless civilian informants, these sorts of things always carried risks, and, for many, faith became a solitary, mental affair.

Some catechesis took place in the confines of a household, to be sure, but children presented a special danger, because they might innocently betray their family while at school—which the regime actively encouraged them to do. As one father remembered the time: "Parents were afraid to teach their children explicit words such as 'love God and neighbor' because a child might unwittingly use them in school," triggering the government's retaliation. Genti Kruja, head of the Department of Islamic Studies at the new Beder University (Tirana), once recounted that as a child overwhelmed with atheist propaganda, he asked his mother directly whether God existed. "Yes, but you must never say I told you," she replied.[102]

While many efforts to skirt the system succeeded, some, sadly, did not. Religious families and individuals caught in a violation at a minimum had their work and educational prospects greatly constrained. Not a few wound up in labor prisons or camps for internally displaced people. The latter did not entail incarcerated conditions per se, but they restricted people with a "bad biography" (in the government's Orwellian jargon) to live in certain areas, usually performing difficult agricultural work, ostracized by those with a "good biography" and compelled to report to local authorities every day.[103]

Perhaps the most tragic and sensational case of the post-1967 era involved the Catholic priest Shtjefen Kurti. Imprisoned in 1967 for opposing the destruction of a church, he was discovered in 1971 to have baptized a child in a labor camp at the request of its mother. For this infraction, he was tried and, unrepentant, executed in 1972.[104] In 1977 another priest, Mark Gjoni, received a sentence of twelve years for possessing Bibles. Comparable stories are not scarce among the Orthodox, Muslim, and Bektashi communities. "A manic religious oppression" took place, as the post-Communist Orthodox archbishop Anastasios ruefully reflected; often "it seemed that it [the government] had succeeded in uprooting religion completely."[105]

Yet all the while, security agents railed against the wily persistence of religion and the difficulty of extirpating it wholly. With a measure of pride in "the brilliant successes which were achieved within an extremely short period in smashing religious centres," a party historian noted in the early 1970s that "the elimination of churches and mosques had not eliminated the religious outlook. Religion has very deep roots. It is interwoven and linked by a thousand threads with backward customs." Yet the struggle, he averred, had to continue until these roots were "unmasked and smashed," a necessary condition for the "building of socialist society."[106] More optimistically, Enver Hoxha in 1973 crowed about "the crushing blow [the state had] dealt to religious dogma, that ancient plague, that poisonous black spider. . . . A cure for cancer has not yet been discovered, but for religion [in Albania] it has been, and if a struggle [continues to be] waged in this direction, consistently and with conviction, the cure will no longer take centuries but a few decades, a few generations."[107]

Hoxha died in 1985. The People's Socialist Republic of Albania collapsed in 1991. "What happened in Albania, dear brothers and sisters, has never happened before in history," Pope John Paul II, with (the Albanian) Mother Teresa at his side, told a crowd gathered in Tirana in 1993. "The State tried to destroy all religious expression in the name of radical atheism, which was universally enshrined in its totalitarian regime."[108]

CHAPTER FIVE

Red Asia

Religion is poison.
—Mao Zedong

They have broken religion.
—The Thirteenth Dalai Lama

IN FEBRUARY 1912, THE LAST QING EMPEROR ABDICATED, ending millennia of Chinese imperial rule, plunging China, and much of Asia with it, into a decades-long conflict over the nature, governance, and future of Asian societies. Warlordism, Western and Japanese imperialism, the Sino-Japanese War, and a vicious civil war eventually gave way to the triumph of the Chinese Communist Party (CCP) in 1949—an epochal event in Asian and world history. Rising from obscurity, the party leader Mao Zedong cut a striking figure at the time, adapting Marxism-Leninism to Asian conditions, bristling with energy, charisma, and the will to power. "Revolution is not a dinner party," he once wrote, but an "act of violence."[1] The ideology that bears his name, Maoism, became one of the most consequential and destructive political forces in the twentieth century, influential not only in Asia but also in Africa, in Latin America, and among leftist radicals in the West. A potent mix of party-building discipline, anti-imperialist rhetoric, nationalism, and "continuous revolution" wedded to Soviet-style Marxism and its eliminationist secularism, Maoism, according to the historian Julia Lovell, "not only unlocks the contemporary history of China, but is also a key influence on global insurgency, insubordination, and intolerance across eighty years."[2]

This chapter considers the implications of Maoism and the Communist triumph in Asia for religious belief and practice. Not surprisingly, China receives the lion's share of attention, both directly before and after the

Revolution of 1949 and especially during the Cultural Revolution (1966–76). The latter witnessed arguably the most furious assault on traditional religious practices in world history, not only across China but also in the Chinese-occupied Himalayan kingdom of Tibet, where Tibet's ancient strains of Buddhism faced near eradication.

China and Tibet will not exhaust our inquiry, however. We shall, initially, glance backward in time at Mongolia, which, breaking from China in 1911, experienced a Soviet-backed Communist revolution in the 1920s, which in turn paved the way for a sweeping attack on Mongolian Buddhism in the 1930s, presaging the Chinese and Tibetan tragedies. Mongolia's dictator at the time, the dreadful, practically forgotten Khorloogiin Choibalsan (1895–1952), simultaneously echoed Stalin and anticipated Mao. In addition, we shall glance forward, taking stock of the bloody hyper-Maoist regime of Pol Pot (1925–98) in Cambodia during the late 1970s. Often lost amid the myriad enormities of this regime was its nearly successful attempt to wipe out traditional Cambodian Buddhism and several minority faiths as well.

Consideration of Mongolia, China, Tibet, and Cambodia merits several preliminary caveats and qualifications. First, whereas in earlier chapters varieties of secularism found themselves dealing principally with the Abrahamic faiths and their religiopolitical configurations, the Asian context presents a different religious palette: Buddhism, Taoist beliefs, shamanism, various redemptive societies, a bewildering smorgasbord of local cults, veneration of ancestor lineages, and Confucian philosophy, in addition to Western-imported versions of Christianity and pockets of Islam, notably in the Xinjiang and Ningxia autonomous regions but also among the Hui minority spread across other parts of China, as well as the Cham minority in Cambodia. Second, as was the case in Russia, the social conditions necessary for the flourishing of Communism, at least according to classical Marxist criteria, were almost wholly unfavorable in Asia, as these regions boasted scant industry, virtually no proletariat, and an overwhelmingly rural population—nomadic, too, in many areas. Influenced by Western thinkers such as Antonio Gramsci and in turn by Mao, Communist leaders in East Asia thus shoehorned Marxism-Leninism to fit local conditions, substituting an oppressed peasantry for a proletariat, making prominent anti-colonial and nationalist rhetoric, emphasizing raw collective willpower over economic determinism, and generously smearing a wide range of opponents, not least religious figures, as "reactionary," "feudal," "imperialistic," or "counterrevolutionary" obstacles to progress.[3] Third, while Communist sensibilities brought with them many discontinuities, one must keep in mind continuities as well: Mao's ability, for example, to benefit from imperial China's strong-central-state tradition and the veneration that its subjects had for the remote emperor (seen as the "Son of Heaven"); the violence that past regimes had visited on religious minorities in efforts to stamp out regional ethnic separatism; anticlerical and "anti-superstition" measures taken during the Republic of China period (1912–49) and even beforehand; and the lashing out against foreign beliefs, as seen, for example, in the anti-Western sentiments informing China's Boxer Rebellion (1900–1901). Fourth, one must bear in mind that the line dividing "religion" and "politics" is blurrier and more confusing in East Asia than the typical Westerner might anticipate. Tibetan and Mongolian lamas, for example, were figures of significant political stature, and their monasteries were major landholders, employers of labor, and dispensaries of charity. Many Asian languages, moreover, even lacked a word for the abstraction "religion" until the late nineteenth century, and then it came by Western importation. Finally, one must firmly dispense with the idea that someone can belong to only one faith. As scholars of Asian religious life have long recognized, plural religious identities were often the rule, not the exception, as Taoist, Buddhist, and Confucian "teachings" (jiao), not to mention other local cultic traditions, have often merged in the same person or collective. In sum, the task of eliminationist secularism to control, degrade, and/or undermine religious belief often encountered conditions in the East rather different from those in the West, even if the methods, responses, and outcomes bear a family resemblance.

MONGOLIA

In 1911, with a nod of support from imperial Russia and chafing under China's recent Sinification efforts, Mongolia—or more properly Outer Mongolia—broke free from the collapsing Qing dynasty, which had ruled all of Mongolia since the seventeenth century. (Southern or "Inner Mongolia" remained under Chinese rule.) The lonesome, windswept landmass briefly reverted to a Buddhist khanate under the leadership of the Bogd Khan, also known as the (eighth) Jebtsundamba Khutuktu, a reincarnated "living Buddha," the top-ranked lama in Mongolia, an office that bore witness to the fact that sixteenth-century Tibetan monk-missionaries of the

Gelug Buddhist lineage had successfully transplanted their faith to Mongolia.[4] The geopolitical situation changed dramatically after the Bolshevik Revolution and during the Russian Civil War (1918–22). For a period, Chinese warlords lay claim to Mongolia, as did the mercurial, adventurous White Russian General Roman von Ungern-Sternberg (1886–1921). To eliminate threats posed by Ungern and China, Bolshevik Red Russia stepped in, supporting Mongolian revolutionary cells, pacifying the region by the middle of 1921. Thereafter, political dissenters faced harsh, often lethal, treatment, and the capital was renamed from Urga or Niislel Khuree to Ulaanbaatar ("Red Hero"). The Bogd Khan was permitted to linger on as a titular figurehead, dying of mysterious circumstances in the Soviet Union in 1924, the year the Mongolian People's Republic received its official name. At this time, Communist authorities connivingly proscribed future reincarnations of the Jebtsundamba Khutuktu.[5] Although the Soviet Union never formally annexed the new country, from its inception it remained a firm friend and ally, administered by the Mongolian People's Revolutionary Party (with Soviet military assistance and Comintern advisers) until the collapse of the Soviet regime in the early 1990s.

Mongolian Communists inherited a complex religious situation, a "priest-ridden society," as one cadre observed: an ecclesiastical-feudal hierarchy with entrenched authority invested in high-ranking lamas who exercised their rule—alongside a lay nobility—through a decentralized network of more than seven hundred monasteries or "lamaseries" housing thousands of temples. Like their European counterparts, these monasteries served as centers of learning and economic activity and dispensers of charity. Alongside the high-ranking lamas—topped by various "reincarnations," the highest of the highest—were numerous middle- and lower-ranking ones from all walks of life. Astoundingly, in a society of about seven hundred thousand people in 1921, around one-third of the adult men counted as lamas of some type. Together, they made up the Mongolian sangha, the all-important sacred brotherhood, one of the three "jewels" (along with the Buddha and the dharma) in classical Buddhist teachings. Not surprisingly, upon assuming power, Mongolian Communists and their Soviet tutors puzzled over "the lama question," or how a relatively small, upstart group of Marxist-Leninist revolutionaries might establish their legitimacy in Mongolia and transform a fundamentally hierarchical, theocratic society (with a largely nomadic and illiterate population) into a modern socialist and secular one.

The challenge was steep. At first, the new regime trod softly on Buddhism, recognizing the deep hold that the lamas had on the Mongolian people. Practically every family had a son in a monastery. Few Mongolians would undertake an important venture without first consulting a lama to find out if the day selected presented "auspicious" conditions. Consequently, a fragile tranquillity prevailed in the early years of the republic. Some lamas even occupied government positions, while social criticism focused more on establishing a "pure" form of Buddhism—one disentangled from temporal political concerns—than abolishing it. As in Buddhist enclaves in the Soviet Union, not a few Communists smiled on the fact that Buddhism could be given an atheistic interpretation.

But in 1924, after the death of the Bogd Khan, things began to change—change that accelerated in an anti-religious direction after a "leftist turn" of the Mongolian Communist Party around 1928 that paralleled developments under Stalin in the Soviet Union. Government and party officials and their Comintern advisers began to work more aggressively toward the political and economic neutralization of the lamas and the creation of a "New Socialist Man." Decrees forbade making donations to monasteries, for instance, and studying at monasteries for those under eighteen. Building on the constitution of 1924, Mongolia's first, a 1926 law separating religion and the state was adopted in an attempt to distinguish social spheres almost wholly fused together in the Tibetan-Mongolian Buddhist heritage.[6] Not only that, the state became a player in the metaphysical realm, categorically outlawing all reincarnations in 1928, as it also forbade the making and exchange of images of reincarnations, which were popular devotional aides. These measures coincided with the government's extensive efforts, in the late 1920s and 1930s, to register and inventory the holdings of monasteries—an initiative that paved the way for punitive taxation, collectivization of property and agriculture, confiscation of possessions, and the redistribution of monasteries' livestock and other forms of wealth.[7]

By the late 1920s, party propaganda became a feature of everyday life, disseminated through organizations such as the Revolutionary Youth League and the Anti-Buddhist League. Pamphlets, books, and crude theatrical productions targeted high-ranking lamas in particular, although sometimes religion itself wound up in the crosshairs. Party officials translated works on religion by Lenin and published booklets bearing such titles as *Ways for the Anti-Buddhist League to Carry Out Propaganda against Religion.*[8] Pilloried as shameful obstacles to certain and imminent progress, lamas were consistently cast as bloodsucking hypocrites and parasites, stuck in a "feudal" mind-set. Posters depicted them as oversized, ravenous tyrants gobbling up smaller figures. Sometimes words and images did not suffice; zealous Communist partisans ransacked stupas, roughed up lamas, intimidated worshippers, gouged out the eyes of Buddhas—to the point even of inviting reprimands from Communist higher-ups for proceeding too fast, too soon.[9]

As Communists heaped criticism and rebuke on higher lamas, they offered lower ones incentives to leave monasteries for secular society. These incentives usually involved promises of education, jobs, deferral or postponement of military duties, and a share in redistributed wealth. "Poor lamas," as one party slogan implored, "leave the temple and monasteries; become lay and work. Lamas who become lay will be given a share of the *jas* [wealth]. Join a cooperative or collective. Lamas who become lay will be free from military duty for three years."[10]

While such appeals attracted some, they alienated others, especially given the fact that early experiments in collectivization and cooperative livestock management on the whole failed abysmally.[11] This failure, combined with fear and frustration with the regime in other areas, reached a high-water mark in 1932 when uprisings broke out against the government in several different places, coming on the heels of several lesser, more localized uprisings. Quashing these with the help of the Soviet Red Army coincided with relaxation of anti-lamaist policies in some areas. Even so, the 1930s witnessed concerted assaults on the cultural front. These included banning the traditional Mongolian script in favor of the Latin and then the Cyrillic alphabet to drive a wedge between Mongolians and their past, as well as attempting to set up an educational system suffused with anticlerical rhetoric while proscribing traditional forms of study in the monasteries. "They have broken religion," the Thirteenth Dalai Lama said when hearing about these actions.[12]

By the mid-1930s, however, it became clear that the position and power of the lamas could not be fully destroyed without more aggressive action. Reviewing statistics sent to him from his Mongolian allies, Stalin himself suggested as much when he met with the Mongolian prime minister, Peljidiin Genden, in 1934, telling him: "It looks like there is a state within your state. One government is Genden's [i.e., socialist] government. The other is the lamas.'"[13] Words preceded actions. And though Genden balked at assailing the lamas (paying for this with his life at the hands of KGB agents in 1937), the Soviets found a willing partner in Khorloogiin Choibalsan, an apostate lama and power-hungry apparatchik who had ascended party ranks in the 1920s and 1930s, after embracing Marxism-Leninism as a young person in Irkutsk (figure 12). Succeeding Genden as prime minister in 1939, Choibalsan served as the founding director of the Revolutionary Youth League before later serving as foreign minister and minister of war, commander and chief of the army, and, not least, director of the Ministry of the Interior, which housed the secret police (Dotood Yaam), responsible for much of the violence in the late 1930s and beyond.[14]

As Choibalsan's star rose in the mid-1930s, legal measures against the lamas escalated. Penalty fees for lamas not joining the military increased tenfold. The law separating religion and the state was tweaked in 1936 to prevent first and second sons of a family from becoming lamas. The tactical use of terror also intensified, a development made possible by amending the criminal code in 1934 to enlarge the number of "counterrevolutionary"

Figure 12. Mongolia's Khorloogiin Choibalsan
around 1925. Photographer unknown. Courtesy of
Wikimedia Commons.

crimes. This turned the members of the Dotood Yaam (often referred to as "Green Hats" because of the headgear they wore) into an incredibly powerful and virtually unmonitored segment of the Mongol state, consisting of informants, researchers, inspectors, and special police. "After 1936, under Choibalsan's supervision, the *Dotood Yaam* become a finely-tuned organization that was charged primarily with the eradication of the Mongolian *Sangha*," as the scholar of Mongolian Buddhism Michael K. Jerryson has summarized.[15]

Three other developments in the mid-1930s tipped the scales toward violence. First, the Japanese invaded mainland China in 1931, setting up the puppet regime of Manchukuo in Manchuria and making their presence felt in Inner Mongolia, where they made appeals to pan-Mongolian nationalism and pan-Buddhist solidarity, often finding a receptive audience among the lamas. Mongolia's Soviet tutors saw this as a dire threat, dreading the possibility of lamas colluding with Japan to bring down the People's Republic. Second, in 1936, following the example of a Soviet study of churches in 1929, the party commissioned another detailed study of Buddhist monasteries, itemizing personnel and material holdings—both studies served as a prelude to what a Mongolian political analyst has termed "genocide."[16] Third, a purge of political opponents (real and imagined) began on the night of 10 September 1937 when security forces arrested sixty-five people and afterward convicted them in show trials, creating a climate of panic and paranoia throughout the country that soon affected the religious establishment. "I have arrested a large group of persons who belong to top leadership," Choibalsan reported to Moscow, "[but] another dimension of [our labor] has been identified—the need to be resolute regarding the counter-revolutionary lamas"—a hint of things to come.[17]

Resolution came in the form of prosecuting a "counter-revolutionary nest" of high-ranking lamas deemed at once intellectually backward and minions of imperial Japan. These lamas—who included Luvsanhaimchig, head of the Yonzon Hamba monastery (among the most important), his deputy, Damdin, Hutagt Tserendorj of the Manjusri monastery, and twenty-one others—were convicted in a high-profile show trial; nineteen of them were then brazenly shot in front of the Central Theatre in downtown Ulaanbaatar between 4 and 7 October 1937. These lamas had numerous disciples who were implicated in subsequent waves of arrests and prosecution, often on the basis of scant criminal evidence. Indeed, this trial opened a floodgate of state-sanctioned violence against the entire Buddhist sangha, already labeled "an irreconcilable enemy of the Mongolian Revolution" at the Eighth Communist Party Congress in 1930.[18]

Numbers alone do not tell the whole story, but in Mongolia's case they leave a searing impression. Although less concentrated violence against lamas had already taken place throughout the 1920s and early 1930s, in a period of eighteen months, from the autumn of 1937 until 1939, thousands of "feudals," the vast majority lamas, were tried and executed in what Choibalsan openly spoke of as a "liquidation."[19] Summary justice was meted out by NKVD-style troikas functioning under an Extraordinary Plenipotentiary Commission set up within the Ministry of the Interior. Around eighteen thousand lamas perished in the bloodbath, and overall deaths of political enemies from this period range from twenty thousand to thirty-five thousand. Astoundingly, in September 1937, according to one estimation, 82,203 lamas resided in the monasteries, but by July 1838 only 562 were left.[20] Those not killed either fled into the countryside or across the border to Inner Mongolia, ended up in prison, found themselves conscripted into the military, or volunteered to exit the sangha and become integrated into the regular workforce, often on state-run cooperatives. High-ranking lamas and reincarnations constituted the state's principal targets, but numerous middle- and lower-ranked lamas were victims as well.

The process of elimination usually involved four steps: arrest, interrogation (including torture), hasty trial, and execution, usually by a bullet or bludgeon to the back of the skull. Investigators received awards for exceeding desired target numbers. Cruelly, lamas themselves often had to do the dirty work. The method of interrogation become fairly routine. Following leads derived from the trial of Luvsanhaimchig and others, prosecutors would go after a senior lama, whose students would then be implicated in an alleged counterrevolutionary plot. Mirroring events in the Soviet Union at the time, promises of leniency if one admitted to crimes were rarely kept but rather served the purpose of a show trial by helping convince the populace that the state was carrying out justice. "Only death could end my suffering. Therefore, I agreed to say anything they wanted," a rare survivor remorsefully said of his experience of interrogation.[21] The whole process begot difficult but efficient work. One Luvsansamdan, who worked at the Ministry of the Interior at the time, admitted in 1962 that "because so many lamas were arrested the prisons were unable to house them all. So, a campaign began to get rid of them. . . . Once or twice a week there would be mass shooting of the lamas. Each time two or three truckloads full of lamas would be killed."[22] Some bodies from this era have been recovered, but most remain missing. In 1992, inspectors excavated a mass grave near Mörön in northern Mongolia containing the remains of around a thousand lamas; their bodies, nearly wholly intact due to the permafrost, revealed sadistic tortures. In 2003, investigators unearthed a similar site near Ulaanbaatar. Convicted lamas not executed usually wound up in the Soviet Gulag or at work camps inside Mongolia, with many never returning home. Generally speaking, younger, able-bodied lamas had the greatest chance of surviving, whereas senior lamas perished practically to a person.

In addition, the Mongolian government forcibly closed and destroyed more than seven hundred monasteries. At monastery after monastery in the late 1930s, Ministry of Interior personnel backed by regular (and sometimes Soviet) troops showed up in trucks to drive lamas out of the monasteries or arrest them. Items inside, including rare works of art and Buddhist scriptures, were then confiscated or destroyed, often in large bonfires on monastery grounds. At the Gandan monastery in Ulaanbaatar, for example, the Migjed Janraisig Buddha (25.5 meters high) was pillaged for its gold and jewels before disappearing, only to surface decades later broken to pieces in Leningrad.[23] The gold and silver wealth of the monasteries became property of the state, while area herders frequently benefited from the distribution of monastery livestock. In a few cases, monks successfully hid sacred items and texts, permitting them to reemerge after the collapse of Communism. Several monasteries were reoutfitted for secular uses, but most were either simply abandoned or burned down. "By July 20 [1938], out of 771 temples and monasteries, 615 have become ash heaps," one Communist underling proudly reported to Moscow, although more compelling assessments today put the total number of closures and destructions closer to eight hundred or even higher.[24] In a nomadic culture, these temples and monasteries often constituted the only stationary structures in an entire region.[25]

The executions and closures cast a pall of fear over society as a whole. "The Green Hats [secret police] came at night to make arrests. . . . I was very afraid," one eyewitness reported; "this fear was present all across the country, especially in adults. Anyone could be arrested; fear was everywhere. If there was ever a knock on the door during the night, we were scared." Some lamas simply disrobed and left their vocations when they saw the writing on the wall. "In 1936 my father was a lama in Bolgan [province]," another eyewitness noted. "After this [the execution of other lamas] happened, he quit being a lama, and went to work as a herdsman in the countryside."[26]

Paralleling events taking place in the Soviet Union and presaging the Chinese Cultural Revolution, the destruction of Mongolian Buddhism in the late 1930s ranks as one of the most extensive but least known religious tragedies of the twentieth century: the virtual annihilation of an entire religious tradition in a matter of months. Noting, too, that all Buddhist ceremonies and holidays were banned after 1937-38, the Hungarian scholar Krisztina Teleki in a study of Ulaanbaatar concluded that Buddhism, at least officially, was almost "totally terminated."[27] As the exigencies of socialist development and education kicked in during the following period, and due to the reticence of and danger for Mongolians to speak about what happened in the 1930s, young people effectively became cut off from their religious heritage. "By the middle of the twentieth century following the reign of terror," as Jerryson has put it, "generations of Mongols were completely removed from their religious history and culture."[28]

Incredibly, in 1961, in a promotional brochure, the Mongolian government had the temerity to recommend its religious policies to socialist-wannabe countries in the developing world: "The experience gained in destroying the structure of lamaseries and resolving the question of the lamas is not only instructive for our Party, but offers a lesson for all countries and their parties where, as in Mongolia, religion is strong."[29]

CHINA

Destructive as Mongolia's policies toward religion were, in terms of sheer numbers they hardly compare to the greater despoliation wrought by Communist China, particularly during the Cultural Revolution. These bitter years, 1966-76, witnessed, in the words of the historians of Chinese religion Vincent Goossaert and David A. Palmer, "the most thorough destruction of all forms of religious life in China and, perhaps, human history."[30] While much blame might be attributed to Mao Zedong and the eliminationist secularism embedded in his particular version of Marxism-Leninism, the destruction also owes its genesis to powerful pre-Communist secularizing currents of thought and reform manifest in the Republic of China (1912-49).

In fact, in the waning years of the Qing dynasty, many elite Chinese intellectuals and reformers had already concluded that religious communities, especially at the messy, popular level, constituted one of the greatest impediments to modernizing the country.[31] And while these same people lamented the humiliation China had endured under European imperialism in the nineteenth century, they nonetheless regularly looked to the West as a model for intellectual and political development, adopting a Western linear or stadial conception of time in particular.[32] Better, Western-style education, many felt, constituted the path forward, and hence arose the "smash temples, build schools" campaign, which targeted local Taoist and Buddhist cults and their "superstitious" or "heterodox" leaders in particular, including many "redemptive societies" (more about them in a moment). Led by Kang Youwei (1858–1927) and his disciple Liang Qichao (1873–1929), and supported by the imperial court, this campaign largely gave Confucianism a pass, interpreting it more as a secular state philosophy and system of social ethics, compatible with modern science and rationality, than as a religion per se.[33]

The campaign reached a milestone with the Temple Confiscation Edict (10 July 1898) during what is called the Hundred Days of Reform. This measure summarily closed thousands upon thousands of local temples and shrines, turning many into schools or other public buildings, while intensifying "anti-superstition" enthusiasm among the intelligentsia. The progressive newspaper *Zhenbao,* for instance, gave voice to many reformers when it editorialized twelve days after the edict that "today's Buddhists and Taoists are really the most heinous criminals on earth. This author feels a deep hatred towards the two religions. . . . But today their buildings, lands, and property are about to be turned over to the good cause; the circumstances are favorable and it seems easy. This is a most happy day for the world!"[34] Such vitriol permeated reformist discourse. In their social criticism, reformers leaned heavily on the distinction between religion (*zongjiao*) and superstition (*mixin*)—Western loan words that had come into Chinese (from Japanese) only at the turn of the century. Reformers extolled the former, usually elevating the ethical far above the cultic, while excoriating the latter, heedless of the fact that one person's superstition might be considered another's religion. While precise numbers are difficult to determine, scholars believe, astoundingly, that only half of the popular temples and shrines operating throughout China in the late nineteenth century were still functioning in the

1930s. And this says nothing about extensive destruction of temple property: statues, art, texts, manuscripts, and the like.[35]

A yet more severe and sweeping anti-religious mentality burst on the scene after the collapse of the Chinese Empire with the May Fourth Movement, a consequential, diffusive reformist campaign set in motion by students in Beijing who on 4 May 1919 protested both the treatment of China in the Versailles Treaty of that year and what they regarded as China's own feckless, behind-the-times leadership. The Nationalist Party (Kuomintang) extended this campaign as its political star rose in the 1920s and 1930s. Whereas Confucian elitism often served as the basis of the smash temples, build schools campaign in 1898, Confucianism itself became a target of reformist ire after 1919; the Chinese Sage's belabored concern with ritual, decorum, and subservience to social superiors, so the argument went, kept China from modernizing intellectually and politically. Confucian wisdom might have served China in the past, but a new day had dawned—one requiring truly radical reforms, even "the possibility of an irrevocable and total break with the past," to remake Chinese culture.[36] "Science" and "democracy" served as the watchwords of what came to be called the New Culture Movement; it found outlets of expression in such cutting-edge journals as *New Youth* and *New Tide,* replete with citations of Descartes, Holbach, Jefferson, Voltaire, Rousseau, Comte, and Marx, among other Western thinkers, including many nineteenth-century European anarchists, widely admired by some Chinese progressives because of their demolitionist attitude toward the past.[37] Above all, as Tu Weiming has written, "it was the Enlightenment mentality exemplified by the revolutionary spirit of the French . . . that dominated the intellectual discourse of the May Fourth generation."[38] Drawing from this spirit, critics held, China needed to develop a more skeptical mind-set, dispensing not only with popular religious enthusiasms but also with mental habits shaped by the inertia of imperial rule and Confucian thought. Writing in *New Tide,* Luo Jialun hailed the "spirit of criticism" as the "creative force" behind Western civilization, before arguing that "this critical spirit has been squelched in China in two ways [,] by autocratic politics and by autocratic thought. Autocratic thought is rooted in Confucianism, propagated by those who don't dare deviate from the sayings of the master."[39] The implication is clear: Confucianism, alongside popular religion, left China incapacitated to fully embrace the modern era.

May Fourth–generation thinking lay behind the Nationalists' official measure "Standards for Preserving and Abandoning Gods and Shrines" (1928), which resulted in numerous temple seizures, property expropriation, and the abrogation of countless popular religious festivals. In a harbinger of the Chinese Communist Party's Red Guards, the Nationalists' youth organizations sent young people out to destroy traditional temples. To accompany these measures, the Nationalists' Department of Propaganda developed a "Superstition Smashing Song" to be sung on the streets by party loyalists:

> This anti-superstition song, what purpose does it serve?
> Because the Chinese folk are more ignorant than wise,
> They do not plan or strive, seeking only dependency
> Losing touch with the real, chasing only illusion.[40]

The late nineteenth-century smash temples, build schools campaign, the May Fourth Movement, and of course the Russian Revolution of 1917 constitute crucial pieces of context to grasp the rise of the Chinese Communist Party and its attitude toward religion. Founded near Shanghai in 1921 by Chinese Marxists and Comintern officials, the CCP shared in the reformist desire to remake society from the ground up.[41] Two of the CCP's key cofounders, Chen Duxiu and Li Dazhao, appropriated both May Fourth and Marxist-Leninist ideas about religion, along with other ideas drawn from other European freethinkers and anarchists. An outspoken atheist and professor at Beijing University, Chen Duxiu argued that all gods are false, certain to disappear with the advance of technology and greater social progress. Li Dazhao admitted that though some faiths had played a progressive role in China's past, their expiration dates had arrived. Both men saw Christianity as a tool for imperialism, and they therefore contributed in the 1920s to anti-Christian campaigns as well as to the formation of organizations such as the Anti-Religious Federation and the Great Federation of Non-Religionists.[42]

The young Mao Zedong shared Duxiu and Dazhao's milieu and mindset.[43] Cutting his intellectual teeth writing polemics against Confucian practices, Mao famously told the Dalai Lama in the 1950s that "all religion is poison."[44] At the same time, his rise to power and especially his experience during the Long March (1934–35) and struggles against Japan led him to develop circumspect views. Recognizing that the Chinese peasantry and various ethnic and religious minorities were needed to strengthen the party's base, he often cautioned moderation, in fact once arguing: "It is the peasants who made the idols [religious belief], and when the time comes they will cast the idols aside with their own hands; there is no need for anyone else to do it prematurely."[45] This wait-and-watch attitude did not extend to Christians and Christian missionary activity, however, which Mao and practically all CCP members loathed as the humiliating ideological offspring of Western imperialism, even if they sometimes countenanced short-term collaborations with individual Christian groups. Nor did it extend to the many salvationist sectarian groups throughout the country, which the CCP saw as inherently counterrevolutionary and hence persecuted mercilessly before and after coming to power in 1949.[46] Nor did it extend to Confucianist thinking, which had virtually no place in Communist thought, as it was regarded by most Communist intellectuals as a ponderous "feudal" obstacle to modernization and secularization.

Shortly after the founding of the People's Republic of China (1949), the new Communist regime drew heavily from Soviet authors on religion, combining the anti-traditionalism already developed among Chinese elites with the Marxist-inspired contempt for all religions. "Long-term eradication, short-term management" might well sum up the early CCP policy toward religion. To this end, in addition to recognizing a narrowly defined religious liberty in the constitution of 1954, a Religious Affairs Bureau was set up to monitor and manage religious communities—a clear case of what I called earlier *conflictual integration*. Under its aegis, five "patriotic associations"— for Buddhism, Taoism, Islam, Protestantism, and Catholicism—came into existence in the 1950s: a fivefold typology testifying to Western influence insofar as each "religion" was largely defined as a discrete social phenomenon in the face of historical realities in China that indicated otherwise. All faith communities, moreover, were expected to cut foreign ties and funding immediately; foreign-born missionaries found themselves hounded out of the country amid a general witch hunt against "class enemies" and "imperialists."[47] The authorities either shut down or took over Christian schools, universities, and hospitals. Among Indigenous Christians, many Protestants proved tractable, agreeing to adhere to the government-prescribed so-called Three-Self Patriotic Principles: that is, an anti-imperialist Chinese church must be self-ruling, self-supporting, and self-propagating. But many others resisted, and as a result often faced harassment and imprisonment—among the best-known cases being that of Watchman Nee (1903–72), arrested in the 1950s and dying in prison in 1972.[48] His "Little Flock" church and several comparable ones persisted in their work but were driven underground, where they faced the disapprobation of government and party officials as well as of more politically cooperative coreligionists.[49]

Catholics arguably presented a thornier problem in the eyes of the CCP.[50] Mortified by the spread of Communism to China, Pope Pius XII worried aloud that a Catholic patriotic association amounted to an unseemly compromise with Caesar. The CCP happily reciprocated the animosity, clearly stating in an internal memorandum: "When the political struggle and the forces of production have reached a high rate . . . then it will become possible to destroy the Catholic Church. This is the objective we aim to reach and it is for this we struggle."[51] In the early 1950s, the government severed ties with Rome, expelling the Vatican's nuncio in Nanjing, Antonio Riberi, along with all foreign bishops and heads of religious orders. It also launched a nationwide crackdown on the Legion of Mary, a Catholic lay service and charitable organization. In the Catholic stronghold of Taiyuan in Shanxi Province, CCP cadres turned the local cathedral into a "living exhibition" of religious obscurantism, going so far as to place priests and nuns in metal cages and compelling the local population to view them.[52]

Recalcitrant Catholic leaders paid a severe price. Francis Xavier Ford, bishop of Kaying, was captured and "reeducated" for eleven months. Martyrs were made of bishops Cyril Jarre (a Franciscan, of Jinan), Leon-Jean-Marie de Smedt (of Xiwanzi), and Alexandre Carlo (of the Paris Foreign Missions Society). Many leading Indigenous Catholics encountered heavy persecution too: notably the high-profile bishop of Shanghai, Ignatius Kung Pin-Mei, who spent thirty years in prison or under house arrest, from the mid-1950s until his release in the 1980s. The vocal anti-Communist Paul Yu Pin was expelled from the country. But this only scratches the surface of thousands of Indigenous Chinese Catholics who are known to have been persecuted or else wound up in the massive system of forced labor and reeducation camps set up throughout the country, generally known as the laogai, "reform through labor"—an often "forgotten gulag" numbering around a thousand sites.[53] Still others were driven into an underground Catholic Church, which has lived, often uneasily, with an officially recognized "patriotic" one until the present.[54]

Yet despite their tribulations, Catholics fared better than the independent salvationist or redemptive societies. Often unrecognized and little understood in the West (except when China's persecution of the Falun Gong has made the headlines), the Chinese religious scene since the Ming dynasty has been awash in what Chinese elites had referred to as "heterodox" societies. Yiguandao (Unity Teaching), Tongshanshe (Fellowship of Goodness), Wanguo daodehui (Universal Morality Society), and Jiugong dao (Nine Palaces Way) were just several of hundreds of such groups present in China in 1949, claiming millions of devoted followers.[55] Despite significant differences in belief and ritual, they had in common an emphasis on apocalyptic expectation, personal salvation, and a proclivity to draw from a smorgasbord of cultic influences. Following in the footsteps of previous regimes but with unparalleled dedication and violence, the CCP went after these societies with a vengeance, beginning with the prerevolutionary decree "Dissolve All Sects and Feudal Superstition Organizations" (January 1949) and thereafter with a speech against "reactionary sects" (*fandong huidaomen*) delivered by Mao in 1950. Practically all were judged inherently disruptive to social unity, counterrevolutionary, and as harboring thick ties to Chinese Nationalists and to Japan. (Some in fact had such ties, but Communists tended to exaggerate the threat.) "The ruthless campaign [by the Communists] to suppress the societies shattered their networks, removed their leaders, and subdued the mass of followers," as the historian S. A. Smith has summed up. Even so, as the Falun Gong illustrates, they have endured—an unpardonable, heavily surveilled exception to state-sanctioned religious belonging or the preferred atheism.[56]

With respect to the state-sanctioned faiths, Buddhism arguably was among the most adversely impacted, materially speaking, in the early years of the People's Republic of China. Among the largest landowners in China, Buddhist monasteries were stung by the early Land Reform Campaign, which abolished their ownership rights and redistributed much of their land; senior abbots were classified as "landlords," and thus "class enemies," and monks as "social parasites."[57] In the several instances where monastic communities resisted, swift police and military intervention involving many casualties effected the government's will. Such episodic violence and the massive loss of land alongside other measures resulted in what the scholar of Chinese Buddhism Holmes Welch once called the attempted "decimation of the Sangha." Other measures included forcing monks to work; compelling them to marry; placing limits on ordinations to enter religious life; dissolution or absorption into the state of Buddhist schools, clinics, and welfare enterprises; appropriating monasteries as edifices for government or military use; and restricting their provision of hospitality to itinerant monks—a venerable tradition in many Asian countries. Yet even those monks who opted for lay life faced discrimination—something they shared with practitioners of other faiths due to a 1950 law that sought to stigmatize "religious or superstitious practitioners," defined as "all those people who for three years immediately prior to liberation, derived the main part of their income from such ... professions as those of clergymen, priests, monks, Taoists, lay Taoists, geomancers, fortune tellers, and diviners." It took five years of "strenuous devotion to labor" to qualify for reclassification and thereby improve one's educational and job prospects.[58] Ten years after the Revolution, the population of the Buddhist monastic community in China had plummeted by 90 percent. By 1961, Welch worried about Buddhism being "virtually eliminated." If government measures are kept up, he elaborated, "Buddhism, just a little less than two thousand years after it arrived in China, will be dead."[59]

Interestingly, during this same period, the CCP undertook the reconstruction of a number of Buddhist monasteries that had fallen into disrepair. But appearances can deceive: typically the purpose of these ventures was to enable central state power to assert its control over a site and transform it into a static museum of the Buddhist past, a decorative bit of cultural heritage, not a living community. "It had the atmosphere of a museum rather than a temple," as one Indian visitor commented in 1953 after a visit to a state-curated Buddhist site. "No monks chanted their hymns. . . . [Religious activity] can operate only within the bounds prescribed by the Communist party and along the lines laid down by the government."[60] Or, as the historian Gregory Adam Scott has sized up the reconstructed sacred sites: they housed "bones and stones but no [actual] Buddhist monks."[61] The CCP put these sites to good diplomatic use as religious showpieces, courting the approval of neighboring Buddhist countries and trying to win international approbation when in fact the sites often bespoke the ruin and dispossession of the sangha, not its ongoing vitality.

Yet not only Buddhists but practically every religious community lost property and wealth in the early years of the regime. "One of the goals of land reform," as the scholar Xiaoxuan Wang has noted, "was to destroy the economic underpinnings of the old society, including religious property. By undermining the economic foundations of religious institutions, however, land revolution had another, more drastic effect: it deterritorialized religious groups on a scale never seen in Chinese history."[62] Most religious institutions were expelled from their traditional sites or at least saw their access to them restricted. Successive campaigns to collectivize agriculture and set up worker communes in the 1950s further disrupted traditional religious life and the communities that sustained it.

These disruptions, however, preceded the tragic Great Leap Forward, during which tens of millions of Chinese perished. In addition to suffering from inept socioeconomic policies and agricultural practices, religious communities faced stepped-up repression, beginning in the late 1950s around the time that Mao, Deng Xiaoping, and Peng Zhen launched the so-called Anti-Rightist Campaign to purge party members—ultimately more than five hundred thousand in number—deemed guilty of "revisionism," that is, being too willing to make concessions to capitalism and insufficiently loyal to party policies and priorities. Concurrent socialist education campaigns sought to deepen religious leaders' commitments to anti-imperialism, patriotism, and anti-rightist thinking. During this process, many religious leaders—unflatteringly designated by the regime as "superstition professionals"—wound up being outed as rightist themselves, notably the Taoist leader Yue Chongdai (1888–1958), who in the mid-1950s had helped establish the Chinese Taoist Association.[63] What is more, CCP tacticians, like their Soviet counterparts, regularly sowed seeds of dissension within religious communities with the goal of having some "patriotic" members of a particular religious community denounce others as insufficiently loyal and cooperative. This took place quite frequently in fact.

Beginning with the second five-year plan in 1958, the CCP imposed greater central planning and collectivization on the entire country. Immense pressure fell on religious leaders to abandon their vocations and participate in the labor of material production; under duress (and sometimes torture) many "confessed" that they had long labored under delusion and misled others. As thousands complied, many sacred buildings were closed, consolidated with others, or else put in the service of pressing economic, political, or military purposes. In the span of a few years, the number of active churches in Beijing fell from sixty-six to four; and in Shanghai, from two hundred to eight.[64] In the municipality of Rui'an, a government survey boasted that zero Buddhist temples and monasteries were active in 1960, in sharp contrast to the four hundred active in 1949.[65] In addition, party officials targeted religious holidays, pilgrimages, and fasts as losses of time and energy that could be better spent on useful labor. A circular called "The Opinions regarding Religious Reformation among the Hui Nationality," prepared by the United Front Work Department, which handled ethnic minorities, illustrates a larger trend. In it, the party stated that frequent and large-scale religious activities among Chinese Muslims constituted a massive "waste of time for work." When Muslim leaders resisted such reforms, they were penalized as "rightists" or "counter-revolutionaries." In Muslim areas, what is more, countless mosques were shuttered and Islamic practices such as prayer, fasting, and circumcision banned as promoting backward and unhelpful mentalities. By the early 1960s, party officials boasted that some areas had become "no-religion prefectures" or "no-religion counties." When the devout complained about their treatment, they were reminded of Premier Zhou Enlai's words to religious leaders in 1957: "Now you should not worry about whether religion can exist or not, but about whether the nation will prosper or not."[66]

Hardly had the Great Leap Forward run aground when a new campaign began—the Socialist Education Movement (1962–66)—to clean up and combat corruption among Communist cadres and to intensify ideological education in the population at large. Often overshadowed by the Great Leap Forward and the Cultural Revolution, this essentially pedagogical movement sought, among other things, to confute religious belief at the popular level by convincing people that it amounted to nothing more than a spiritual weapon used by the ruling classes to maintain oppression.[67] In certain respects, one might regard the Socialist Education Movement as a minor prelude to the Cultural Revolution, which continued its pungently anti-religious emphasis and obsession with reeducation for a "new society." Nowhere is this seen better than in the "Eliminate Superstition" program, begun in 1963, that sought through local exhibitions in Shanghai aimed at young people to pit "religion" against "science" in a zero-sum game, pointing out to visitors the manifest superiority of the latter and the delusory, counterrevolutionary nature of the former.[68] For these exhibitions, the CCP's Science Popularization Publishing House developed a series of posters for mass consumption. Cleverly illustrated and often unintentionally quite comical, they included such titles as "The exploiting classes fabricate gods and ghosts to dominate the people"; "Reactionary and evil elements use old customs to engage in destructive activities"; "Exposing the trick of the 'Buddhist master'"; "There is no 'heavenly palace' or 'jade emperor' in the sky"; and, not least, "Let everyone eradicate superstition."[69]

Of course, anti-religious measures became more intense, violent, and extensive during the Cultural Revolution, which claimed hundreds of thousands of Chinese lives beginning in 1966. This massive upheaval might well represent the most effective manipulation of youthful idealism since the medieval Children's Crusade. Ever since the disaster of the Great Leap Forward, Mao had fretted about his power ebbing. The economic devastation and the lives lost from starvation due to the Great Leap could not be ignored by even the most loyal functionary. Relations with the Soviet Union, moreover, had soured since the mid-1950s. Khrushchev had criticized the excesses of Mao's mentor and ally, Stalin, which in effect amounted to criticism of Mao as well. In a preemptive strike against real and imagined enemies within the party, Mao appointed his wife, the former actress Jiang Qing, to instigate a purge. Beijing's mayor, the chief of staff of the People's Liberation Army, and the director of the Propaganda Department numbered among the first victims. On 4 August 1966, Mao made a conspicuous display of his own vigor by swimming across the Yangtze River, to great popular acclaim. Shortly thereafter, the "Decision Concerning the Great Proletarian Cultural Revolution," a sixteen-point document prepared by Mao, was broadcast on the radio and published in major newspapers; it called for "a more intensive and extensive new stage" of socialist development, focusing attention on the "ideological sphere . . . to transform the spiritual aspect of the whole society." "Our objective," the document continues in the patois of historical materialism, "is to struggle against and overthrow those persons in authority who are taking the capitalist road, to criticize and repudiate the reactionary bourgeois academic 'authorities' and the ideology of the bourgeoisie and all other exploiting classes and to transform education, literature and art and all other parts of the superstructure not in correspondence with the socialist economic base."[70] In mid-August, several rallies took place in Tiananmen Square involving millions of students whipped into a frenzy of progressivist zeal and party devotion. Soon mobilized into a mass, student-led paramilitary movement known collectively as the Red Guards, and drawing inspiration from Mao's famous *Little Red Book,* they were exhorted to search out and destroy the so-called four olds—old thoughts, old cultures, old customs, and old habits. Practically all surviving religious structures in China found themselves caught up in the fury that followed.

The Red Guards' rampage destroyed or closed down all religious sites throughout the country. The Bureau of Religious Affairs and the individual religious associations under its authority were dismantled and their leaders persecuted. Sacred buildings from all traditions were razed completely, statues of gods and other artifacts broken to pieces, sacred texts incinerated.[71] Some people took great risks to preserve items, but criminal charges followed those caught secretly hiding scripture or devotional objects; violators faced "struggle sessions," labor camp, or imprisonment. Red Guards made it a priority to confiscate religious items belonging to households and families. A report from one team encountering ground-level popular piety gives some indication of the aims and scope of destroying the four olds: "Within only a few days, ancestral altars, stovetop shrines, old tablets, clay statues of divinities, old doorplates have been destroyed spontaneously . . . now all 150 households in the Brigade have put up Chairman Mao's posters in each of their homes. They [also] turned the tablets that used to hold ancestral altars into Chairman [Mao] quotation boards. Every house has hung one up. Members of Xu'nan and Xubei Brigade voluntarily demolished thirty-five clay and wooden statues of divinities in [various temples]."[72] "Superstition professionals" were targeted as the personification of the four olds and, alongside outspoken laity, humiliated by being forced to make public confessions and subject themselves to self-criticism and struggle sessions. A defining feature of the Cultural Revolution, these sessions involved the public shaming of those accused of counterrevolutionary behavior, with the goal of extracting confessions and deterring undesirable behavior in others. They included such things as having the accused's face smeared with ink, forcing him or her to bark like a dog, and/or wear ridiculous, demeaning clothing. One Christian preacher, Shu Chengqian of Rui'an, remembered being forced to wear plaques around his neck labeling him a "leader of superstition" and "a special agent of imperialism" while he walked around the town receiving kicks, blows, and spittle from fellows citizens who either believed in the Cultural Revolution or else (as was often the case) were too afraid not to conform to prescribed expectations.[73] In one Chinese Catholic village, the devout were made to kneel for days, eat dirt, and sign statements of apostasy with sentences such as "Since I was a child my breast has been full of superstitious poison."[74] Similar scenes played out repeatedly, especially in 1966 and 1967, with the accused, after being coerced to recant, often winding up injured, dead, or in labor/reeducation camps. Experiencing the shame of such sessions and the prospect of enduring dishonor resulted in thousands of suicides across China.[75]

Anti-Confucianism surged during the Cultural Revolution. Authorities banned *The Analects* of Confucius, a pillar of Chinese civilization, and subjected many Confucian scholars to struggle sessions, imprisonment, and torture, while thousands of Confucian temples and shrines were vandalized or destroyed. Not least, in Confucius's hometown, Qufu, Red Guards and Mao's lieutenants trashed Confucius's gravesite and the surrounding cemetery in November 1966, disinterring what were believed to be family members and hanging their shriveled corpses from trees. So antithetical to his own ideology did Mao regard Confucius that he began a special "Criticize Confucius" campaign in the mid-1970s, the last major campaign of his life, which doubled as a ploy to take down opponents whom he judged too reactionary in their thinking.[76]

Geographically, the Cultural Revolution was a pan-China affair, affecting the Han ethnic majority as well as numerous minority peoples, located especially in the western regions, most of whom had already experienced extensive harassment and Sinification policies since the 1950s. In Xinjiang, home of Uyghur Muslims, all religious services were categorically prohibited after 1966; individuals caught practicing their faith received fines and punishment. As in other places, mosques, numbering in the thousands in this vast area, were closed, destroyed, or repurposed. To add insult to injury, authorities turned several mosques into pigsties, thus poking fun at Muslim taboos against pork. The greater the symbolic value of a place, the greater the chance that it was desecrated and/or put to nonreligious uses. The Great Mosque of Xi'an, built in 1384 under the Ming dynasty, for instance, became a steel factory.[77] In addition, several Muslim uprisings were crushed, including that of the Shadian Incident in the province of Yunnan, in which sixteen hundred Hui Muslims were massacred and many more homes destroyed in late July and August 1975.[78]

In Inner Mongolia, the Cultural Revolution's impact on Tibeto-Mongolian Buddhism compares to the devastation that Outer Mongolia experienced under Khorloogiin Choibalsan in the 1930s. A poster affixed to one Buddhist temple in the region succinctly summed up the general Communist attitude to Buddhism there: "Buddhism is like an ulcer that absorbs the vital energy of the people and prevents them from flourishing." On 28 August 1968, two hundred Red Guards pillaged the Great Monastery of Gegen Süme, hauling out thousands of Buddhist statues, destroying thirty-five made of stone, and vandalizing the architecture, leaving the site a ruin. Similar scenes played out at many other sites, with the aim of "the methodical destruction of [Inner Mongolia's] religious patrimony," as the scholar of Mongolian Buddhism Isabelle Charleux has summed up.[79] Lamas not imprisoned or slain had to join the mundane workforce.

In Tibet, the "Land of Snows" and the spiritual spawning ground of Mongolian Buddhism, the desecrations were even worse—both before and during the Cultural Revolution—with clear echoes in China's present-day policies toward Tibet.

TIBET

Whether Tibet belongs to China or deserves independent nationhood is of course a long-disputed geopolitical matter. The horrendous treatment of Tibet and its Buddhist traditions under Mao, however, is indisputable. In October 1950, shortly after the Chinese Communist Revolution, People's Liberation Army (PLA) troops arrived in the isolated Himalayan kingdom, making short work of Tibetan resistance. Several years later, Beijing cajoled Tibet's government, headed by the young Dalai Lama, to accept a Seventeen-Point Agreement that placed Tibet under Chinese authority, ending its de facto independence since the fall of the Qing dynasty, disempowering and later forcibly retiring the Kashag, Tibet's ruling council that had been founded under the Qing. Like Mongolia, Tibet was a monastic civilization, boasting more than six thousand monasteries and thousands of highly revered lamas of various ranks within a population of around four million. Political and religious authority were joined at the hip. At first, the CCP took a gradualist approach, trying to win over elites and according some respect to the Dalai Lama and the Panchen Lama, respectively the two highest offices in Tibetan Buddhism. But fear of and resentment against China ran deep in Tibetan society, and co-opting Buddhist elites proved no easy task. In the mid-1950s, when China stepped up class warfare and land reform, as well as efforts to combat "feudal superstition" in the eastern parts of the Tibetan Plateau known as Amdo and Kham, rebellions broke out and soon spread to other areas.

In suppressing these rebellions, the PLA included violence against traditional religious life as part of its arsenal. Numerous monasteries were closed or destroyed and senior lamas humiliated, maimed, and not infrequently killed in brutal struggle sessions or else packed off to labor camps. In February 1956, around three thousand monks took refuge in Chatreng's Sampheling monastery (one of the largest monasteries in Kham, the head of which, Trijang Rinpoche, had tutored the Dalai Lama). The PLA decided not to storm the monastery and risk heavy casualties. Instead, a plane was called in to bomb it, leaving it in ruins, with survivors either surrendering or fleeing deeper into Tibet. A similar aerial bombing brought destruction to nearby Lithang monastery, once home of the Seventh Dalai Lama. To terrified Tibetans, many of whom had never before seen an airplane, the bombings heralded a famous eighth-century prophecy stating, "When the iron bird flies and horses run on wheels, the Tibetan people will be scattered across the world." As refugees poured westward, news of atrocities began to circulate, eventually reaching the Dalai Lama, who recounted in his memoirs: "Slowly, from the reports of refugees, we began to receive a clearer impression of the terrible things. . . . The Chinese were using artillery and bomber aircraft, not only against guerrillas when they could find them, but also against the villages and monasteries. . . . Lamas and the lay teachers of the people were being humiliated, imprisoned, killed, and even tortured. Land was confiscated. Sacred images, books of scriptures, and things of holy significance to us, were broken up, derided, or simply stolen."[80]

By 1959 the conflict reached Lhasa, inciting its inhabitants to rise up against the PLA. Responding with massive force, the PLA attacked the city and shelled the outlying Norbulingka Palace, the summer residence of the Dalai Lama. Worried about his own life, the Dalai Lama, dressed as a commoner, narrowly escaped and fled to India on 17 March 1959, with around eighty thousand Tibetans soon following on a dangerous, cold trek through the Himalayas.[81] Thereafter, the PLA sealed the border and stepped up the conflict, at the cost of thousands of lives, and soon established martial law throughout Tibet. Of course, the Dalai Lama remains in exile in India until the present, while China—which once referred to the former Nobel Peace Prize laureate as "the root of the most reactionary, darkest, cruelest, and most barbaric serfdom"—denies him entry into China and criminalizes the display of his image.[82]

The years between 1959 and 1966 witnessed intrusive reforms and repression in Tibet. China permitted the window dressing of ostensibly allowing Tibet its own leaders—the Panchen Lama, who was more acquiescent to

Beijing than the Dalai Lama, and the politically agile, reform-minded Nga-poi Ngawang Jigme, who chaired the committee of the Tibet Autonomous Region after its creation in 1965. But real power lay with the PLA's military control committee, under General Zhang Guohua, and ultimately with the CCP in Beijing. In addition to snuffing out pockets of rebellion throughout society, the CCP abandoned all remaining efforts to appeal to Tibet's elites and concentrated attention on implementing a comprehensive program of class conflict and religious persecution. Characterizing Tibet's entire past as a nightmare of "feudal serfdom" and "backward superstition," the party initiated major land reforms, stripping power from aristocrats and lamas in a policy euphemistically called "the warm embrace of the motherland" and setting up state-run collective farms, most of which failed spectacularly and lethally due to the flawed centralized decision-making and unsound agri-cultural techniques that characterized the Great Leap Forward as a whole.[83] Those who resisted reforms were subjected to struggle sessions, sent to labor and reeducation camps, or executed. Thousands of monasteries, some that had operated continuously for centuries, were suddenly shut down, their residents evicted and their treasures plundered, sold off, or shipped to China. To be sure, Tibet's lower classes welcomed some reforms and the general principle of equality, but they were profoundly shaken that the changes appeared inextricably bundled with a relentless assault on their religious heritage.[84]

As reforms failed and the devastation to Buddhism became apparent, the Panchen Lama bravely penned and submitted to Beijing the so-called Seventy-Thousand Character Petition in 1962, leveling trenchant criti-cisms of CCP behavior and itemizing various violations and abuses within Tibet.[85] At first the letter was guardedly accepted by Beijing authorities, but the CCP soon sided with the military staff in Tibet, who condemned the letter as a "poisoned arrow." Consequently, the Panchen Lama, who had sought to work with Beijing, faced weeks of intense struggle sessions before being confined to the feared Qincheng prison, where political pris-oners languished in solitary confinement, subjected to psychological and physical torture. Later placed under house arrest and once reported as dead, the Panchen Lama won his freedom only in the 1980s, several years after the death of Mao.

Difficult as things were in Tibet in the early 1960s, the Cultural Revo-lution inaugurated a more devastating round of violence and repression.

Carried out by Red Guards (made up of both young Tibetans and Han Chinese) and often working through the institution of "neighborhood committees," this round of attack demolished practically everything left of traditional culture, seen as it was through the harsh lenses of the four olds. "Completely smash the old world! We demand to be masters of the new world," as one Red Guard banner in Tibet aptly characterized the moment, quoting Mao.[86] Or, to cite selectively from a leaflet issued by the Red Guards of the Teacher Training College of the Tibet Autonomous Region, the path ahead for Tibet should include the following: "All observance or religious festivals should be abolished"; "all large and small chortens [stupas] must be destroyed"; "all mani walls, prayer flags and incense burners should be destroyed"; "no one should recite prayers, circumambulate, prostrate"; and "all monasteries and temples apart from those that are protected by the government should be converted for general public use."[87] "In Lhasa," as one Tibetan ruefully remembered the onset of the Cultural Revolution in the city, "all the sacred statues, scriptures, and images . . . [were] destroyed, and people's houses had been searched and they were made to carry whatever sacred images or religious paraphernalia they had through the streets in public humiliation processions. . . . Now as I contemplated how the Chinese had flung away the disguise of 'freedom of religion' policy and gotten down to the basics of Communist practice, I started shivering with anxiety as though I had caught malaria."[88]

The furious assault on remaining religious structures began with the sacking of Lhasa's Jokhang temple, a rich artistic shrine of deities and bodhisattvas, a veritable "Sistine Chapel" of Tibetan Buddhism, dating from the mid-seventh century during the reign of the Songtsen Gampo, who is widely credited with bringing Buddhism to Tibet from India. In an orgy of destruction, Red Guards carried out Buddhist manuscripts, piled them high in the courtyard and burned them. They vandalized and smashed statues, including the ancient Jowo statue, said to have been blessed by the Buddha himself, arguably the most potent emblem of Tibetan Buddhism. As one perpetrator later remembered: "When we arrived there [on 24 August 1966], there were still worshipers doing full prostrations in front of the Jokhang. We pasted big-character [propaganda] posters on them. And we glued posters onto the two statues of the protector deities by the main entrance of the Jokhang. . . . On that day most of what the students did was to smash up prayer wheels and then to burn prayers and texts pulled out from inside the wheels."[89]

Following precedent in other Communist lands, the Jokhang became a museum of superstition, garishly displaying "four old" objects gathered from temples and stupas around Lhasa.[90] The despoliation of the Jokhang set off a countrywide wave of destruction of sacred structures, in which all but thirteen of the some six thousand documented monasteries—centuries-old centers of literacy, learning, thangka painting, sculpture, embroidery, meditation, music, dance, chanting, and ritual—were wrecked, often with the use of explosives. While some monasteries were quite small, set in desolate places, others—such as Samye, Tibet's first monastery, or the great Ganden

Figure 13. Ruins of Ganden monastery (Tibet), damaged after the Chinese invasion of Tibet in 1959 and again during the Chinese Cultural Revolution. Photographed by Tashio. Courtesy of Wikimedia Commons.

monastery near Lhasa (figure 13), established by the founder of the Gelug Order, the monastic lineage of the Dalai Lama, and once supporting five thousand monks—were architectural treasures of immense cultural and religious significance.

As monasteries fell, persecution intensified against leading figures of pre-Communist Tibet, lamas foremost. Throughout Tibet, thousands upon thousands of vowed religious faced cruel struggle sessions, during which they had to wear dunce caps and carry placards itemizing their putative errors and crimes. Denounced, shamed, beaten, and spat upon in mass assemblies, they also marched forlornly in "humiliation parades" organized by neighborhood committees, police, and military personnel. Entire monastic communities were sent to the coal mines. In Lhasa, struggle sessions frequently took place in the Sungchöra, once the famous debating forum just outside the Jokhang temple. Red Guards branded lamas and other reactionary elements with the Chinese phrase "ox-demon-snake-spirits," which amounts to the most despicable cultural "other" imaginable. "The number of religious figures who were attacked in these struggle sessions during the Cultural Revolution was staggering," writes Tsering Woeser of her native Tibet; "because of their role in guiding all living beings on the path of liberation, they are traditionally seen as one of the three jewels of the religion. . . . You could say that lamas are in fact the soul of spirit of Tibet. . . . The slander and scorn that religion was subject to in Tibet during the Cultural Revolution was unprecedented; it . . . [almost] completely eliminated the faith important to so many Tibetans." Or, as one surviving lama movingly remembered his humiliation: "During a *thamzing* [struggle session], I was made to wear a tall, pointed hat and my monk's robes. . . . All manner of badges and ritual instruments were pinned to my robes to make me look ridiculous. I was paraded twice through the Lhasa marketplace to the music of trumpets and gongs and the insults of the Red Guards. . . . I had to bend over with my eyes looking down, and they would start beating and criticizing me. . . . [But] I was one of the lamas who suffered the least. The proof is that I am still alive today to tell you about it."[91] By the late 1970s, Tibet's monastic population had been reduced by about 93 percent.[92]

Destroying monasteries and humiliating lamas did not exhaust the Red Guards' repertoire. As was the case throughout China, so-called big-character posters appeared everywhere, denouncing the four olds and promoting a bright Communist future. Read one poster: "Unless you attack them, reactionary things will not collapse on their own. It's just like the principle of floor-cleaning. Dust won't remove itself until the broom does its work." Tibetans gained merit by squealing on their neighbors who exhibited religious behavior, even those quietly praying or meditating at home. Prayer flags—Tibet's signature feature of everyday piety—were strictly banned, along with other objects of devotion. Practically every major religious holiday and festival was abolished, including the Monlam Chenmo or the Great Prayer Festival, a major, weeklong event of piety, circumambulating stupas, and celebration, which had taken place annually since 1409. What is more, many places, buildings, and streets received new names, canceling the past, promoting the future. Authorities even required people, if their names smacked too much of the past, to adopt new ones. "Back then," as one woman remembered, "we were . . . required to change our names, we were told that our Tibetan names were tainted by feudal superstition and were therefore signs of the Four Olds. . . . You could choose the name you wanted to change to, but it had to be approved by the Bureau's Political Affairs Office."[93] The Barkhor, or Circumambulation Street in central Lhasa—a reference to the pilgrimage route—became Establish-the-New Avenue, while the Dalai Lama's summer palace, Norbulingka, became People's Park. Finally, Mao's name and image became almost instantaneously ubiquitous after 1966, replacing those of the Dalai Lama and Avalokitesvara, the bodhisattva of compassion believed to be reincarnated as the Dalai Lama, and sometimes of the historical Buddha himself, Siddhartha Gautama. Take, for instance, how Communists modified the lyrics from *East of the Sun*, a popular Tibetan folk song, during the Cultural Revolution.

Original:

East of the Sun
There's a palace of gold.
In the palace built of gold
Is Vajrasattva, the Adamantine Buddha.

South of the Sun
There's a palace built of silver.
In the palace built of silver
Is Amitabha, the Buddha of Endless Light.

The version developed during the Cultural Revolution:

East of the Sun
There's a palace built of gold.
In the palace built of gold
Is our great leader Mao Zedong.

South of the Sun
There's a palace built of silver.
In the palace built of silver
Is our great Chinese Communist Party.[94]

The death of Mao and the emergence of new Chinese leadership in the late 1970s brought a sudden halt to the excesses of the Cultural Revolution, widely recognized today as a "cultural genocide," in addition to its heavy human costs. Since that time, Buddhism has incrementally regained a public presence in Tibet, although it remains heavily surveilled and bureaucratically manipulated. And one cannot undo the past's enormous material losses, to say nothing of the extensive disruption and cost in human lives. Credible estimates of unnatural deaths among Tibetans since the Chinese occupation range as high as hundreds of thousands and now include hundreds of self-immolations by protesting Tibetans monks.[95] During the 1950s and 1960s, it is estimated that at any given time one in every ten Tibetans resided in a labor/reeducation camp. Finally, the difficult question of memory remains a disquieting reality for Tibetans, evocatively described by the historian Tsering Shakya: "For them [Tibetans] the trauma of the Cultural Revolution would linger in their minds, and the evidence of the appalling destruction of Tibet's cultural heritage would haunt the Tibetan landscape. The people who lived through the period still express their incomprehension and describe it as the time [when] 'the sky fell to the earth.'"[96]

CAMBODIA

As the sky collapsed on Tibetan Buddhism in the 1950s and 1960s, tumultuous events unfolded in Cambodia. Gaining its independence from France in 1953, the kingdom of Cambodia under King Norodom Sihanouk eked out a short, unimpressive existence, expiring when its prime minister, Lon Nol, staged a coup d'état in 1970 and took over the reins of government. Between 1970 and 1975, a bloody civil war ensued, pitting Nol's forces (backed by the United States, then mired in the Vietnam War and given to indiscriminate bombing) against Sihanouk's regime, supported by the North Vietnamese and a new, hyper-Maoist revolutionary group, the Khmer Rouge, which slithered into existence in the early 1960s in the jungles of eastern Cambodia, hiving off from Ho Chi Minh's Indochinese Communist Party (f. 1930). Its reign formally began on 17 April 1975 when Khmer Rouge forces took the capital, Phnom Penh, establishing Democratic Kampuchea, soon sidelining Sihanouk as a hapless figurehead. As is well known, from 1975 until 1979, the Khmer Rouge, led by the mercurial, enigmatic Pol Pot, perpetrated one of the bloodiest political crimes in modern history, killing nearly two million (more than 20 percent) of its own citizens in "an attempt to implement total Communism in one fell swoop."[97]

Like many of the Khmer Rouge's early leaders, Pol Pot (born Saloth Sar) had studied in France in the 1950s. An undistinguished student, he and other future leaders had become members of the French Communist Party and were involved in several Marxist reading circles. The Communist triumph in China in 1949 had created a magical moment for Asian radicals, providing a sense of immense, world-historical possibility. In addition to reading the writings of Mao, especially *On New Democracy,* Pol Pot pored over Stalin's *History of the Communist Party of the Soviet Union,* also reading several French writers, notably Rousseau, as well as the Russian anarchist Peter Kropotkin, whose *Great French Revolution* glamourized Robespierre and the Jacobin stages of the French Revolution.[98] A potent mélange of these influences hitched to a xenophobic Cambodian nationalism and lust for domination, the Khmer Rouge positioned itself by the mid-1970s to impose its will on Cambodian society.

Its time in power started with the execution of surrendering officials of the former government and the brutal emptying of the capital and other major cities in an effort to build a classless agrarian utopia. Astoundingly, Phnom Penh went from two million people to practically none within a matter of days. Black-clad soldiers forcibly marched millions of people into the countryside and put them to work as virtual slaves digging canals, building roads, tending crops. Seeing the family as a feudal holdover, they did not hesitate to break apart families, pressing children into labor brigades and military units. Anyone who criticized the new arrangement risked torture and death by a blow to the head. Rather quickly, gross mismanagement of the economy led to shortages of food, medicine, and basic supplies, and untold numbers of Cambodians succumbed to disease and starvation, not infrequently headed off by suicide. "The form of Communism that they [Cambodians] faced was perhaps the worst of all, and the liquidation of such a terrible past is an almost intolerable burden," as Jean-Louis Margolin has summed up the Khmer Rouge experience.[99]

And what of the religious sphere? Theravada Buddhism arrived in Southeast Asia in the third century B.C.E. and by the twelfth century C.E. had become the state religion in Kampuchea (the ancient name of Cambodia later revived by the Communists). Over time, its fortunes waxed and waned, with a notable revival of Buddhism taking place after independence from France in 1953—a political changing of the guard largely supported by the sangha. A Buddhist pagoda or temple (wat) and monastery stood in nearly every village—the center of the community's activities, a haven for the pious, aged, and destitute. By 1969, when the Kampuchean population crested at seven million, an estimated 3,369 monasteries and 65,062 saffron-wearing monks could be found throughout the country, along with countless *achars*, lay Buddhist ritual specialists.[100] During the civil war, Buddhists' allegiance was divided, as both sides courted Buddhist leaders and the full anti-religious intentions of the Khmer Rouge trailed behind other pressing matters.[101]

Although roughly 90 percent of the Cambodian population was Buddhist, a small Christian minority, mainly dating from the French colonial experience, existed as well, along with a still older Muslim community, restricted mainly to the Cham people, a Malayo-Polynesian-speaking minority in Cambodia and southern Vietnam descended from the once powerful Champa Kingdom, which had converted from Hinduism to Islam in the seventeenth century. Cham Muslims tended to live in closed communities, concentrated especially in Kampong Cham province and in Takeo and Kampot along the country's southern coastline.

Following the script of other Communist countries, revolutionary Democratic Kampuchea, albeit an avowed atheist state, paid lip service to "the right to worship" in the constitution adopted in 1976, but tellingly singled out "reactionary religion" as "strictly forbidden" (article 20).[102] Shortly after the Khmer Rouge seized power on 17 April 1975, the writing was already on the wall for Cambodian Buddhism. The very next day in fact, Huot Tat, the highest-ranking monk in the country and a critic of the new regime (figure 14), was taken from his monastery in Phnom Penh to Oudong and promptly killed. A month later, on 20 May, the new regime summoned all regional leaders, civilian and military, for a five-day meeting in the northern suburbs of the former capital to map out the road ahead. No paper record of this meeting survives, but participants' memories corroborate what took place. In an eight-point plan, Pol Pot's item 4 was: "Defrock all Buddhist monks and put them to work growing rice." Heng Samir, a cadre studying military affairs, remembered it this way: "Monks, they said, were to be disbanded. They had to be wiped out (*lup bombat*). . . . I heard Pol Pot say this myself. . . . He said no monks were to be allowed, no festivals were to be allowed any more, meaning 'wipe out religion.'" Another individual, Nuoin Chea, affirmed this recollection, adding: "Wats [temples] would not be allowed."[103]

Figure 14. Huot Tat, the supreme patriarch of the Maha Nikaya Buddhist order of Cambodia, murdered by the Khmer Rouge in April 1975. Photographer unknown. Courtesy of Wikimedia Commons.

These prescriptions for action, however, arguably only set in motion previous sayings of Pol Pot, which in addition to repeating Marx's famous line on the opiate of the masses included remarks such as "Monks are parasites" and "Monks are tapeworms gnawing at the bowels of society."[104]

The coerced disrobing of monks began in the summer of 1975. As one monk from Takeo Province remembered the process: "They told us to disrobe . . . but we refused and some monks were sent elsewhere [executed?] for this. But in the end they came with guns and forced us to disrobe. Fifteen monks disrobed with me. There were no monks after that." In September 1975, a self-congratulatory party memorandum crowed about the achievement: "Ninety to ninety-five percent of the monks have disappeared, in the sense that the majority of the monks have abandoned religion. Monasteries, which were pillars for the monks, are largely abandoned. The foundation pillars of Buddhism are abandoned, the people have stopped going to the monasteries, stopped having festivals and concentrate only on making dams and canals, etc."[105] Deprived of monasteries, former monks and achars faced prohibitions against chanting, lighting incense candles, collecting alms, shaving their heads, or practicing meditation. Penalties for doing these things could be lethal. Pali, the sacred language of Theravada Buddhism, was everywhere suppressed.

The disrobing process coincided with forcing monks into the regular labor force, compelling some to marry and others to take up military duties. Marriage and military service directly contravened a monk's vows upon ordination, and in Theravada Buddhism the monastic rule of discipline (vinaya) and ideal of nonviolence (ahimsa) prevented monks from engaging in many labors that risked harming sentient life. Doing such activities under coercion thus came as a profound rupture to the traditional monastic vocation. Although many complied, feeling they had few options to do otherwise, some risked fleeing the country to Laos, Vietnam, and especially Thailand, where a large monastic refugee community came into existence, enduring there until the downfall of the Khmer Rouge regime in 1979.[106] Those who defied orders and did not flee invariably wound up dead or sent to one of several labor and reeducation camps that largely followed the Chinese model.[107] Unaccustomed to hard manual labor, many monks perished from exhaustion or injury.

Temples, pagodas, stupas, Buddha images, murals, sacred texts, and other forms of religious material culture suffered considerable harm after

1975, although some destruction had already taken place during the civil war (1970–75). An estimated 1,968 temples (of around 4,000) were completely destroyed by 1979.[108] Authorities dismantled some to use their materials for party-directed building projects. Golden Buddhas, not surprisingly, were coveted for their melted-down value, while destroyed cement statues provided raw materials for new constructions. "If you demolish a statue of Buddha, you will gain a sack of cement" went a well-attested slogan of the regime, making clear its value system, although some statutes—whether from ideological disregard or efforts to spare—wound up in rivers and ravines—some of which have been recovered. Others were sold off, winding up in foreign art markets. Numerous instances of book burnings also occurred under the Khmer Rouge, with highly valued, traditional palm-leaf manuscripts incinerated in the process.

In a few instances, so-called pagoda demolition teams, made up of prisoners working with sledgehammers, often sleeping on-site, came into existence for the express purpose of dismantling sacred buildings. Unnerved by the work forced upon him, one Buddhist testified after the collapse of the regime that under his breath he prayed while destroying temples around Khsach Kandal: "Please Buddha, do not accuse me; I was ordered to do it."[109] Such workers were told that their labor served two purposes: to provide the regime with necessary building materials and to ensure that future generations never knew Cambodia even had a Buddhist heritage.

Structures not destroyed became rice-storage facilities, livestock farms, arms depots, schools, medical facilities, barracks, prisons, and, not least, execution centers. Wat Kaich Roteh in Moung Ruessei district functioned as a holding place for intellectuals. Once these prisoners were slain and cremated, locals were enjoined to use their ashes as fertilizer. Since 1979, investigators have discovered mass graves at many sites of temples, stupas, and monasteries. "Buddhist ritual sites associated with mountains and caves exercised a special fascination for those engaged in mass murder," the scholar of Cambodian Buddhism Ian Harris once observed, taking stock of the post-regime fact-finding and exhumation process.[110]

Determining exactly how many monks perished under the Khmer Rouge is an inexact science. Collectively, they represented a possible threat of opposition, an alternative hierarchy of values, a sphere of authority outside the scope of the state, and as such a "special class" deserving surveillance and often lethal attention. In some areas, one may speak of almost complete liquidation, making the recollection of an elderly monk from Phnom Penh, who survived the ordeal, apposite: "Only two [out of a previous one thousand], including myself, came [back] and joined the monkhood [in Unnalom, Phnom Penh]. There are a few more who remain as laymen; perhaps ten or fewer that I have met. There were many learned monks in Unnalom monastery. They all have disappeared; I'm sure they died. If they were not killed, they would have died of starvation or sickness."[111] Nationwide, it is estimated that only about two thousand monks, from a previous number of about sixty-five thousand in 1975, survived to witness the collapse of the regime in 1979. Of those unaccounted for, the Khmer Rouge's successor regime, the People's Republic of Kampuchea, gave the figure of 25,168 monks dying by violent executions, usually from an iron bar's blow to the back of the skull—the preferred way of killing. Some scholars have offered higher figures, some lower, suggesting that this number might be roughly accurate. But all can agree that this period ranks as an exceedingly dark time for Theravada Buddhism, the virtual destruction of a nation's religion in a matter of years. "For centuries, the Buddhist wat or temple was the center of village life, the source of learning, the reservoir and transmitter of Cambodian culture," but then, as the scholar Karl D. Jackson has summed up, "[the] Khmer Rouge policy toward Buddhism constituted one of the most brutal and thoroughgoing attacks on religion in modern history."[112]

Even so, Cambodian Christians and Muslims arguably had it worse. During the Khmer Rouge period, mortality rates among the small Protestant and Catholic communities approached 50 percent, although many simply fled the country.[113] Associated with French colonialism, the Catholic cathedral in Phnom Penh was dismantled piece by piece after 1975, its stones and bricks used to reinforce dams for nearby rice-paddy farming. Other churches experienced comparable destruction. Contact with Western missionaries or Vietnamese Catholics spelled severe punishment or death.

Although the Khmer Rouge despised all minorities, it reserved special venom for the Cham minority (the country's largest), not least because of its Muslim faith and proclivity to offer the regime resistance. Chams' lives, faith, and material culture consequently faced almost total eradication by the late 1970s, the logical conclusion of a process that began with the execution of the grand mufti and the hakim of the Nur ul-Ihsan Mosque in Phnom Penh (built in 1813) and several other Muslim dignitaries in the summer of 1975. In addition, all Muslim prayers and holidays were proscribed, all mosques vandalized and/or destroyed, and all distinctive clothing forbidden. On several occasions, Muslims encountered a choice between raising pigs and eating pork or being put to death—a somewhat ironic demand, since practically all types of meat disappeared from people's diets during the Khmer Rouge years. After mid-1978, the government began systematically exterminating Cham villages, killing women and children as well as men.[114] Roughly ninety thousand Cham perished in the late 1970s from a population that stood at about two-hundred-and-fifty thousand in 1975. "The systematic extermination of the Cham community and [its] religious leaders, let alone the large-scale massacres of tens of thousands of ordinary Chams," the scholar Ben Kiernan has concluded, "are further evidence of the genocidal intent of the regime."[115]

Begun in the Soviet Union and Mongolia, then continued in China and Tibet under Mao and in Cambodia under Pol Pot, the Communist, state-sponsored assault on Buddhism, as well as on other faith traditions, ranks as one of the most extensive religious tragedies of the twentieth century.

CONCLUSION

Deliver my soul from the sword.
—Psalm 22:20

PERMIT THE REITERATION OF A POINT MADE IN THE Introduction: combative secularism and eliminationist secularism, as I have defined them, should not be conflated. The former presents more of an anticlerical than an anti-religious posture and did not launch a frontal attack against religion as such, while eliminationist secularism sometimes did—or at least it more readily had that potential, tethered as it was to an ideology in which the decline (and eventual extinction) of belief served as a bellwether of revolutionary progress and its resilience presented a vexing political problem.

Still, combative and eliminationist secularism shared some things in common. In addition to authoritarian tendencies, exponents of both often possessed an unflappable certainty about being on the "right side of history" and confidence in the tutelary capacity of the modern state, exorcized of obscurantism, to subdue and/or manage dissenters. If the former did this in more of a Voltairean-Comtean register and the latter in a Marxist-Leninist or Maoist one, an Enlightenment-derived stadial conception of historical progress powerfully informed both visions. Stadial historical conscious-ness in turn lent itself to interpretations of social reality marked by sharp divisions between "us" (the forces of progress) and "them" (the forces of reaction), the latter meriting opposition and control and, at least from the standpoint of eliminationist secularism, disappearance, whether hastened by deliberate action or through the putatively inexorable laws of history.

In accounting for ideological state-sponsored violence of the twentieth century, scholars have preponderantly focused on racism and anti-Semitism (Hitler, Goebbels, . . .) and class warfare (Lenin, Stalin, Mao, . . .) as the principal culprits. Hannah Arendt's conceptualization of "totalitarianism," although controversial in some quarters, has served as a helpful analytic tool as well.[1] Far from denying these approaches, this book aims to complement them by flagging ideological secularism, or at least some militant variants thereof, as a contributing factor as well. Still, this claim requires several final caveats and qualifications.

For starters, one should of course not conclude that secularism *exhaustively* explains the instances of violence given in this book. Other factors come into play as well, as I have made clear all along. In addition to Maoist anti-religious sentiment, for example, China possessed a long-standing historical interest in subduing Tibet politically. In this case and others, moreover, it can sometimes be difficult to disentangle whether regimes targeted religion, ethnicity, political dissent, or separatism, although these realities were often complexly amalgamated.

Then, there is the question of nationalism. Both French Third Republic-style secularism and modern Turkish nationalism informed Kemalism in Turkey in the 1920s and 1930s. Similarly, although echoing the secularist universalism of Lenin, Albania's Enver Hoxha championed his own local brand of nationalism, rhapsodizing about ancient "Illyricum" as an areligious idyll before marauding empires—Byzantium (Orthodoxy), the Austro-Hungarian Empire (Catholicism), and the Ottoman Empire (Islam)—despoiled the land. While not without a measure of truth, this amounts to a partial reading of history that, once put into practice, ran roughshod over the beliefs and customs of actual Albanians. But the broader point stands: whether in China, Turkey, Albania, or elsewhere, one should not expect to find unalloyed secularism as the sole causal agent in explaining violence. History is messier and more complicated than that. But even when they were not in the driver's seat shaping affairs, secularist ideologies often supplied a modern, sophisticated-sounding ideological posture, appealing to "progress," "science," or "historical necessity," to augment and confer legitimacy on more visceral (national) political motivations.

Opponents and victims of secularist ideologies, furthermore, should not necessarily be regarded as innocent lambs, for they often committed misdeeds as well. Franco's fighters in the Spanish Civil War, for example, gave as good as they got, as did the Catholic Cristeros in Mexico—to offer but two examples. And not every priest, monk, lama, rabbi, or imam confronted with the hostility of secularist regimes responded by "turning the other cheek," although, remarkably, not a few actually did, while others compromised or collaborated with authorities, sometimes to the peril of more intransigent coreligionists. In addition, some of the attitudes and practices that mistreated religious communities sought to defend—the subservient role of women, a stratified social order, nostalgia for the old order—admittedly do not sit well with most modern Westerners today. Conversely, the same secularist regimes perpetrating violence often championed what we might regard as meritorious ideas—equality, literacy, women's rights—even if their implementation often came without genuine democratization and sometimes with methods that would have made Robespierre jealous.

One must add that many secularist policies ultimately failed and/or led to ironic outcomes. Although officially banned in Kemalist Turkey and for periods in most Soviet Muslim-majority republics, Sufi masters continued to exercise significant social authority, if clandestinely. Stalin and his henchmen widely expected a census in 1937 to confirm a steep decline in religious belief. When this did not happen, he had the census results suppressed and removed questions about religious belief from future censuses.[2] Underground religious communities cropped up in practically all countries given to repressive secularism, often succeeding in turning disgruntlement over religious policies into more broad-based political dissent and human-rights advocacy. Among several examples, recall the influential *samizdat* journal *Chronicle of the Lithuanian Church* (f. 1972). Its writers documented antireligious persecution and human-rights abuses and with the help of Western partners conveyed their findings beyond the Iron Curtain.[3] Catholicism not only did not decline in Poland during the Soviet era, it arguably became more tightly entwined with Polish national identity. Considerable evidence suggests, too, that the secularist excesses of the Mexican Revolution in the early twentieth century did not degrade but rather fanned the flames of popular religious sentiment.[4]

At the level of "lived religion," rank-and-file believers often persisted with their religious practices in the face of harsh repression or else came up with resourceful work-arounds to circumvent a regime's strictures. In 1959, for example, Soviet authorities banned pilgrimages to a site in Kirov Oblast on the banks of the Velikaya River where an icon of Saint Nicholas was believed to have mysteriously appeared in the fourteenth century. Even after the destruction of the site and the refusal of intimidated clergy to participate, the Orthodox laity continued to travel there, insistently defying authority.[5] Evangelicals and Pentecostals in Ceauşescu's Romania often met secretly in rural, remote locations. In an even more restrictive Albania, the devout during the Cold War made trips to a popular pilgrimage site north of Tirana, Kisha e Shna Ndout, furtively and at night.[6]

What is more, atheist propaganda, journalism, and education in Communist countries rarely succeeded as their implementors hoped. Many people might have toed the party line publicly, but only from a desire to make life more tolerable for themselves and their families. Some resisted more courageously. Communist newspapers during the Cold War frequently complained about the whack-a-mole difficulty of stamping out religious belief. An exasperated writer for the official Soviet newspaper *Pravda* (3 October 1964), for example, complained that after forty-seven years of indoctrination, atheism remained far from the norm. "Where do they [religious believers] come from?" the writer fulminated, continuing: "The question is not a simple one. When the believer is a person in his declining years, it may perhaps be explained. But what if he is a 'slave of the Lord' at seventeen? A Baptist with a graduation certificate? How does this happen?"[7] "In developed socialism, religion . . . [persists as] the gravest obstacle of the ideological purification of society," echoed a Czech Communist news source.[8] These types of utterances pervaded Communist discourse in the second half of the twentieth century. Conversions from atheism to faith especially flummoxed Communist authorities, leading them in several cases to confine such subversive individuals in psychiatric hospitals.[9]

Weary of ideological intimidation and repression, religious actors played a significant role in fomenting dissent in the late 1980s, contributing substantially to the collapse of the entire Soviet bloc. "Much to the surprise of many," the cultural anthropologist Catherine Wanner has written, "the final years of the Soviet Union's rule coincided with a religious revival that quickly took root in the USSR's fifteen republics [and in Eastern Europe too]. Religion rapidly emerged as a rallying force for change . . . to effectively galvanize larger groups in protest against Soviet rule."[10] Catalyzed by the charismatic papacy of John Paul II (r. 1978–2005), the Catholic Church played a significant role in this process, as has been well documented.[11]

In another type of historical reversal, some of the most brutal attempts to repress religion contributed in a few cases to religion's resurgence, if of a different or altered kind. In Mongolia, for instance, the scorched-earth policies toward Buddhism in the twentieth century created a cultural vacuum, which Christian missionaries have partially filled since the collapse of Communism in the early 1990s. Mongolia has witnessed the significant growth of Pentecostal and other forms of Christianity, including Latter-day Saints, as have many other former Soviet republics.[12] Something similar could be said of China after Mao. "Hundreds of millions of Chinese," the veteran journalist of China Ian Johnson wrote in 2017, "are consumed with doubt about their society and turning to religion and faith [of various kinds] for answers that they do not find in the radically secular world constructed around them."[13] And as is widely documented, the rise of Islamism, whether of meek or militant varieties and often in stark contrast to traditional Muslim practices, has gone hand in hand with the humiliation of Muslims living under the authoritarian secularist-nationalist policies of Kemalist provenance once exported throughout much of the Islamic world in the twentieth century.[14] If not as extreme as the Turkish case, Tunisia under Habib Bourguiba and Iran under the shahs are two additional examples, reflecting to various degrees the Kemalist combative-secularist prototype and engendering comparable reactions—the Iranian case in 1978–79 being the most explosive globally.[15]

One might be forgiven for wishing that the violence toward religious communities by secularist regimes has been comprehensively marked in the previous pages and it is now a thing of the past. Sadly, this is not the case.

Knowledge of religious life in North Korea, because of its extreme insularity, is spotty. But all indications suggest that the "hermit kingdom"—in keeping with the repressive conditions afflicting the population at large—ranks among the most extreme cases of eliminationist secularism, despite the fact that Pyongyang was once known as the "Jerusalem of the East" due to the heavy concentration of Christian missionary work there.[16] Following the Soviet example, the government has permitted a few Potemkin temples and churches in Pyongyang and several shell religious organizations to bolster claims that it respects religious freedom. But escapees, intelligence agencies, and scholars alike attest to a regime of cruel persecution, in which the "expression of religion has been almost completely suppressed."[17] Shortly after World War II, all religious communities in North Korea were stripped of their property under the rule of Kim Il Sung and forced to endure "the campaign of thought for state-building," which prioritized the elimination of "superstition." People deemed "dangerous" to the regime were subsequently placed in fifty-one categories: numbers 37, 38, and 39 indicated, respectively, Protestants, Buddhists, and Catholics. By 1950, every Catholic priest or religious in the country had been exiled or slain, or had simply disappeared—the case of the prelate Francis Hong Yong-ho being the most prominent.[18] During the Korean War, the regime repressed or killed other religious leaders and their followers, excoriating their putative ideological criminality and ties to the West. The tragedy continues. According to the Database Center for North Korean Human Rights, the early 2000s witnessed some of the highest instances of anti-religious repression on record.[19]

While not as insular or ideologically rigid as North Korea, the Communist states of Laos and Vietnam—collectively populated by no fewer than a hundred million people—also score extremely poorly on human-rights records in religious matters. Since the establishment of these countries as complete Communist states in 1975 (with North Vietnam under Ho Chi Minh's Communist rule since 1954), the general Marxist-Leninist anti-religious bias of the governments had applied in principle to all faith communities. But the legacy of the Vietnam War has made the situation in both countries especially trying for Christians, whether Catholic or Protestant, who are found especially among ethnic minorities and often accused of harboring execrable Western ties and sympathies. "Earlier in this period [after 1975]," as the scholar of the region Reginald E. Reimer has summed up, "a good part of the oppression was of the 'smash' variety involving various forms of coercion and violence. More recently it has been dominated by the 'squeeze' variety, employing both social opposition and a plethora of complicated and arbitrarily enforced regulations administered by large bureaucracies focused on controlling religion."[20] Security forces in both countries have special units dedicated to surveilling and constraining the actions of religious communities. Both governments blame religiously inspired dissidents for the collapse of Communism in Eastern Europe and the Soviet Union—a fate they want to avoid. As in other Communist countries, Laos and Vietnam have made provision for "officially recognized" religious bodies, condemning those who refuse to register to a life in the margins. According to the Human Rights Watch 2021 World Report on Vietnam, "Police monitor, harass, and sometimes violently crack down on [unregistered] religious groups. . . . [They] face constant surveillance, harassment, and intimidation . . . [and] are subject to public criticism, forced renunciation of faith, detention, interrogation, torture, and imprisonment."[21]

One must not forget Cuba in the Western Hemisphere. When the dictatorship of Fulgencio Batista gave way to the dictatorship of Fidel Castro in 1959, the Catholic Church found itself in the new regime's crosshairs, even though most clergy happily said goodbye to Batista-era corruptions. Things went from bad to worse after the botched Bay of Pigs affair in 1961. Catholic periodicals were shut down, church properties seized, and all religious colleges closed, including the Bethlehem Jesuit College, where Castro received his education. "Let the Falangist priests start packing their bags," Castro declared in September 1961, contriving the arrests of many priests and forcing hundreds to leave the country.[22] Others wound up slain as dissidents or forced into labor camps. After rule by decree for a decade and half, 1976 witnessed the promulgation of a Cuban constitution that officially committed the party-state to "atheism"—later changed to "secularism"—even as it paid lip service to religious freedom. Always numerous among political dissenters, religious figures have experienced a cruel fate in Cuba, such as that of Pedro Luis Boitel, a practicing Catholic who refused to join the Communist Party, wound up incarcerated, and died in 1972 after being tortured in the Castillo del Príncipe fortress; or that of Armando Valladares, an evangelical Christian who refused to genuflect to Castro and suffered a twenty-two-year imprisonment, movingly recounted in his memoir *Against All Hope*.[23] For most of the regime's existence, indication of religious practice denied one access to higher education after turning sixteen, while unregistered "house churches," once discovered, predictably triggered intervention by the State Security Department, the so-called Red Gestapo. Although the collapse of the Soviet Union (which bankrolled Cuba) and the death of Castro have ameliorated conditions for the devout in Cuba, much of the improvement should be seen as a tactical necessity born of desperation. In 2016, the government showed its true colors, shutting down Las Damas de Blanco (the Ladies in White), a group of spouses and other female relatives of jailed or vanished dissidents, many of them Catholic, who met for Mass on Sundays in Havana followed by silent protest. Perhaps one believer put it best when, describing the relatively improved recent conditions, she noted: "Church members [in Cuba today] are still tied to a choke chain, but the leash is [now] just a little longer."[24]

Of the remaining Communist regimes in the world today, however, nowhere is the situation for religious practitioners, at least in terms of scale, bleaker than in China, home now to almost one-fifth of humanity. Although significant religious growth has occurred there since the late twentieth century, and although the official apparatus of a State Administration for

Religious Affairs (SARA)—a major instance of *conflictual integration*—presiding over five "patriotic" religious bodies seeks to control and not categorically forbid religion, all signs in recent years point to a gradual tightening of the screw for religious communities. In "Document 19," a 1982 statement on religion that still governs party religious policy, the CCP recognized that "old thinking and habits cannot be thoroughly wiped out in a short period," before confidently proclaiming that "religion will eventually disappear from human history."[25] In the short term, according to a Freedom House report on China, the Chinese government aims to manage and when possible opportunistically exploit faith communities for its own purposes, even as it selectively maltreats or bans some forms of religious expression with "long-term asphyxiation" as the final aim for all. Several years after coming to power, current Communist Party chairman Xi Jinping made clear that all CCP cadres must be "unyielding Marxist atheists," even as he increased measures to "Sinicize" all religious communities, insisting that they evince unswervingly patriotic and socialist stances in the public sphere.[26] At the Twentieth Congress of the CCP in October 2022, the party-state went so far as to convey to religious leaders that "Sinicization" implied, sooner or later, coming around to a "Marxist view of religion."[27]

The situation with Muslims—mainly Uyghurs but also ethnic Uzbeks, Kazakhs, Kyrgyz, and Huis—in the vast western Xinjiang region has been, of course, an acute area of contemporary concern; many countries and the United Nations have used the term "genocide" or "crimes against humanity" to describe China's actions there.[28] Since 2017, in the name of fighting terrorism, more than one million Muslims have been arbitrarily interned in hundreds of so-called vocational education and training centers. Those not detained have been subjected to intense surveillance (with the help of eerie biometric technologies and GPS tracking devices) as well as restrictions on religious practice, forced labor, sexual abuse, and coerced sterilization. The CCP bans growing long beards and wearing the hijab in public. As during the Cultural Revolution, numerous religious grave sites and thousands of mosques have been shut down or demolished in recent years, often on the pretext of shoddy or unsafe construction. Many people, finally, have simply gone missing, their families having no idea of what happened to them and in many cases being too afraid to ask.[29]

Hong Kong and Tibet also remain areas of special concern. Since the transfer of the former port colony from British to Chinese hands in 1997, basic liberties, including religious freedom, have incrementally withered, accelerating in recent years, as evidenced by the arrest and trial of Cardinal Joseph Zen, a plucky champion of religious freedom and a harsh critic of the government's stranglehold over "official" Catholicism in his city.[30] While Tibetan Buddhism flickered to life again following Mao's death, the long shadows of the Cultural Revolution have in some respects never gone away on the "Roof of the World," and in recent years the situation has worsened. Mentioning the Dalai Lama or displaying his image remain criminal offenses. In 1995 Chinese officials abducted the Panchen Lama—recognized as a legitimate reincarnation by the Dalai Lama—when he was six years old, and his whereabouts still remain unknown. "Religious practice is carefully managed and increasingly restricted in Tibet," as Freedom House's 2022 Report on Tibet summarizes. "The government's efforts to 'Sinicize' Tibetan Buddhism have accelerated in recent years, with officials requiring lamas to pledge loyalty to the government and socialism above their religious beliefs, denounce the Dalai Lama, and attend increasingly long political indoctrination sessions."[31] Monastery schools have been closed down, dissenters languish in prison, and surveillance is ubiquitous. Self-immolation among protesting Tibetan monks has perhaps slackened in recent years only due to the government's cruel treatment of past immolators' closest family members and friends.

Sadly, Xinjiang, Hong Kong, and Tibet represent extreme instances of a much broader phenomenon, affecting millions upon millions of people. Not just in these areas but all across China, and despite the government's effort to celebrate some religious traditions as a form of "heritage," "religious practitioners [in China] live under the permanent threat of politically motivated prosecution and conviction," according to a recent Amnesty International report.[32]

In light of the onslaught of violence directed at religious communities by modern secularist regimes, it merits asking again what accounts for the persistence in the West of the commonplace that religion is inherently violent and that secularism is the appropriate, liberating solution? Put differently, why the curious blind spot among many educated Westerners with respect to violence committed under the aegis of ideological secularism?

As indicated in the Introduction, many academic treatments of modern secularism suffer from a limited focus on the North Atlantic world—concentrating on (Lockean) passive secularism, perhaps with an occasional nod to French-style laïcité as a strident variant. The Canadian philosopher Charles Taylor's influential (and very long) *A Secular Age* (2007) is an especially egregious example—commendably erudite but preponderantly and ponderously Eurocentric. Lesser achievements of comparable outlook abound, sometimes adding to blinkeredness of standpoint a simplistic tale of secularist triumphalism. But if one provincializes the North Atlantic world and aims for a broader, global perspective, the full unsettling reality of secularist violence comes into view. "The scholarship on secularization and secularism," note Tam T. T. Ngo and Justine B. Quijada in their perceptive *Atheist Secularism and Its Discontents,* "still largely remains within the Western world," resulting in the strange reality that "state-sponsored atheism, a political project that dominated half the globe in the twentieth century, is [astoundingly] not usually considered a form of secularism."[33] Or, as the historian Adeeb Khalid puts it in his magisterial *Central Asia:* "The Soviet experience of the battering of religion by the party-state occupies little space in general histories of secularization, which continues its focus on the gradual differentiation of the realms of religion and the state [in the West] through long-term social change. The Soviet method of violent repression of religion was to be replicated in several places in the mid-twentieth century. . . . That violence is also part of the history of secularization in the modern world and the one most relevant to Central Asia."[34] To be fair, the study of secularism has to some degree become more globalized in recent years, but this is really only among a handful of academic experts, who nonetheless still often do not connect the dots to see the big picture due to the exigencies of period and regional scholarly specialization.[35] In the penumbral academic world of journalism, Western-centric blinkeredness and triumphalism with respect to secularism appear imperturbable.

One must take into consideration, too, that in explaining Marxism-Leninism numerous Western scholars and intellectuals, given to unexamined assumptions about religion's inherent violence and secularism's curative potential, have reassuringly sought to define Communism as a surrogate for religion or as a "political religion," pointing out similarities, say, between Christian promises of an afterlife and Communist promises of a classless society or between the medieval cult of the saints and the cultlike devotion paid to Communist leaders. This type of analysis is not without some explanatory power, to be sure, as I indicated earlier. But as the anthropologist of secularism Sonja Luehrmann has helpfully countered:

"Metaphors that assimilate Communism to religion disguise what Communist ideologues saw as a distinguishing feature [of their labor]: . . . a focus on the humanly achievable rather than trust in divine help."[36] Communist anti-religious violence, then, cannot adequately be explained simply as violence done in the name of yet another religion, ersatz religion, or quasi-religion. Such lines of inquiry stretch the definition of religion beyond reasonable boundaries while failing to account for and, in some respects exculpating, misdeeds resolutely tied to immanent, stadial, Enlightenment-rooted conceptions of history and society.

What is more, admitting violence done in the name of secularism perhaps strikes too close to home for many Western elites. It complicates a reflexive "master narrative" about the nature of modernity as onward-and-upward deliverance from religious obscurantism and past "wars of religion."[37] It is for this reason, as the scholar of secularism José Casanova perceptively conjectures, that "contemporary Europeans . . . prefer selectively to forget the more inconvenient recent memories of secular ideological conflict [in the twentieth century] and retrieve instead the long-forgotten memories of the religious wars of early-modern Europe," in an effort to understand the emergence of their world and their place in it. "One may suspect," Casanova continues, "that the function of such selective historical memory is to safeguard the perception of the progressive achievements of Western secular modernity, offering a self-validating justification of the secular separation of religion and politics as the condition for modern, liberal democratic politics."[38] Put differently, the ample violence committed by modern states hitched to forms of ideological secularism in the twentieth century simply does not cohere with how modernity was supposed to have turned out, and hence it is simply elided, disowned, or interpreted in a manner—that is, Marxism-Leninism was after all really just another "religion"—that permits the conventional narrative to remain undisturbed.

A comparable reality pertains to the asymmetry in educated Western attitudes toward Nazism—curiously usually labeled "right-wing" despite its manifold socialist economic commitments—and toward the various Communist states and the enormous violence perpetrated by each. At some level, violence is violence, and arguments about "moral equivalence" can quickly become tedious and beside the point. Yet Nazism (seen as racist and atavistic) undeniably has elicited more moral attention and remembrance than Communism (seen as egalitarian and universalistic in its aspirations). This is true despite the fact, as the Bulgarian-French historian Tzvetan Todorov observes, that Communist violence "lasted longer . . . spread more widely, to almost every continent, and was not confined to the European theater; and it killed an even greater number of people."[39] Quantitatively, credible estimates range as high as reckoning Nazism responsible for around twenty-five million deaths in the twentieth century; Communism for around eighty-five to one hundred million.[40] The status of being an ex-Nazi, furthermore, carries an ineradicable moral stigma, whereas that of being an ex-Communist—say, the French philosopher Jean-Paul Sartre, the Mexican artist Diego Rivera, or the Chilean poet Pablo Neruda—does not. Along similar lines, the Pulitzer Prize–winning historian Anne Applebaum once recalled Western tourists in Prague in the years after the collapse of Communism happily decking themselves out in Communist paraphernalia, most of whom "would be sickened by the thought of wearing a swastika." She and many others, moreover, have remarked on the relative lack of attention filmmakers have devoted to Soviet and Chinese concentration camps in comparison to Nazi ones. In large part, as Applebaum surmises, the discrepant attitudes suggest that "to condemn the Soviet Union too thoroughly would be to condemn a part of what some of the Western left once held dear as well."[41] Or, as the historian Tony Judt trenchantly stated, "To many Western European intellectuals, Communism was a failed variant of a common progressive heritage," and thus presumably gets graded on a forgiving curve.[42]

Similar dynamics perhaps help explain scholarly inattention to secularist anti-religious and anticlerical violence in the modern era. During the Cold War, the McCarthyite anti-Communist fervor of the political right often included blanket denunciations of "godless Communism" tied to sensationalized stories of religious persecution. Not surprisingly, polite society recoiled from such rhetoric, which admittedly often did not help its cause and often overreached—not least in the unconscionable penchant to tag all anti-segregationists and other liberals as "Communists."[43] The problem with maintaining this stance now, however, is that the "archival revolution" since the 1990s—in which Soviet-era sources of information have become more accessible—has in significant measure vindicated more measured anti-Communists' appraisal of Communist anti-religious activity.[44] The same political dynamics go a long way in explaining why many progressive Westerners took at face value Communists' attempts to parry the charges of such malfeasance. As we have seen, in official Communist discourse, authorities hardly ever stated that they targeted religion as such; accusations instead were expressed in, and in part camouflaged by, an elaborate smoke screen of Marxist-Leninist-speak. Officials thus spoke of cracking down on "counterrevolutionaries," "feudals," "reactionaries," "bourgeois sympathizers," and the like—terms acceptable to and even embraced within Western progressive circles.[45]

Permit me to conclude by emphatically restating that focusing on violence in the name of militant ideological secularism neither denies nor excuses violence in the name of religious belief. Disputing this regrettable reality is not the purpose this book, although I have raised an eyebrow at the supposition that religion is somehow *inherently* violent. The theologian David Bentley Hart might have put it best when he wrote, "As a historical force, religion has been neither simply good nor simply evil but has merely reflected human nature in all its dimensions."[46] Perhaps something similar applies to secularism and the various uses to which it has been put by modern regimes. At the very least, a tour d'horizon of secularist violence in global perspective holds the promise of bringing greater nuance and circumspection to fraught debates about the nature of religion, politics, modernity, and violence. Which secularism, whose religion, where, and under what conditions, we might more discerningly ask. Failure to do so comes at the price of enormous forgetfulness, dishonoring those who experienced persecution and detrimental to a considered and capacious understanding of the modern age.

Notes

INTRODUCTION

1. Douglas G. Jacobsen and Rhonda Hustedt Jacobsen, *The American University in a Postsecular Age* (Oxford: Oxford University Press, 2014), and Thomas Albert Howard, *The Faiths of Others: A History of Interreligious Dialogue* (New Haven: Yale University Press, 2021), 1–16, 235–57. See also the issue of the *Hedgehog Review* devoted to "After Secularization" (vol. 8, 2006), edited by Slavica Jakelić.

2. Hector Avalos, *Fighting Words: The Origins of Religious Violence* (Amherst, NY: Prometheus, 2005), 18.

3. Richard Dawkins et al., *The Four Horsemen: The Discussion That Sparked an Atheist Revolution* (London: Bantam Press, 2019).

4. "General Assembly Proclaims 22 August International Day for Victims of Violence Based on Religion, Other Beliefs" at https://www.un.org/press/en/2019/ga12147.doc.htm (accessed on 16 October 2020).

5. William T. Cavanaugh, *The Myth of Religious Violence: Secular Ideology and the Roots of Modern Conflict* (Oxford: Oxford University Press, 2009), 3.

6. Janet R. Jakobsen, "Is Secularism Less Violent Than Religion?" in Elizabeth A. Castelli and Janet R. Jakobsen, *Interventions: Activists and Academics Respond to Violence* (New York: Palgrave, 2006), 58.

7. Jürgen Osterhammel, *The Transformation of the World: A Global History of the Nineteenth Century,* trans. Patrick Camiller (Princeton: Princeton University Press, 2009), 873ff., 904–5.

8. I borrow and adapt the terms from Ahmet T. Kuru, *Secularism and State Policies Toward Religion: The United States, France, and Turkey* (Cambridge: Cambridge University Press, 2009); Jean Baubérot, *Histoire de la laïcité en France* (Paris: Presses universitaires de France, 2007); and Sonja Luehrmann, "Soviet Atheism and Its Aftermath," in Phil Zuckermann and John R. Shook, eds., *Oxford Handbook of Secularism* (Oxford: Oxford University Press, 2017), 231–48.

9. Baubérot, *Histoire de la laïcité en France,* 41.

10. Linde Lindkvist, *Religious Freedom and the Universal Declaration of Human Rights* (Cambridge: Cambridge University Press, 2017).

11. Of course, this does not attempt to exonerate regimes adopting passive secularism from other forms of violence. What is more, in their foreign policy, these regimes have sometimes happily supported regimes committed to combative or eliminationist secularism.

12. Dipesh Chakrabarty, *Provincializing Europe: Postcolonial Thought and Historical Difference* (Princeton: Princeton University Press, 2000).

13. Rita Hermon-Belot, *Aux sources de l'idée laïque: Révolution et pluralité religieuse* (Paris: O. Jacob, 2015), 157–89.

14. David A. Bell, "The French Revolution, the Vendée, and Genocide," *Journal of Genocide Research* 22 (2020): 19–25.

15. Michael Burleigh, *Earthly Powers: The Clash of Religion and Politics from the French Revolution to the Great War* (New York: HarperCollins, 2005), 252.

16. Joseph Moody, "French Anticlericalism: Image and Reality," *Catholic Historical Review* 56 (1971): 646.

17. Jean Baubérot, "La laïcité française et ses mutations," *Social Compass* 45 (1998): 181–82.

18. Many socialists—some on principle, others as a matter of political expediency—supported the Social Democratic Party of Germany's Gotha Program of 1875 and the Erfurt Program of 1891, both of which simply declared religion to be a private matter (*Privatsache*). Lenin and many others eventually repudiated this point of view. Moreover, some figures, notably Proudhon, spoke of socialism as the realization of Christian ethics, even if it meant the abolition of traditional Christianity as a metaphysical system. On the Gotha Program, Lenin's repudiation of it, Proudhon's thought, and other trajectories of secularist-leftist thought vis-à-vis religion in the nineteenth century, see especially James H. Billington, *Fire in the Minds of Men: Origins of the Revolutionary Faith* (New Brunswick, NJ: Transaction, 1998), 5, 18, 182, 185–86, 227–28, 252, 302–3, 465.

19. Pierre-Joseph Proudhon, *Idée générale de la révolution au XIX siècle* (Paris: Garnier Frères, 1851), 185.

20. Traugott Koch, "Revolutionsprogramm und Religionskritik bei Karl Marx," *Zeitschrift für Theologie und Kirche* 68 (1971): 61–62.

21. Noted in James C. Scott, *Seeing Like a State: How Certain Schemes to Improve the Human Condition Have Failed* (New Haven: Yale University Press, 1998), 205.

22. Roland Boer, "Spiritual Booze and Freedom: Lenin on Religion," *Journal of Marxism and Interdisciplinary Inquiry* 6 (2013): 102.

23. Jonathan Israel, *Radical Enlightenment: Philosophy and the Making of Modernity, 1650–1750* (Oxford: Oxford University Press, 2001).

24. Leszek Kolakowski, *Is God Happy? Selected Essays* (New York: Basic Books, 2013), 36.

25. Karen Armstrong, *Fields of Blood: Religion and the History of Violence* (New York: Alfred A. Knopf, 2014), 262–339.

26. Monica Duffy Toft, Daniel Philpott, and Timothy Samuel Shah, *God's Century: Resurgent Religion and Global Politics* (New York: W. W. Norton, 2011), 71–79.

27. Wilfred Cantwell Smith, *The Meaning and End of Religion* (Minneapolis: Fortress Press, 1991 [1962]).

28. Ernst Feil, *Religio: Die Geschichte eines neuzeitlichen Grundbegriffs vom Frühchristentum bis zur Reformation*, vol. 1 (Göttingen: Vandenhoeck and Ruprecht, 1986), 105–11.

29. Tomoko Masuzawa, *The Invention of World Religions: Or, How European Universalism Was Preserved in the Language of Pluralism* (Chicago: University of Chicago Press, 2005), 61–71.

30. Jonathan Z. Smith, *Imagining Religion: From Babylon to Jonestown* (Chicago: University of Chicago Press, 1982), xi.

31. Talal Asad, *Formations of the Secular: Christianity, Islam, Modernity* (Stanford: Stanford University Press, 2003), 192.

32. Israel, *Radical Enlightenment.* Cf. Margaret C. Jacob, *The Secular Enlightenment* (Princeton: Princeton University Press, 2019).

33. Saba Mahmood, *Religious Difference in a Secular Age: A Minority Report* (Princeton: Princeton University Press, 2016), 3. See also Charles Taylor, *A Secular Age* (Cambridge, MA: Belknap Press of Harvard University Press, 2007), and Ashis Nandy, "The Politics of Secularism and the Recovery of Religious Tolerance," in Rajeev Bhargava, ed., *Secularism and Its Critics* (New Delhi: Oxford University Press, 1998), 321–44.

34. Cavanaugh, *Myth of Religious Violence,* 13, 120–21.

35. See, inter alia, Eric Voegelin, *Die Politischen Religionen* (Munich: Fink, 1996 [1938]), and Emilio Gentile, *Politics as Religion,* trans. George Staunton (Princeton: Princeton University Press, 2006), 1–4.

36. Philippe Burrin, "Political Religion: The Relevance of a Concept," *History and Memory* 9 (1997): 330–31.

37. Benedict Anderson, *Imagined Communities: Reflections on the Origin and Spread of Nationalism,* rev. ed. (Verso: London, 2016), 9–12. On the powerful contributions of religious forces to nationalism in the nineteenth century, see Hugh McLeod, "Christianity and Nationalism in Nineteenth-Century Europe," *International Journal for the Study of the Christian Church* 15 (2015): 7–22.

38. Taylor, *A Secular Age,* 21, and Henri de Lubac, *The Drama of Atheist Humanism,* trans. Anne E. Nash, Edith Riley, and Mark Sebane (San Francisco: Ignatius, 1995 [1949]), 14.

39. José Casanova, "The Secular, Secularization, Secularisms," in Craig Calhoun et al., eds., *Rethinking Secularism* (Oxford: Oxford University Press, 2011), 59.

40. Burrin, "Political Religion," 329.

41. Leszek Kolakowski, *Main Currents of Marxism,* vol. 3, trans. P. S. Falla (Oxford: Oxford University Press, 1978), 54.

42. See, e.g., Gabriel Marcel, *Le mystère de l'être* (Paris: Aubier, 1951).

43. Yves Labbe, "La théologie négative dans la théologie des religions," *Revue des sciences religieuses* 72 (1998): 469–84.

44. Denis R. Janz, *World Christianity and Marxism* (New York: Oxford University Press, 1998), 6–10.

45. Quoted in Bohdan R. Bociurkiw, "Lenin and Religion," in Leonard Schapiro et al., eds., *Lenin: The Man, the Theorist, the Leader* (New York: Praeger, 1987), 119.

46. Leszek Kolakowski, *Modernity on Endless Trial* (Chicago: University of Chicago Press, 1990), 9.

47. On this distinction, see Shannon Craigo-Snell, "Kairos in the Chronos: A Rahnerian View," *Philosophy and Theology* 23 (2011): 301–25.

48. Max Weber, *Wissenschaft als Beruf* (Berlin: Duncker und Humblot, 1967 [1918]).

49. Ernest Gellner, "The Struggle to Catch Up," *Times Literary Supplement* (9 December 1994): 14.

50. Thomas Nipperdey, *Germany from Napoleon to Bismarck,* trans. Daniel Nolan (Princeton: Princeton University Press, 1996), 20.

51. Jacques Maritain, *The Person and the Common Good,* trans. John J. Fitzgerald (Notre Dame: University of Notre Dame Press, 1947), 93.

52. Pillot quoted by Billington, *Fire in the Minds of Men,* 252.

53. On some of the latest literature, see Elizabeth Frazer and Kimberly Hutchings, *Violence and Political Theory* (Ann Arbor: Polity, 2020).

54. Hannah Arendt, *On Violence* (New York: Harcourt, 1969), 53–56.

55. Arendt, *On Violence,* 55.

56. See, e.g., James A. Kapaló and Kinga Povedák, eds., *The Secret Police and the Religious Underground in Communist and Post-Communist Europe* (London: Routledge, 2022).

ONE

1. Quoted in Nicholas Wiseman, *Recollections of the Last Four Popes and of Rome in Their Times* (London: Hurst and Blackett, 1858), 223.

2. Wiseman, *Recollections of the Last Four Popes,* 219.

3. Darrin M. McMahon, *Enemies of the Enlightenment: The French Counter-Enlightenment and the Making of Modernity* (Oxford: Oxford University Press, 2001), 153–88.

4. René Rémond, *Religion and Society in Modern Europe,* trans. Antonia Nevill (Malden, MA: Blackwell, 1999), 81.

5. Frédéric Lambert, *Théologie de la république: Lamennais, prophète et législateur* (Paris: Harmattan, 2001), and C. B. Hastings, "Hugues-Félicité Robert de Lamennais: A Catholic Pioneer of Religious Liberty," *Journal of Church and State* 30 (1988): 321–25.

6. Brian E. Vick, *The Congress of Vienna: Power and Politics after Napoleon* (Cambridge, MA: Harvard University Press, 2014), 162.

7. John T. Noonan, *The Church That Can and Cannot Change: The Development of Catholic Moral Teaching* (Notre Dame: University of Notre Dame Press, 2005), 146.

8. The journal ran only from October 1830 to November 1831. See Ruth L. White, *L'Avenir de La Mennais: Son rôle dans la presse de son temps* (Paris: Klinckseck, 1974).

9. From *L'Avenir* as cited in Hastings, "Hugues-Félicité Robert de Lamennais," 321.

10. Owen Chadwick, *A History of the Popes, 1830–1914* (Oxford: Oxford University Press, 1998), 12–30.

11. Thomas J. Shelley, "Mutual Independence: Church and State in Belgium, 1825–1846," *Journal of Church and State* 32 (1990): 49–63.

12. J. F. Maclear, ed., *Church and State in the Modern Age: A Documentary History* (New York: Oxford University Press, 1995), 130.

13. George Athan Billias, *American Constitutionalism Heard Round the World, 1776–1989* (New York: New York University Press, 2016), 156, and J. A. Hawgood, "Liberalism and Constitutional Developments," in J. P. T. Bury, ed., *New Cambridge Modern History,* vol. 10 (Cambridge: Cambridge University Press, 1971), 19.

14. Billias, *American Constitutionalism Heard Round the World,* 156–57.

15. Linde Lindkvist, *Religious Freedom and the Universal Declaration of Human Rights* (Cambridge: Cambridge University Press, 2020).

16. See the U.N. Universal Declaration of Human Rights at https://www.un.org/en/universal-declaration-human-rights/ (accessed on 15 July 2020).

17. Cornelis de Jong, *The Freedom of Thought, Conscience and Religion or Belief in the United Nations (1946–1992)* (Antwerp: Intersentia, 2000).

18. Noonan, *The Church That Can and Cannot Change*, 155. See especially John Courtney Murray, *We Hold These Truths: Catholic Reflections on the American Proposition* (London: Sheed and Ward, 1961).

19. John W. O'Malley, *What Happened at Vatican II* (Cambridge, MA: Belknap Press of Harvard University Press, 2008), 211-18, 254-58, 287-88.

20. Heinrich Denzinger, ed., *Enchiridion symbolorum definitionum et declarationum de rebus fidei et morum / Compendium of Creeds, Definitions, and Declarations on Matters of Faith and Morals*, 43rd ed. (San Francisco: Ignatius, 2012), 930-31 (translation modified).

21. Ahmet Kuru, *Secularism and State Policies toward Religion: The United States, France, and Turkey* (Cambridge: Cambridge University Press, 2009), 11.

22. The *Kulturkampf* in Germany bears some resemblance to the conflicts generated by combative secularism, but the Prussian state, instigating and prosecuting it, was more religious (Protestant) in character than France's Third Republic. See Michael B. Gross, *The War against Catholicism: Liberalism and the Anti-Catholic Imagination in Nineteenth-Century Germany* (Ann Arbor: University of Michigan Press, 2008).

23. To be sure, Western ideas and some reforms borne from them had penetrated Muslim societies beforehand. See, e.g., Bernard Lewis, *The Shaping of the Modern Middle East* (New York: Oxford University Press, 1994), and Indira Falk Gesink, *Islamic Reform and Conservatism: Al-Azhar and the Evolution of Modern Sunni Islam* (London: Tauris, 2010).

24. See, e.g., Ulrich L. Lehner, *Enlightened Monks: The German Benedictines, 1740-1803* (Oxford: Oxford University Press, 2013), and Dale Van Kley, *Reform Catholicism and the International Suppression of the Jesuits in Enlightenment Europe* (New Haven: Yale University Press, 2018).

25. Alexis de Tocqueville, *The Old Regime and the French Revolution*, trans. Stuart Gilbert (New York: Random House, 1955), 6.

26. Voltaire, *Oeuvres complètes de Voltaire*, vol. 26 (Paris: Garnier Frères, 1877-85), 298.

27. On the larger theme of Enlightenment rationality and anti-Judaism, see especially Markus Kneer, *Die dunkle Spur im Denken: Rationalität und Antijudaismus* (Paderborn: Schöningh, 2003), 109-20.

28. Quoted in Gertrude Himmelfarb, *The Roads to Modernity: The British, French, and American Enlightenments* (New York: Alfred A. Knopf, 2004), 152.

29. Peter Gay, *Voltaire's Politics: The Poet as Realist* (Princeton: Princeton University Press, 1959), 272. Voltaire's own views were given voice still earlier in what the historian Jonathan Israel has called the "Radical Enlightenment." See Jonathan Israel, *Radical Enlightenment: Philosophy and the Making of Modernity, 1650-1750* (Oxford: Oxford University Press, 2001).

30. Charles A. Gliozzo, "The *Philosophes* and Religion: Intellectual Origins of the Dechristianization Movement in the French Revolution," *Church History* 40 (1971): 282.

31. Robert Zaretsky, *Catherine and Diderot: The Empress, the Philosopher, and the Fate of the Enlightenment* (Cambridge, MA: Harvard University Press, 2019)

32. Jean le Rond D'Alembert, *Sur la destruction des Jésuites en France* (Edinburgh: Chez J. Balfour, 1765).

33. Chadwick, *The Popes and European Revolution*, 345–90, and Kley, *Reform Catholicism and the International Suppression of the Jesuits*.

34. Derek Beales, *Prosperity and Plunder: European Catholic Monasteries in the Age of Revolution, 1650–1815* (Cambridge: Cambridge University Press, 2002), 192.

35. Beales, *Prosperity and Plunder*, 228

36. Thomas Albert Howard, *God and the Atlantic: America, Europe, and the Religious Divide* (Oxford: Oxford University Press, 2011), 4.

37. G. Lefebvre, "Les recherches relatives à la vente des biens nationaux," *Revue d'histoire moderne et contemporaine* 3 (1928): 188–219.

38. From the encyclical *Charitas* (13 April 1791) in Claudia Carlen, ed., *The Papal Encyclicals*, vol. 1 (Ann Arbor: Pierian Press, 1990), 177.

39. Jean Baubérot, *Histoire de la laïcité française* (Paris: Presses universitaires de France, 2000), 14, and Claude Langlois, "La rupture entre l'Église catholique et la Révolution," in François Furet and Mona Ozouf, eds., *The French Revolution and the Creation of Modern Political Culture, vol. 3, The Transformation of Political Culture, 1789–1848* (Oxford: Oxford University Press, 1989), 375–99.

40. Barbara Estelle Beaumont, *La restauration des monastères de Dominicaines en France au dix-neuvième siècle* (Rome: Istituto storico domenicano, 2002), 28–30.

41. Jacques Villemain, *Génocide en Vendée, 1793–1794* (Paris: Cerf, 2020), and Mark Levene, *Genocide in the Age of the Nation-State: The Rise of the West and the Coming of Genocide* (London: I. B. Taurus, 2005), 118.

42. Tocqueville, *Old Regime and French Revolution*, 3, 155–56.

43. Monica Duffy Toft, Daniel Philpott, and Timothy Samuel Shah, *God's Century: Resurgent Religion and Global Politics* (New York: W. W. Norton, 2011), 65.

44. See Michael Broers, *The Politics of Religion in Napoleonic Italy: The War against God, 1801–1814* (New York: Routledge, 2007), and Thomas Albert Howard, *The Pope and the Professor: Pius IX, Ignaz von Döllinger, and the Quandary of the Modern Age* (Oxford: Oxford University Press, 2019), 16–19, 24–29.

45. Beales, *Prosperity and Plunder*, 275.

46. Ulrich Hufeld, *Der Reichsdeputationshauptschluss von 1803: Eine Dokumentation zum Untergang des Alten Reiches* (Cologne: Böhlau, 2003), 69–119.

47. Liubov Melnikova, "Orthodox Russia against 'Godless' France: The Russian Church and the 'Holy War' of 1812," in Janet M. Hartley et al., eds., *Russia and the Napoleonic Wars* (New York: Palgrave Macmillan, 2015), 187–88, 195.

48. Donny Gluckstein, *The Paris Commune: A Revolution in Democracy* (Chicago: Haymarket, 2011), 155, and Alec Mellor, *Histoire de l'anticléricalisme français* (Paris: H. Veyrier, 1978), 282–84. The Communards received brutal retaliation with the collapse of the Commune—a series of events known in French as *semaine sanglante* (bloody week) that took place in May 1871.

49. Emile Poulat, *Liberté, laïcité: La guerre des deux France et le principe de la modernité* (Paris: Cerf, 1987).

50. Paul Farmer, *France Reviews Its Revolutionary Origins: Social Politics and Historical Opinion in the Third Republic* (New York: Octagon, 1973), 22ff.

51. Michel Winock, "Comment la France a inventé la laïcité," *L'histoire* 289 (2004): 40–49.

52. Laurent Fedi, "Lien social et religion positiviste chez les penseurs de la Troisième République," *Revue des sciences philosophiques et théologiques* 87 (2003): 127–50, and Mary Pickering, "Positivism in European Intellectual, Political, and Religious Life," in Warren Breckman and Peter Gordon, eds., *Cambridge History of Modern European Thought: The Nineteenth Century*, vol. 1 (Cambridge: Cambridge University Press, 2019), 159–62.

53. Michael Burleigh, *Earthly Powers: The Clash of Religion and Politics from the French Revolution to the Great War* (New York: HarperCollins, 2003), 230.

54. Lionel Gossman, "Michelet and the French Revolution," in Furet and Ozouf, eds., *The French Revolution and the Creation of Modern Political Culture*, vol. 3, 639–64.

55. Joseph M. Moody, *The Church as Enemy: Anticlericalism in Nineteenth-Century French Literature* (Washington, DC: Corpus, 1968), 120–23, 221.

56. Hugh McLeod, *Secularisation in Western Europe, 1848-1914* (New York: St. Martin's Press, 2000), 61–62.

57. On Ferry's debt to positivism, see L. Legrand, *L'influence du positivisme dans l'oeuvre scolaire de Jules Ferry* (Paris: Rivière, 1961).

58. Milorad N. Vuckovic, "The Suppression of Religious Houses in France in 1880," *Canadian Catholic Historical Association Report* 28 (1961): 17–18.

59. J. F. Maclear, ed., *Church and State in the Modern Age: A Documentary History* (New York: Oxford University Press, 1995), 276–77.

60. Frederick Brown, *For the Soul of France: Culture Wars in the Age of Dreyfus* (New York: Alfred A. Knopf, 2010).

61. Jean Sévillia, *Quand les catholiques étaient hors la loi* (Paris: Perrin, 2005), 13–16, 105ff., 146. See also Christian Sorrel, *La République contre les congregations: Histoire d'une passion française, 1899-1904* (Paris: Cerf, 2003).

62. Maclear, ed., *Church and State in the Modern Age*, 304–10.

63. Quoted in Baubérot, *Histoire de la laïcité française*, 87.

64. According to the Concordat, the state managed church properties on the church's behalf.

65. This paragraph draws generously from Kuru, *Secularism and State Policies toward Religion*, 150–53.

66. Sévillia, *Quand les catholiques étaient hors la loi*, 168–69.

67. Jean-Michel Duhart, *La France dans la tourmente des inventaires: La separation des Églises et de l'État* (Tours: Alan Sutton, 2001), 90–91.

68. Baubérot, *Histoire de la laïcité française*, 82.

69. Olivier Roy, *Secularism Confronts Islam* (New York: Columbia University Press, 2007), 18.

70. Sévillia, *Quand les catholiques étaient hors la loi*, 168–69.

71. Duhart, *La France dans la tourmente des inventaires*, 34, 40.

72. Implied long beforehand, the term "laïcité" first appeared only in the 1946 French constitution. The Catholic Church resigned itself to accept the 1905 law only in the 1920s once the French government had agreed to relax enforcing some of its measures.

73. Robert C. Bowles, "The Reaction of Charles Fourier to the French Revolution," *French Historical Studies* 1 (1960): 350.

74. Gareth Stedman Jones, "European Socialism from the 1790s to the 1890s," in Breckman and Gordon, eds., *Cambridge History of Modern European Thought*, vol. 1, 196–209.

75. D. G. Charlton, "New Creeds for Old in Nineteenth-Century France," *Canadian Journal of Theology* 8 (1962): 269.

76. On Proudhon, Bakunin, and the surprisingly extensive hatred of God in the nineteenth century, see Bernard Schweizer's enlightening *Hating God: The Untold Story of Misotheism* (Oxford: Oxford University Press, 2011), 40–51. On the religious elements in Proudhon, see Henri de Lubac's engaging treatment of his thought: *Proudhon et christianisme* (Paris: Cerf, 2011).

77. Quoted in Moody, *Church as Enemy*, 114.

78. Proudhon, *Idée générale de la révolution au XIX siècle* (Paris: Garnier Frères 1851), 185.

79. Mikhail Bakunin, *Dieu et l'État* (Geneva: Cafiero et Reclus, 1882), 35, 58.

80. Nicolas Berdyaev, *The Origins of Russian Communism* (Ann Arbor: University of Michigan Press, 1960), 45–57. See also Victoria Frede, *Doubt, Atheism, and the Nineteenth-Century Russian Intelligentsia* (Madison: University of Wisconsin Press, 2011).

81. Isaiah Berlin, *Russian Thinkers* (New York: Penguin, 1978), 139.

82. Jacek Uglik, "Ludwig Feuerbach's Conception of the Religious Alienation of Man and Mikhail Bakunin's Philosophy of Negation," *Studies in Eastern European Thought* 62 (2010): 19–28.

83. For a summary of Hegel's religious thought, see Claude Welch, *Protestant Thought in the Nineteenth Century, 1799–1800*, vol. 1 (New Haven: Yale University Press, 1972), 86–107.

84. On Hegel and strands of Hegelian thought prior to Marx, see John Edward Toews, *Hegelianism: The Path toward Dialectical Humanism, 1805–1841* (Cambridge: Cambridge University Press, 1980), and Warren Breckman, "The Young Hegelians: Philosophy as Critical Praxis," in Breckman and Gordon, eds., *Cambridge History of Modern European Thought*, vol. 1, 88–110.

85. Bruno Bauer, *Die Posaune des jüngsten Gerichts über Hegel den Atheisten und Antichristen: Ein Ultimatum* (Leipzig, 1841).

86. Van A. Harvey, "Ludwig Feuerbach and Karl Marx," in Ninian Smart, ed., *Nineteenth-Century Religious Thought in the West*, vol. 1 (Cambridge: Cambridge University Press, 1985), 293–94.

87. Ludwig Feuerbach, *The Essence of Christianity*, trans. George Eliot (New York: Harper, 1957), 14, 25, and Ludwig Feuerbach, "Grundsätze der Philosophie der Zukunft," *Sämmtliche Werke*, vol. 2 (Leipzig: Wieland, 1846), 248, 273.

88. Friedrich Engels, *Ludwig Feuerbach und der Ausgang der klassischen deutschen Philosophie* (Berlin: J. H. W. Dietz, 1946 [1888]), 14.

89. Karl Marx, *Writings of the Young Marx on Philosophy and Society*, trans. L. D. Easton and K. H. Guddat (New York: Anchor, 1967), 205.

90. Quoted in Traugott Koch, "Revolutionsprogramm und Religionskritik bei Karl Marx," *Zeitschrift für Theologie und Kirche* 68 (1971): 59.

91. N. Lobkowicz, "Karl Marx's Attitude toward Religion," *Review of Politics* 26 (1964): 326.

92. Marx, "Zur Kritik der hegelschen Rechtsphilosophie" (1843), in Marx and Engels, *Werke* (Berlin: Dietz, 1974), 378–79, and Marx and Engels, *On Religion* (Mineola, NY: Dover, 2008), 41–42 (emphases in original, translation modified).

93. Marx, "Zur Judenfrage," *Werke*, vol. 1 (Berlin: Dietz, 1974), 352.

94. Marx and Engels, *On Religion*, 63, 69–72.

95. Victoria Smolkin, *A Sacred Space Is Never Empty: A History of Soviet Atheism* (Princeton: Princeton University Press, 2018), 10–11. On various editorial liberties taken in publishing the *German Ideology* by the Soviet Marx-Engels Institute in Moscow, see Terrell Carver and Daniel Blank, *Political History of the Editions of the Marx and Engels "German Ideology" Manuscripts* (New York: Palgrave Macmillan, 2014). In essence, the Soviet edition made Marx and Engels's materialist theory of history more systematic than it actually was.

96. Marx and Engels, *On Religion*, 74. See too the critical edition of Gerald Hubmann and Ulrich Pagel, eds., *Karl Marx und Friedrich Engels: Deutsche Ideologie zur Kritik der Philosophie* (Berlin: De Gruyter, 2018).

97. While Engels shared in Marx's criticism of religion, he felt that under certain conditions religion could be a progressive force in human history (such as the German Peasants' War of 1525) or at least the cultural medium through which oppressed classes struggled to express their class identity. See Michael Löwy, "Friedrich Engels on Religion and Class Struggle," *Science and Society* 62 (1998): 79–87.

98. David McClellan, *Karl Marx: His Life and Thought* (New York: Harper and Row, 1973), 110, 116, 139, passim.

99. Rüdiger Reitz, *Christen und Sozialdemokratie: Konsquenzen aus einem Erbe* (Stuttgart: Radius, 1983), see especially chapters 1 and 2.

100. John Molony, *The Worker Question: A New Historical Perspective on "Rerum Novarum"* (London: Gill and Macmillan, 1991).

101. Jacqueline Turner, *The Labour Church: Religion and Politics in Britain, 1890–1914* (London: I. B. Tauris, 2018).

102. In making this claim, one must also recognize that some Continental voices expressly sought to reconcile Christianity and socialism too. Ferdinand Lasalle (1825–64) would be an example. See Burleigh, *Earthly Powers*, 261–63.

103. Jochen-Christoph Kaiser, *Arbeiterbewegung und organisierte Religionskritik: Proletarische Friedenverbände in Kaiserreich und Weimarer Republik* (Stuttgart: Klett-Cotta, 1981), 31.

104. Albert Dulk, "Religion," *Vorwärts* 58 (19 May 1878) as quoted in Vernon L. Lidtke, "August Bebel and German Social Democracy's Relation to the Christian Churches," *Journal of the History of Ideas* 27 (1966): 251.

105. Delos B. McKown, *The Classical Marxist Critiques of Religion: Marx, Engels, Lenin, Kautsky* (The Hague: Martinus Nijhoff, 1975), 122ff. See also Max Geiger, "August Bebels Stellung zum Christentum und religiösem Sozialismus," *Theologische Zeitschrift* 46 (1990): 20–63. In making their critiques, socialists would sometimes pit a putatively primal "spirit" of Christianity against the miscreant reactionary nature of actual churches. Others, following Engels, conceded that sometimes certain forms of religious expression had contributed unwittingly to progressive historical development.

106. Quoted material from Burleigh, *Earthly Powers*, 265–66.

107. See Wilhelm Hohoff and August Bebel, *Christentum und Sozialismus: Eine religiöse Polemik zwischen Herrn Kaplan Hohoff in Hüffe und August Bebel* (Berlin, 1892), at https://www.marxists.org/deutsch/archiv/bebel/1874/02/christentum.html (accessed on 6 September 2022). See also Carl Strikwerda, "The Divided Class: Catholics versus Socialists in Belgium, 1880–1914," *Comparative Studies in Society and History* 30 (1980): 333–59.

108. See Claudia Verhoeven, "Rethinking Revolution: Radicalism at the End of the Long Nineteenth Century," in Breckman and Gordon, eds., *Cambridge History of Modern European Thought,* vol. 1, 474–80, 485–89, 491–92; Billington, *Fire in the Minds of Men,* 386ff., 419ff.; and Michael Burleigh, *Sacred Causes: The Clash of Religion and Politics from the Great War to the War on Terror* (New York: Harper Perennial, 2006), 40–42.

109. Roland Boer, "Religion and Socialism: A. V. Lunacharsky and the God-Builders," *Political Theology* 15 (2014): 188–209.

110. The letter dates from late November 1913; see *Lenin's Collected Works,* vol. 35, trans. Andrew Rothstein (Moscow: Progress, 1976), 127–29.

111. Alain Besançon, *Les origins intellectuelles du Léninisme* (Paris: Calmann-Lévy, 1977), 90–93.

112. As quoted in Bociurkiw, "Lenin and Religion," 110. For a general view on this topic, see Roland Boer, *Lenin, Religion, and Theology* (New York: Palgrave Macmillan, 2013).

113. Quoted in Bociurkiw, "Lenin and Religion," 108.

114. On Russian radicalism and the example of the French Revolution, see Dmitry Shlapentokh, *The French Revolution in Russian Intellectual Life, 1865–1905* (Westport, CT: Praeger, 1996), 101–46, and Stéphane Courtois, "De la revolution française à la revolution d'Octobre," in Renaud Escande, ed., *Le livre noir de la revolution française* (Paris: Cerf, 2008), 397–402.

115. Lenin, "The Attitude of the Workers' Party to Religion," in Lenin, *Collected Works,* vol. 15, 411.

116. Lenin, "The Attitude of the Workers' Party to Religion," in Lenin, *Collected Works,* vol. 15, 405.

117. Lenin, *Collected Works,* vol. 17 (122) and vol. 35 (325), and Bociurkiw, "Lenin and Religion," 109.

TWO

1. Christopher Clark and Wolfram Kaiser, eds., *Culture Wars: Secular-Catholic Conflict in Nineteenth-Century Europe* (Cambridge: Cambridge University Press, 2003).

2. Wolfram Kaiser, "'Clericalism—that is our Enemy!' European Anticlericalism and the Culture Wars," in Clark and Kaiser, eds., *Culture Wars,* 175. Of course, reactionary forces often had binary vision as well.

3. See the Federal Constitution of the United Mexican States of 1857 at World History Commons (accessed on 19 April 2022). See also E. V. Niemeyer, *Revolution at Querétaro: The Mexican Constitutional Convention of 1916–1917* (Austin: University of Texas Press, 1974).

4. Brian Hamnett, *A Concise History of Mexico* (New York: Cambridge University Press, 1999), 221–33.

5. G. de la Fuete, "Clericalismo y anticlericalismo en México, 1810–1938," *Ayer* 27 (1997): 39–65, and Roberto di Stefano, *Pasiones anticlericales: Un recorrido iberoamericano* (Bernal, Argentina: Universidad Nacional de Quilmes Editorial, 2013).

6. T. G. Powell, "Priests and Peasants in Central Mexico: Social Conflict during *La Reforma,*" *Hispanic American Historical Review* 57 (1997): 296–313.

7. John Lynch, *New Worlds: A Religious History of Latin America* (New Haven: Yale University Press, 2022), 211–15.

8. Alan Knight, "The Mentality and Modus Operandi of Revolutionary Anticlericalism," in Matthew Butler, ed., *Faith and Impiety in Revolutionary Mexico* (New York: Palgrave Macmillan, 2007), 29.

9. Paula Cortes-Rocca, "Positivism in Latin America," in Sangeeta Ray et al., eds., *Encyclopedia of Postcolonial Studies* (Oxford: Blackwell, 2016), 1–9.

10. Quoted in Jeffrey Klaiber, S.J., "Anticlericalism in the Nineteenth and Early Twentieth Centuries," in Lee M. Penyak and Walter J. Petry, eds., *Religion and Society in Latin America* (Maryknoll, NY: Orbis, 2009), 163.

11. Prada, "Slaves of the Church," trans. Cathleen Carris, *PMLA* 1283 (2013): 765–77.

12. Lynch, *New Worlds,* 345.

13. Ben Fallow, "Religion and Revolution, Mexico: 1910–1940," in William Beezley, ed., *Mexican History* (Oxford Handbooks Online, 2020).

14. E. V. Niemeyer Jr., "Anticlericalism in the Mexican Constitutional Convention of 1916–1917," *Americas* 11 (1954): 42–49.

15. Quoted from an interview Obregón gave on 20 February 1915 in David C. Bailey, "Alvaro Obregón and Anticlericalism in the Revolution of 1910," *Americas* 26 (1969): 190.

16. Michael Burleigh, *Sacred Causes: The Clash of Religion and Politics, from the Great War to the War on Terrorism* (New York: Harper Perennial, 2006), 124. It merits mentioning that under Calles and with his support, the non-Roman Iglesia Católica Apostólica Mexicana came into existence in 1925. Largely a pawn of the government, it was exempted from the harsh measures but never gained popular traction and ceased to exist in 1931.

17. Quoted material taken from Adrian A. Bantjes, "Idolatry and Iconoclasm in Revolutionary Mexico: The De-Christianization Campaigns, 1929–1940," *Mexican Studies/Estudios Mexicanos* 13 (1997): 108.

18. Former Cristeros lashed out at the government as well. On the Cristero War, see especially the classic work of Jean Meyer, *La Christiada,* 3 vols. (Mexico City: Siglio XXI, 1973–74), and Julia Grace Darling Young, *Mexican Exodus: Emigrants, Exiles, and Refugees of the Cristero War* (New York: Oxford University Press, 2019).

19. Lynch, *New Worlds,* 252, and Young, *Mexican Exodus,* 125–54.

20. On Pro's execution and its larger significance, see Marisol López-Menéndez, *Miguel Pro: Martyrdom, Politics, and Society in Twentieth-Century Mexico* (Lanham, MD: Lexington Books, 2016).

21. Adrian A. Bantjes, "The Regional Dynamics of Anticlericalism and Defanaticization in Revolutionary Mexico," in Butler, ed., *Faith and Impiety in Revolutionary Mexico,* 113.

22. Bantjes, "Regional Dynamics of Anticlericalism," 117.

23. Adrian A. Bantjes, "Burning Saints, Molding Minds: Iconoclasm, Civic Ritual, and the Failed Cultural Revolution," in William H. Beezley et al., eds., *Rituals of Rule, Rituals of Resistance: Public Celebrations and Popular Culture in Mexico* (Wilmington, DE: SR Books, 1997), 268–69.

24. Bantjes, "Idolatry and Iconoclasm in Revolutionary Mexico," 99–101.

25. Adrian A. Bantjes, "The War Against Idols: The Meanings of Iconoclasm in Revolutionary Mexico, 1910–40" in Anne McClanan and Jeff Johnson, eds., *Negating the Image: Case Studies in Iconoclasm* (Burlington, VT: Ashgate, 2005), 53.

26. Graham Greene, *The Power and the Glory* (New York: Penguin, 2015), 26.

27. See *Acerba animi* (29 September 1932) at vatican.va (accessed on 19 April 2022).

28. Bantjes, "Burning Saints, Molding Minds," 270.

29. Bantjes, "Idolatry and Iconoclasm," 111.

30. Bantjes, "The Regional Dynamics of Anticlericalism," 118.

31. Young, *Mexican Exodus*, 42-46.

32. Ben Fallaw, "The Seduction of Revolution: Anticlerical Campaigns against Confession in Mexico, 1914-1935," *Journal of Latin American Studies* 45 (2013): 91-120.

33. Bantjes, "The Regional Dynamics of Anticlericalism," 115.

34. Bantjes, "Idolatry and Iconoclasm," 119-20.

35. Donald J. Mabry, "Mexican Anticlericals, Bishops, Cristeros, and the Devout in the 1920s: A Scholarly Debate," *Journal of Church and State* 20 (1967): 82.

36. Graham Greene, *The Lawless Roads* (New York: Penguin, 2006), 118.

37. For the numbers, see the groundbreaking study of Antonio Montero Moreno, *Historia de la persecución religiosa en España* (Madrid: Editorial cattolica, 1961). See also Gabriele Ranzato, "Dies irae: La persecuzione religiosa nella zona Repubblicana durante la Guerra Civile Spagnola (1936-39)," *Movimento operaio e socialista* 11 (1988): 195-220.

38. Robert Royal, *The Catholic Martyrs of the Twentieth Century* (New York: Herder and Herder, 2000), 125.

39. Lisa Dittrich, *Antiklerikalismus in Europa: Öffentlichkeit und Säkularisierung in Frankreich, Spanien und Deutschland (1848-1914)* (Göttingen: Vandenhoeck und Ruprecht, 2014), 91-115.

40. R. A. H. Robinson, "The Religious Question and the Catholic Revival in Portugal, 1900-1930," *Journal of Contemporary History* 12 (1977): 345-62.

41. Michael Burleigh, *Sacred Causes: The Clash of Religion and Politics, from the Great War to the War on Terror* (New York: Harper Perennial, 2007), 134.

42. Julio de la Cueva, "The Assault on the City of Levites: Spain," in Clark and Kaiser, eds., *Culture Wars: Secular-Catholic Conflict in Nineteenth-Century Europe*, 181-201.

43. Joan Connelly Ullman, *Tragic Week: A Study of Anticlericalism in Spain* (Cambridge, MA: Harvard University Press, 1968).

44. Feliciano Montero García, "La question religieuse en Espagne au 20e siècle," *Revue d'histoire* 127 (2015): 248.

45. Noted in Paul Preston, *The Spanish Holocaust: Inquisition and Extermination in Twentieth-Century Spain* (New York: W. W. Norton, 2012), 10.

46. José M. Sánchez, "The Spanish Church and the Second Republic and Civil War, 1931-1939," *Catholic Historical Review* 82 (1996): 661-68.

47. Frances Lannon, *Privilege, Persecution, and Prophecy: The Catholic Church in Spain, 1875-1975* (Oxford: Oxford University Press, 1996), 181.

48. Quoted in Julio de la Cueva, "Religious Persecution, Anticlerical Tradition and Revolution: On Atrocities against the Clergy during the Spanish Civil War," *Journal of Contemporary History* 33 (1998): 368.

49. As quoted in Mary Vincent, "'The Kings of the Kingdom': Religious Violence in the Spanish Civil War, July-August 1936," in Chris Ealham and Michael Richards, eds.,

The Splintering of Spain: Cultural History of the Spanish Civil War, 1936–1839 (Cambridge: Cambridge University Press, 2011), 69.

50. Julio de la Cueva, "Violent Culture Wars: Religion and Revolution in Mexico, Russia, and Spain," *Journal of Contemporary History* 53 (2018): 517–19.

51. From the *Solidaridad Obrera* (15 August 1936) and *La Batalla* (19 August 1936) as cited in Sánchez, *The Spanish Civil War as a Religious Tragedy*, 38.

52. Julius Ruiz, *The "Red Terror" and the Spanish Civil War: Revolutionary Violence in Madrid* (Cambridge: Cambridge University Press, 2012), 13.

53. Manuel Pérez Ledesma, "Studies in Anticlericalism in Contemporary Spain," *International Review of Social History* 46 (2001): 248.

54. Royal, *Catholic Martyrs of the Twentieth Century*, 109, and De la Cueva, "Violent Culture Wars," 519.

55. Sánchez, *Spanish Civil War as a Religious Tragedy*, 31.

56. The interviewer was the historian Quintín Aldea as conveyed in De la Cueva, "Religious Persecution," 361.

57. Cedric Salter, *Try-Out in Spain* (New York: Harper and Brothers, 1943), 19–20.

58. Bruce Lincoln, "Revolutionary Exhumations in Spain, July 1936," *Comparative Studies in Society and History* 27 (1985): 241–42.

59. M. Álvarez Tardío and R. Villa Gracía, "El impacto de violencia anticlerical en la primavera de 1936 y la respuesta de las autoridades," *Hispania sacra* 65 (2013): 683–764.

60. *Daily Telegraph* (19 July 1936) as cited in Sánchez, *The Spanish Civil War as a Religious Tragedy*, 46.

61. George Orwell, *Homage to Catalonia* (London, 1938), 106. Orwell's searing book was most controversial for revealing the Stalinist Communist elements' brutal suppressions of their anarchist and Trotskyist allies, but it also told uncomfortable truths about the Republican side in general.

62. José María Gironella, *The Cypresses Believe in God*, trans. Harriet de Onís (New York: Alfred A. Knopf, 1955), 929.

63. Ernest Hemingway, *For Whom the Bell Tolls* (New York: Charles Scribner's Sons, 1940), 135.

64. Maria Thomas, "Political Violence in the Republican Zone of Spain during the Spanish Civil War: Evolving Historical Perspectives," *Journal of Contemporary History* 52 (2017): 143–46.

65. Preston, *Spanish Holocaust*, 267.

66. Sánchez, *Spanish Civil War as a Religious Tragedy*, 26.

67. De la Cueva, "Religious Persecution," 369.

68. An anonymous Republican as cited in Burleigh, *Sacred Causes*, 135.

69. Preston, *Spanish Holocaust*, 14, 19.

70. Şükrü Hanioğlu, *Atatürk: An Intellectual Biography* (Princeton: Princeton University Press, 2011), 134–35, 158–59, and Andrew Mango, *Atatürk: The Biography of the Founder of Modern Turkey* (New York: Overlook, 2002), 396.

71. Ralph Stehly, "De Bonaparte à l'état Islamique," *Revue des sciences religieuses* 90 (2016): 17.

72. Taner Akçam, *The Young Turks' Crime against Humanity: The Armenian Genocide and Ethnic Cleansing in the Ottoman Empire* (Princeton: Princeton University Press, 2012).

73. Abdullahi Ahmed An-Na'im, *Islam and the Secular State: Negotiating the Future of Shari'a* (Cambridge, MA: Harvard University Press, 2008), 187. At the same time, one should be wary of idealizing the empire in light of such events as the Hamidian massacres of 1894–97, during which tens of thousands of Armenians lost their lives due to imperial persecutions. See Ronald Grigor Suny, "The Hamidian Massacres, 1894–1897: Disinterring a Buried History," *Études arméniennes contemporaines* 11 (2018): 125–34.

74. Pierre-Jean Luizard, *Laïcité autoritaires en terres d'Islam* (Paris: Fayard, 2008), 33–46. See also Vedit Inal, "The Eighteenth and Nineteenth Century Ottoman Attempts to Catch Up with Europe," *Middle Eastern Studies* 47 (2011): 725–56.

75. Bernard Lewis, *The Emergence of Modern Turkey*, 3rd ed. (New York: Oxford University Press, 2002), 210–38.

76. François Georgeon, *Aux origines du nationalisme turc: Yusuf Akçura (1876–1935)* (Paris: Éditions ADPF, 1908), 16–30.

77. Quoted from a speech in 1924 in Niyazi Berkes, *The Development of Secularism in Turkey* (Montreal: McGill University Press, 1964), 464.

78. Pankaj Mishra, *From the Ruins of Empire: The Intellectuals Who Remade Asia* (New York: Farrar, Straus and Giroux, 2012), 282.

79. Hakan Özoğlu, *From Caliphate to Secular State: Power Struggle in the Early Turkish Republic* (Santa Barbara: Praeger, 2011).

80. Gail Minault, *The Khilafat Movement: Religious Symbolism and Political Mobilization in India* (New York: Columbia University Press, 1982).

81. Lewis, *Emergence of Modern Turkey*, 263.

82. Michael Provence, *The Last Ottoman Generation and the Making of the Modern Middle East* (New York: Cambridge University Press, 2017), 154–55.

83. Paul Stirling, "Religious Change in Republican Turkey," *Middle East Journal* 12 (1958): 396.

84. Lewis, *Emergence of Modern Turkey*, 266.

85. Ahmet Kuru, *State Policies Toward Religion: The United States, France, and Turkey* (Cambridge: Cambridge University Press, 2009), 222, and Elizabeth Özdalga, *The Veiling Issue, Official Secularism and Popular Islam in Modern Turkey* (Surrey: Curzon, 1998), 27.

86. Mango, *Atatürk*, 442.

87. Quoted material taken from Kuru, *State Policies toward Religion*, 221.

88. J. D. Norton, "Bektashis in Turkey," in Denis MacEoin and Ahmed Al-Shani, eds., *Islam in the Modern World* (London: Croom Helm, 1983), 79.

89. Hülya Küçük, "Sufi Reactions against the Reforms after Turkey's National Struggle: How a Nightingale Turned into a Cow," in Touraj Atabaki, ed., *The State and the Subaltern: Modernization, Society, and the State in Turkey and Iran* (London: I. B. Tauris, 2007), 123–42.

90. Camilla T. Nereid, "Kemalism and the Catwalk: The Turkish Hat Law of 1925," *Journal of Social History* 44 (2011): 722–24.

91. Berkes, *Development of Secularism in Turkey*, 466, 477; Kuru, *Secularism and State Policies toward Religion*, 218; and Nathan Spannaus, "Religion in the Service of the State: Diyanet and Republican Turkey," in Masooda Bano, ed., *Modern Islamic Authority and Social Change*, vol. 1,

Evolving Debates in Muslim-Majority Countries (Edinburgh: Edinburgh University Press, 2018), 306–07.

92. Berkes, *Development of Secularism in Turkey*, 466–67.

93. Stirling, "Religious Change in Republican Turkey," 402.

94. Şükrü Hanioğlu, *Atatürk*, 153.

95. Lewis, *Emergence of Modern Turkey*, 279.

96. Nevzet Çelik, "From Secularism to *Laïcité* and Analyzing Turkish Authoritarian *Laiklik*," *Insight Turkey* 20 (2018): 198.

97. Esposito, *Islam and Politics*, 97.

98. Amélie Barras, *Refashioning Secularism in France and Turkey: The Case of the Headscarf Ban* (London: Routledge, 2016).

99. Abdullahi Ahmed An-Na'im, *Islam and the Secular State: Negotiating the Future of Shari'a* (Cambridge, MA: Harvard University Press, 2008), 198.

100. Sumantra Bose, *Secular States, Religious Politics: India, Turkey, and the Future of Secularism* (Cambridge: Cambridge University Press, 2018), 39. See also Erik Jan Zürcher, *Political Opposition in the Early Turkish Republic: The Progressive Republican Party, 1924–1925* (Leiden: Brill, 1991), 80–94.

101. Yael Navaro-Yashin, *Faces of the State: Secularism and Public Life in Turkey* (Princeton: Princeton University Press, 2002), 202.

102. Angel Rabasa and F. Stephen Larrabee, *The Rise of Political Islam in Turkey* (Santa Monica: Rand Corporation, 2008), 32.

103. Bose, *Secular States*, 218–19.

104. Karen Armstrong, *Fields of Blood: Religion and the History of Violence* (New York: Alfred A. Knopf, 2014), 318.

105. An-Na'im, *Islam and the Secular State*, 183.

106. Luizard, *Laïcité autoritaires*, 7.

107. Mustafa Akyol, "Turkey's Troubled Experiment with Secularism," *Century Foundation* (25 April 2019).

108. Andrea Mura, "A Genealogical Inquiry into Early Islamism: The Discourse of Hasan al-Banna," *Journal of Political Ideologies* 12 (2012): 62.

THREE

1. N. Bukharin and E. Preobrazhensky, *The ABC of Communism: A Popular Explanation of the Program of the Communist Party of Russia*, trans. Eden and Cedar Paul (Ann Arbor: University of Michigan Press, 1966 [1919]), 248.

2. William Husband, "Soviet Atheism and Russian Orthodox Strategies of Resistance, 1917–1932," *Journal of Modern History* 70 (March 1998): 74–107.

3. From a writing published on 19 June 1963, as quoted in Michael Bourdeaux, *Patriarch and Prophets: Persecution of the Russian Orthodox Church Today* (London: Macmillan, 1969), 23.

4. Richard Pipes, *A Concise History of the Russian Revolution* (New York: Vintage, 1995), 333.

5. Victoria Smolkin, *A Sacred Space Is Never Empty: A History of Soviet Atheism* (Princeton: Princeton University Press, 2018), 25.

6. J. F. Maclear, ed., *Church and State in the Modern Age: A Documentary History* (New York: Oxford University Press, 1995), 331–33, and Dimitry V. Pospielovsky, *Soviet Anti-Religious Campaigns and Persecutions* (New York: St. Martin's Press, 1988), 2–4.

7. Smolkin, *A Sacred Space Is Never Empty*, 28.

8. Richard Madsen, "Religion under Communism," in S. A. Smith, ed., *Oxford Handbook of the History of Communism* (Oxford: Oxford University Press, 2014), 587.

9. See Felix Corley, ed., *Religion in the Soviet Union: An Archival Reader* (New York: New York University Press, 1996), 24.

10. The February Revolution allowed for the abolition of the Holy Synod, a governmental office created under Peter the Great to control the church, and made way for the restoration in 1917 of a Church Council (*Sobor*), which voted to reinstate the Moscow Patriarchate in the person of Tikhon as leader of the Russian Orthodox Church.

11. Pospielovsky, *Soviet Anti-Religious Campaigns and Persecutions*, 27.

12. On the fate of Orthodox nuns: Mary Grace Swift, *More Than Nameless Martyrs: The Nun, the Hammer, the Sickle* (unpublished manuscript, circa 1988), box 1, folder 1. Accession #07-08, Women Religious Imprisoned under Eastern Communism Collection. Archives, Catholic Theological Union, Chicago.

13. Pospielovsky, *Soviet Anti-Religious Campaigns and Persecutions*, 4–9.

14. Quoted in S. A. Smith, "Bones of Contention: Bolsheviks and the Struggle against Relics," *Past and Present* 204 (2009): 175.

15. Jonathan W. Daly, "'Storming the Last Citadel': The Bolshevik Assault on the Church, 1922," in Vladimir N. Brovkin, ed., *The Bolsheviks in Russian Society: The Revolution and the Civil Wars* (New Haven: Yale University Press, 1997), 238–40.

16. Quoted in Richard Pipes, *Russia under the Bolshevik Regime* (New York: Alfred A. Knopf, 1993), 351–52.

17. James Ryan, "Cleansing NEP Russia: State Violence against the Orthodox Church in 1922," *Europe-Asia Studies* 65 (2013): 1820.

18. Nicholas Werth, "A State against Its People: Violence, Repression, and Terror in the Soviet Union," in Stéphane Courtois et al., eds., *The Black Book of Communism: Crimes, Terror, Repression*, trans. Jonathan Murphy and Mark Kramer (Cambridge, MA: Harvard University Press, 1999), 126.

19. Pipes, *Russia under the Bolshevik Regime*, 354–56.

20. Archival evidence has suggested that Tikhon's statement was likely doctored to make it look more supportive of the regime than it actually was. See Pipes, *Russia under the Bolshevik Regime*, 346.

21. See Geraldine Fagan, "'There Are Things in History That Should Be Called by Their Proper Names': Evaluating Russian Orthodox Collaboration with the State," in Dominic Erdozain, ed., *The Dangerous God: Christianity and the Soviet Experiment* (Dekalb: Northern Illinois University Press, 2017), 187–209.

22. V. I. Lenin, "On the Significance of Militant Materialism," in *Lenin's Collected Works*, vol. 33, trans. David Skvirsky and George Hanna (Moscow: Progress, 1972), 229.

23. Boleslaw Szczesniak, ed., *The Russian Revolution and Religion: A Collection of Documents Concerning the Suppression of Religion by the Communists, 1917-1925* (Notre Dame: University of Notre Dame Press, 1959), 49.

24. Pospielovsky, *Soviet Anti-Religious Campaigns and Persecutions*, 19ff., and Smolkin, *A Sacred Space Is Never Empty*, 32–33.

25. The All-Union Leninist Young Communist League, or Komsomol, was a political youth organization. Having members aged fourteen to twenty-eight, it served as the final stage of three Soviet Youth Organizations, the others being the Young Pioneers (up to the age of fourteen) and Little Octoberists (up to the age of nine). See Isabel Tirado, "The Komsomol's Village Vanguard: Youth and Politics in the NEP Countryside," *Russian Review* 72 (2013): 427–46.

26. Marianna Shakhnovich, "Comparative Religion and Anti-Religious Museums of Soviet Russia in the 1920s," *Religions* 11 (2020): 1–11. On the league in general, see especially Daniel Piers, *Storming the Heavens: The Soviet League of the Militant Godless* (Ithaca: Cornell University Press, 1998). See also Roland Elliott Brown, ed., *Godless Utopia: Soviet Anti-Religious Propaganda* (London: Murray and Sorrell Fuel, 2019).

27. Michael Burleigh, *Sacred Causes: The Clash of Religion and Politics, from the Great War to the War on Terror* (New York: Harper Perennial, 2006), 50–51.

28. Glennys Young, *Power and the Sacred in Revolutionary Russia: Religious Activists in the Village* (University Park: Pennsylvania State University Press, 1997), 108.

29. Jörg Baberowski, *Der rote Terror: Die Geschichte des Stalinismus* (Munich: Deutsche, 2003), 112–13.

30. Joseph Stalin, *Works*, vol. 10 (Moscow: Foreign Languages, 1955), 138–39.

31. Gregory L. Freeze, "The Stalinist Assault on the Parish, 1929–1941," in Manfred Hildermeier and Elisabeth Müller-Luckner, eds., *Stalinismus vor dem Zweiten Weltkrieg* (Munich: Oldenbourg, 1998), 209–14.

32. Quoted in Daniel Peris, *Storming the Heavens: The Soviet League of the Militant Godless* (Ithaca: Cornell University Press, 2019), 127.

33. Young, *Power and the Sacred in Revolutionary Russia*, 259.

34. Freeze, "Stalinist Assault on the Parish," 209.

35. On the 1929 law, see Maclear, ed., *Church and State in the Modern Age*, 260–63.

36. In the new scheme, on a rotating basis, an individual worked five days and had the sixth day off, but because this process was staggered, work went on continuously.

37. Quoted in Freeze, "Stalinist Assault on the Parish," 216.

38. Quoted material in Pospielovsky, *Soviet Anti-Religious Campaigns and Persecutions*, 64.

39. Robert Conquest, *Religion in the U.S.S.R.* (New York: Praeger, 1968), 25. On Soviet higher education and religion generally, see Michael David-Fox, *Revolution of the Mind: Higher Learning among the Bolsheviks, 1918–1929* (Ithaca: Cornell University Press, 2016).

40. Julie deGraffenried, "Combating God and Grandma: The Soviet Antireligious Campaigns and the Battle for Childhood," in Erdozain, ed., *The Dangerous God: Christianity and the Soviet Experiment*, 32–50.

41. Anna Dickinson, "Quantifying Religious Oppression: Russian Orthodox Church Closures and Repression of Priests, 1917–1941," *Religion, State and Society* 28 (2000): 329–31

42. "Old Russia's Icons: Symbols Being Destroyed by the Bolsheviks Permeated the Nation's Life for Ages," *New York Times* (20 April 1930).

43. See Alexandra Guzeva, "How Did the Soviets Use Captured Churches?" (29 January 2019), at https://www.rbth.com/history/329913-orthodox-churches-soviet-union (accessed on 14 June 2021).

44. David E. Powell, *Antireligious Propaganda in the Soviet Union: A Study of Mass Persuasion* (Cambridge, MA: MIT Press, 1975), 93.

45. Titus D. Hewryk, ed., *The Lost Architecture of Kiev* (New York: Ukrainian Museum, 1982).

46. Alexander N. Yakovlev, *A Century of Violence in Soviet Russia*, trans. Anthony Austin (New Haven: Yale University Press, 2002), 167.

47. On this document, "NKVD Order 00447," see Rolf Binner and Marc Junge, "Vernichtung der orthodoxen Geistlichen in der Sowjetunion in den Massenoperationen des Großen Terrors 1937–1938," *Jahrbücher für Geschichte Osteuropas* 52 (2004): 515–33. It is reprinted in English in J. Arch Getty and Oleg V. Naumov, *The Road to Terror: Stalin and the Self-Destruction of the Bolsheviks, 1932–1939*, trans. Benjamin Sher (New Haven: Yale University Press, 1999), 473–74.

48. Richard Pipes, *Communism: A History* (New York: Modern Library, 2001), 66.

49. Pospielovsky, *Soviet Anti-Religious Campaigns and Persecutions*, 68.

50. Corley, ed., *Religion in the Soviet Union*, 115.

51. Pospielovsky, *Soviet Anti-Religious Campaigns and Persecutions*, 76–78, 90–91.

52. A separate body was created for other religious communities: the Council for the Affairs of Religious Cults. In 1963, it merged with the Council for the Russian Orthodox Church to become a single Council for Religious Affairs. See John Anderson, "The Council for Religious Affairs and the Shaping of Soviet Religious Policy," *Soviet Studies* 43 (1991): 689–710.

53. The All-Union Society for the Dissemination of Scientific and Political Knowledge (known by its acronym, Znanie) was founded as successor to the League of the Militant Godless.

54. Moscow Patriarchate, *The Truth about Religion in Russia*, trans. E. N. C. Sergeant (London: Hutchison, 1942).

55. Smolkin, *A Sacred Space Is Never Empty*, 67–71.

56. Quoted in David A. Lowrie and William C. Fletcher, "Khrushchev's Religious Policy, 1959–1964," in Richard H. Marshall, ed., *Aspects of Religion in the Soviet Union, 1917–1967* (Chicago: University of Chicago Press, 1971), 133–34.

57. Quoted in Pospielovsky, *Soviet Anti-Religious Campaigns and Persecutions*, 127.

58. Smolkin, *A Sacred Space Is Never Empty*, 87.

59. Victoria Smolkin, "Cosmic Enlightenment: Scientific Atheism and the Soviet Conquest of Space," in James T. Andrews and Asif A. Siddiqi, eds., *Space Exploration and Soviet Culture* (Pittsburg: University of Pittsburg Press, 2011), 159–94.

60. Conquest, *Religion in the U.S.S.R.*, 50, 55.

61. Smolkin, *A Sacred Space Is Never Empty*, 76.

62. Andrew B. Stone, "'Overcoming Peasant Backwardness': The Khrushchev Antireligious Campaign in the Rural Soviet Union," *Russian Review* 67 (2008): 296–320.

63. Lowrie and Fletcher, "Khrushchev's Religious Policy, 1959–1964," 128, 144–45.

64. Nikita Struve, *Christians in Contemporary Russia* (London: Scribner, 1967), 305. See also Greg Wilkinson, "Political Dissent and 'Sluggish' Schizophrenia in the Soviet Union," *British Medical Journal* 293 (13 September 1986): 641–42.

65. Philip Walters, "A Survey of Soviet Religious Policy," in Sabrina Petra Ramet, ed., *Religious Policy in the Soviet Union* (Cambridge: Cambridge University Press, 1993), 21.

66. Bohdan R. Bociurkiw, "Religion in the USSR after Khrushchev," in John W. Strong, ed., *The Soviet Union under Brezhnev and Kosygin: The Transition Years* (New York: Van Nostrand Reinhold, 1971), 149.

67. See especially Emily B. Baran, *Dissent on the Margin: How Jehovah's Witnesses Defied Communism and Lived to Preach about It* (New York: Oxford University Press, 2014).

68. Quoted in Bourdeaux, *Patriarch and Prophets*, 18.

69. Walters, "A Survey of Soviet Religious Policy," in Ramet, ed., *Religious Policy in the Soviet Union*, 25.

70. John Anthony McGuckin, *The Eastern Orthodox Church: A New History* (New Haven: Yale University Press, 2020), 224.

71. See Keith Armes, "Chekists in Cassocks: The Orthodox Church and the KGB," at http://www.demokratizatsiya.org/Dem%20Archives/DEM%2001-04%20armes.pdf (accessed on 26 April 2023).

72. Adeeb Khalid, *The Politics of Muslim Cultural Reform: Jadidism in Central Asia* (Berkeley: University of California Press, 1998).

73. Terry Martin, *The Affirmative Action Empire: Nations and Nationalities in the Soviet Union, 1923–1939* (Ithaca: Cornell University Press, 2001), 10–11.

74. Ivar Spector, *The Soviet Union and the Muslim World, 1917–1958* (Seattle: University of Washington Press, 1959), 15–17.

75. Conquest, *Religion in the U.S.S.R.*, 68–69.

76. Quoted in Conquest, *Religion in the U.S.S.R.*, 68.

77. In diminished form, the uprising persisted until the 1930s. See Baymirza Hayit, *Basmatschi: Nationaler Kampf Turkestans in den Jahren 1917 bis 1934* (Cologne: Dreisam, 1993).

78. Quoted in Geoffrey Wheeler, "Islam and the Soviet Union," *Middle Eastern Studies* 13 (1977): 40.

79. Michael Kemper, "The Soviet Discourse on the Origin and Class Character of Islam, 1923–1933," *Die Welt des Islams* 49 (2009): 1–48.

80. Congress Report as quoted in Conquest, *Religion in the U.S.S.R.*, 70.

81. Shoshana Keller, "The Central Asian Bureau: An Essential Tool in Governing Soviet Turkestan," *Central Asian Survey* 22 (2003): 281–97, and Adeeb Khalid, *Islam after Communism: Religion and Politics in Central Asia* (Berkeley: University of California Press, 2007), 67–68.

82. Walter Kolarz, *Religion in the Soviet Union* (London: Macmillan, 1961), 412.

83. On Soviet education and Islam, see Sonja Luehrmann, *Secularism Soviet Style: Teaching Atheism and Religion in a Volga Republic* (Bloomington: Indiana University Press, 2011), and Erich W. Bethmann, *The Fate of Muslims under Soviet Rule* (New York: American Friends of the Middle East, 1958), 15–16.

84. Kolarz, *Religion in the Soviet Union*, 412.

85. Fanny Bryan, "Anti-Islamic Propaganda: *Bezbozhnik*, 1925–35," *Central Asian Survey* 5 (1986): 29–47, and Y. Ro'i, "The Task of Creating the New Soviet Man: 'Atheistic Propaganda' in the Soviet Muslim Areas," *Europe-Asia Studies* 36 (1984): 26–44.

86. Cloé Drieu, "Cinema, Local Power and the Central State: Agencies in Early Anti-Religious Propaganda in Uzbekistan," *Die Welt des Islams* 50 (2010): 532–58.

87. Devin Deweese, "Islam and the Legacy of Sovietology: A Review Essay of Ro'i's *Islam in the Soviet Union*," *Journal of Islamic Studies* 13 (2002): 298–330.

88. Noted in "Moslems Tell of Persecution at Reds' Hands: Thousands Slain, Exiled; Mosques Desecrated," *Chicago Tribune* (17 October 1950).

89. Shoshana Keller, *To Moscow, Not Mecca: The Soviet Campaign against Islam in Central Asia, 1917–1941* (Westport, CT: Praeger, 2001), 115.

90. Quoted in Keller, *To Moscow, Not Mecca,* 116.

91. Ahmed Rashid, *Jihad: The Rise of Militant Islam in Central Asia* (New Haven: Yale University Press, 2002), 39.

92. Alexandre Bennigsen and Chantal Lemercier-Quelquejay, *Les Musulmans oubliés: L'Islam en Union soviétique* (Paris: F. Maspero, 1981), 126–56.

93. A villager quoted from an oral interview in Marianne Kamp, "Where Did the Mullahs Go? Oral Histories from Rural Uzbekistan," *Die Welt des Islams* 50 (2020): 521–22.

94. Allen J. Frank, *Gulag Miracles: Sufis and Stalinist Repression in Kazakhstan* (Vienna: Austrian Academy of Sciences Press, 2019), and Anne Applebaum, *Gulag: A History* (New York: Anchor, 2003), 298–99.

95. Adeeb Khalid, *Central Asia: A New History from the Imperial Conquests to the Present* (Princeton: Princeton University Press, 2021), 218.

96. Eren Murat Tasar, "Soviet Policies toward Islam," in Philip E. Muehlenbeck, ed., *Religion and the Cold War: A Global Perspective* (Nashville: Vanderbilt University Press, 2012), 163.

97. Khalid, *Islam after Communism,* 76–77.

98. Jeff Eden, *God Save the USSR: Soviet Muslims and the Second World War* (Oxford: Oxford University Press, 2021).

99. Marie Broxup, "Islam and Atheism in the North Caucasus," *Religion in Communist Lands* 9 (1981): 40.

100. Brian Glyn Williams, "The Hidden Ethnic Cleansing of Muslims in the Soviet Union: The Exile and Repatriation of the Crimean Tatars," *Journal of Contemporary History* 37 (2002): 323–47.

101. Robert Conquest, *The Soviet Deportation of Nationalities* (London: Macmillan, 1960), 58. Considerable repatriation took place under Khrushchev's de-Stalinization program. See also Norma M. Naimark, *Stalin's Genocides* (Princeton: Princeton University Press, 2010).

102. Kolarz, *Islam in the Soviet Union,* 430.

103. Noted in Ali Kantemir, "The Moslems," in Nikolai K. Deker and Andrei Lebed, eds., *Genocide in the USSR: Studies in Group Destruction,* trans. Oliver J. Frederiksen (New York: Scarecrow, 1958), 200.

104. Khalid, *Islam after Communism,* 94.

105. Khalid, *Islam after Communism,* 81.

106. Muhammet Koçak, "Official and Unofficial Islam in the Soviet Union during the Cold War," *Journal of Turkish History Researches* 3 (2018): 117.

107. Frank, *Gulag Miracles.*

108. Khalid, *Islam after Communism,* 14.

109. Sylvain Boulouque, "Communism in Afghanistan," in Courtois et al., eds., *Black Book of Communism*, 725. See also Pervez Hoodbhoy, "Afghanistan and the Genesis of Global Jihad," *Peace Research* 37 (2005):15–30.

110. Edmund Silberner, *Kommunisten zur Judenfrage: Zur Geschichte von Theorie und Praxis des Kommunismus* (Opladen: Westdeutscher, 1983), 16–42.

111. Nora Levin, *The Jews in the Soviet Union since 1917*, vol. 1 (New York: New York University Press, 1988), 57.

112. Masha Gessen, *Where the Jews Aren't: The Sad and Absurd Story of Birobidzhan, Russia's Jewish Autonomous Region* (New York: Schocken, 2016).

113. Zvi Gitelman, *A Century of Ambivalence: The Jews of Russia and the Soviet Union, 1881 to the Present*, 2nd ed. (Bloomington: Indiana University Press, 2001), 1–57.

114. Joshua Rothenberg, "Jewish Religion in the Soviet Union," in Lionel Kochan, ed., *The Jews in Soviet Russia since 1917*, 3rd ed. (Oxford: Oxford University Press, 1978), 177.

115. Kolarz, *Religion in the Soviet Union*, 380.

116. Léon Leneman, *La tragédie des Juifs en U.R.S.S.* (Paris: Desclee de Brouwer, 1959), 38.

117. Quoted in David E. Fishman, "Judaism in the USSR, 1917–1930: The Fate of Religious Education," in Yaacov Ro'i, ed., *Jews and Jewish Life in Russia and the Soviet Union* (Ilford, England: Frank Cass, 1995), 252.

118. Pipes, *Russia under the Bolshevik Regime*, 365, and Aryeh Y. Yodfat, "The Closure of Synagogues in the Soviet Union," *East European Jewish Affairs* 3 (1973): 48–56.

119. Anonymously quoted in B. Z. Goldberg, *The Jewish Problem in the Soviet Union* (Westport, CT: Greenwood, 1982), 26.

120. Due to an international outcry, his sentence was commuted, and he was ultimately allowed to emigrate.

121. Antony Polonsky, *The Jews in Poland and Russia, vol. 3, 1914–2008* (Oxford: Littman Library of Jewish Civilization, 2012), 269.

122. Rothenberg, "Jewish Religion in the Soviet Union," 178.

123. Quoted in Fishman, "Judaism in the USSR, 1917–1930: The Fate of Religious Education," in Ro'i, ed., *Jews and Jewish Life in Russia and the Soviet Union*, 259.

124. Quoted material in Heinz-Dietrich Löwe, "Reconstructing in the Image of Soviet Man: The Jews in the Soviet Union, 1917–1941," *Cahiers slaves* 11 (2010): 277–78.

125. Kolarz, *Religion in the Soviet Union*, 375.

126. Robert Weinberg, "Demonizing Judaism in the Soviet Union in the 1920s," *Slavic Review* 67 (2008): 127–28.

127. Mordechai Altshuler, *Religion and Jewish Identity in the Soviet Union, 1941–1964*, trans. Saadya Sternberg (Waltham, MA: Brandeis University Press, 2012), 103–4.

128. Zvi Gitelman, "The Evolution of Jewish Culture and Identity in the Soviet Union," in Yaacov Ro'i and Avi Becker, eds., *Jewish Culture and Identity in the Soviet Union* (New York: New York University Press, 1991), 65.

129. Löwe, "Reconstructing in the Image of Soviet Man," 274.

130. On the work of the committee generally, see Arno Lustiger, *Stalin and the Jews: The Red Book: The Tragedy of the Soviet Jews and the Jewish Anti-Fascist Committee* (New York: Enigma, 2003).

131. Diana Dumitru, "From Friends to Enemies? The Soviet State and the Jews in the Aftermath of the Holocaust," in Katreřina Čapková et al., eds., *Jewish Lives under Communism: New Perspectives* (New Brunswick, NJ: Rutgers University Press, 2022), 71-90.

132. Leonid Smilovitsky, "Jews under Soviet Rule: Attempts by Religious Communities to Renew Jewish Life during the Postwar Reconstruction Period: The Case of Belorussia, 1944-1953," *Cahiers du Monde Russe* 49 (2008): 506-11.

133. Piet Buwalda, *They Did Not Dwell Alone: Jewish Emigration from the Soviet Union* (Baltimore: Johns Hopkins University Press, 1997), 139-97.

134. Rothenberg, "Jewish Religious Life in the Soviet Union," in Lionel Kochan, ed., *The Jews in Soviet Russia since 1917*, 3rd ed. (Oxford: Oxford University Press, 1978), 168.

135. Quoted in Gitelman, *A Century of Ambivalence*, 195 (emphasis in original).

136. Quoted in Goldemann, "The Jews," in Deker and Lebed, eds., *Genocide in the USSR*, 106-7.

137. Conquest, *Religion in the U.S.S.R.*, 117.

138. See "Buddhism," in *Great Soviet Encyclopedia*, vol. 4 (New York: Macmillan, 1973), 136.

139. Hans Bräker, *Der Buddhismus in der Sowjetunion im Spannungsfeld zwischen Vernichtung und Überleben* (Cologne: Bundesinstitut für ostwissenschaftliche und internationale Studien, 1982), 3-6.

140. Geraldine Fagan, "Buddhism in Postsoviet Russia: Revival or Degeneration?" *Religion, State and Society* 29 (2001): 9-10.

141. John Snelling, *Buddhism in Russia: The Story of Agvan Dorzhiev, Lhasa's Emissary to the Tsar* (London: Bega, 2002).

142. Quoted in Kolarz, *Religion in the Soviet Union*, 455.

143. Nicholas N. Poppe, "The Buddhists," in Deker and Lebed, eds., *Genocide in the USSR*, 186.

144. Melissa Chakars, *The Socialist Way of Life in Siberia: Transformation in Buryatia* (Budapest: Central European University Press, 2014), 73.

145. Fagan, "Buddhism in Postsoviet Russia," 10.

146. This is from A. M. Tennissons, a Western convert to Buddhism. Quoted in Ernst Benz, *Buddhism or Communism: Which Holds the Future of Asia?* trans. Richard and Clara Winston (New York: Doubleday, 1965), 174.

147. Chakars, *Socialist Way of Life in Siberia*, 74.

148. Kolarz, *Religion in the Soviet Union*, 464-66.

149. James Forsyth, *A History of the People of Siberia: Russia's North Asian Colony, 1581-1990* (Cambridge: Cambridge University Press, 1992), 281.

150. Quoted in Eva Jane Fridman, *Sacred Geography: Shamanism among the Buddhist Peoples of Russia* (Budapest: Akadémiai Kiadó, 2004), 239.

151. Kolarz, *Religion in the Soviet Union*, 462-64; Conquest, *Deportation of Nationalities*, 94; and Pavel Polian, *Against Their Will: The History and Geography of Forced Migrations in the USSR* (Budapest: Central European Press, 2004), 144-45. See also Elza-Bair Guchinova, "'All Roads Lead to Siberia': Two Stories of the Kalmyk Deportation," *Forum for Anthropology and Culture* 3 (2006): 239-85.

152. Quoted material in Dorzha Arbakov, "The Kalmyks," in Deker and Lebed, ed., *Genocide in the USSR*, 35.

153. Chakars, *Socialist Way of Life in Siberia*, 74.

154. Fridman, *Sacred Geography*, 237.

155. Quoted in Janis Sapiets, "Buddhists Struggle for Survival in the USSR," *Religion in Communist Lands* 2 (1974): 5.

156. Bräker, *Der Buddhismus in der Sowjetunion*, 20–21.

157. Fagan, "Buddhism in Postsoviet Russia," 10.

158. Quoted in Poppe, "The Buddhists," in Deker and Lebed, eds., *Genocide in the USSR*, 191.

159. From a speech on 1 July 1991 quoted in Ivan Sablin, "Soviet and Buddhist: Religious Diplomacy, Dissidence, and the Atheist State, 1945–1991," *Journal of Religion* 99 (2019): 58.

160. The Armenian Catholic Church should not be confused with the Armenian Apostolic Church, an oriental Orthodox Church and the dominant church in Armenia. It, too, experienced considerable oppression during the early Soviet era; its churches were razed and repurposed; its clergymen harassed, imprisoned, and killed. Most notoriously, the leader of the Armenian Apostolic Church, Catholicos Khoren I (r. 1932–38), was in all likelihood murdered by Soviet agents in 1938. See Edward Alexander, "The Armenian Church in Soviet Policy," *Russian Review* 14 (1955): 357–62.

161. Christopher Lawrence Zugger, *The Forgotten: Catholics of the Soviet Empire from Lenin through Stalin* (Syracuse, NY: Syracuse University Press, 2001), 107–10.

162. Robert Royal, *Catholic Martyrs of the Twentieth Century: A Comprehensive World History* (New York: Herder and Herder, 2000), 48–49.

163. As reported in Francis McCullagh, *The Bolshevik Persecution of Christianity* (London: E. P. Dutton, 1924), 221.

164. Paul Mailleux, S.J., "Catholics in the Soviet Union," in Richard H. Marshall et al., eds., *Aspects of Religion in the Soviet Union, 1917–1967* (Chicago: Chicago University Press, 1971), 363.

165. Paul Lesourd, *Entre Rome et Moscou: Le jésuite clandestin, Mgr. Michel d'Herbigny* (Paris: P. Lethieleux, 1976).

166. Quoted in Nadezhda Teodorovich, "The Roman Catholics," Deker and Lebed, eds., *Genocide in the USSR*, 213.

167. Zugger, *Forgotten Catholics of the Soviet Union*, 257.

168. Mailleux, "Catholics in the Soviet Union," 364.

169. Report on the Volga Germans as cited in Teodorovich, "The Roman Catholics," 214.

170. Quoted in Irina Osipova, *Se il mondo vi odia: Martiri per la fede nel regime sovietico* (Rome: La Case di Matriona, 1997), 33.

171. Arūnas Streikus, "The History of Religion in Lithuania since the Nineteenth Century," in Milda Alisauskiene and Ingo W. Schröder, eds., *Religious Diversity in Post-Soviet Society: Ethnographies of Catholic Hegemony and the New Pluralism in Lithuania* (Farnham: Ashgate, 2012), 45–46.

172. Pranas Dauknys, "The Resistance of the Catholic Church in Lithuania against Religious Persecution," *Litunas* 31 (1985): 2.

173. Arūnas Streikus, "The Roman Catholic Church in Lithuania and Its Soviet Past," in Lucian Turcescu and Lavinia Stan, eds., *Churches, Memory and Justice in Post-Communism* (Cham, Switzerland: Palgrave Macmillan, 2021), 207, and Arūnas Streikus, *The Church in Soviet Lithuania* (Vilnius: Genocide and Resistance Research Centre of Lithuania, 2019), 13.

174. On Lithuanian resistance, see Arūnas Streikus, ed., *The Unknown War: Anti-Soviet Armed Resistance in Lithuania and Its Legacies* (New York: Routledge, 2022).

175. Vilma Narkute, "The Confrontation between the Lithuanian Catholic Church and the Soviet Regime," *New Blackfriars* 87 (2006): 465, and Pranas Dauknys, *The Resistance of the Catholic Church in Lithuania against Religious Persecution* (Rome: Pontificia Studiorum Universitas A.S. Thomas Aquinas, 1984), 43.

176. Arūnas Streikus, "Der Berg der Kreuze," in Joachim Bahlcke et al., eds., *Religiöse Erinnerungsorte in Ostmitteleuropa: Konstitution und Konkurrenz im nationalen- und epochen-überergreifenden Zugriff* (Berlin: Akademie, 2013), 223–31.

177. Royal, *Catholic Martyrs*, 252–53.

178. Its contents in English translation are available online at https://lkbkronika.lt/en/

179. The following account draws especially from Bohdan R. Bociurkiw, *The Ukrainian Greek Catholic Church and the Soviet State (1939–1950)* (Edmonton: Canadian Institute of Ukrainian Studies Press, 1996).

180. Bohdan R. Bociurkiw, "The Uniate Church in the Soviet Union: A Case Study in Church Policy," *Canadian Slavonic Studies* 7 (1965): 89–90.

181. Bociurkiw, *Ukrainian Greek Catholic Church and the Soviet State*, 102–47.

182. Bociurkiw, *Ukrainian Greek Catholic Church and the Soviet State*, 148–88, 221–22, 237.

183. Bociurkiw, "The Uniate Church in the Soviet Union: A Case Study in Church Policy," 113.

FOUR

1. Tony Judt, *Postwar: A History of Europe since 1945* (New York: Penguin, 1945), 129–96.

2. John Connelly, *From Peoples to Nations: A History of Eastern Europe* (Princeton: Princeton University Press, 2020), 508.

3. Anne Applebaum, *Iron Curtain: The Crushing of Eastern Europe* (New York: Anchor, 2013), 256.

4. Helmut David Baer, *The Struggle of Hungarian Lutherans under Communism* (College Station: Texas A&M University Press, 2006), 16.

5. Vladimir M. Rodzianko, "The Golgotha of the Orthodox Church in Yugoslavia," *Eastern Churches Quarterly* 10 (1953): 71.

6. "Basic Guidelines of the NKVD for the Countries in the Soviet Orbit (Moscow, June 1947)," as quoted in Paul Caravia et al., *The Imprisoned Church: Romania, 1944–1989* (Bucharest: Romanian Academy; National Institute for the Study of Totalitarianism, 1999), 13.

7. Quoted material in Applebaum, *Iron Curtain*, 151–52, 258, 269. The Information Bureau of the Communist and Workers' Parties, or Cominform, was the official central organization of the International Communist Movement from 1947 to 1956, a successor to the Third International, otherwise known as Comintern, which ceased meeting in 1935.

8. Adam Somorjai, "La Chiesa Cattolica in Ungheria," in Jan Mikrut, ed., *La Chiesa cattolica e il comunismo in Europa Centro-Orientale e in Unione Sovietica* (Verona: Gabrielli editori, 2016), 578.

9. Cardinal Mindszenty's "Last Pastoral Letter" (18 November 1948), in J. F. Maclear, ed., *Church and State in the Modern Age: A Documentary History* (New York: Oxford University Press, 1995), 418.

10. Quoted in Albert Galter, *The Red Book of the Persecuted Church* (Westminster: New Press, 1957), 138.

11. Zsuzsánna Magdó, "The Socialist Sacred: Religion, Atheism, and Culture in Communist Romania, 1948–1989," Ph.D. diss., University of Illinois at Urbana-Champaign, 2016, 131.

12. Adolf Fugel, *Christen unterm Roten Stern: Dokumentationen, Berichte, Lebensbilder* (Freiburg im Breisgau: Herder, 1984), 82–85.

13. See, e.g., Paul Caravia et al., *The Imprisoned Church: Romania, 1944–1989* (Bucharest: Romanian Academy; National Institute for the Study of Totalitarianism, 1999), 14–18.

14. Michael Burleigh, *Sacred Causes: The Clash of Religion and Politics, from the Great War to the War on Terrorism* (New York: Harper, 2007), 331, 335.

15. Owen Chadwick, *The Christian Church in the Cold War* (London: Penguin, 1992), 37.

16. Pedro Ramet, *Cross and Commissar: The Politics of Religion in Eastern Europe and the USSR* (Bloomington: Indiana University Press, 1987), 71.

17. Alexander Tomsky, "'Pacem in Terris' Between Church and State in Czechoslovakia," *Religion in Communist Lands* 10 (1982): 278.

18. Robert Royal, *The Catholic Martyrs of the Twentieth Century* (New York: Herder and Herder, 2000), 221, and Chadwick, *Christian Church in the Cold War*, 30.

19. Agata Mirek, "The Labour Camps for Nuns Which Functioned between 1954 and 1956 in Poland," in Martina Fiamová and Pavol Jakubčin, eds., *Persecution of Churches in the Communist Countries in Central and Eastern Europe* (Bratislava: Ústav Pamäti Národa, 2010), 98–109.

20. See Vicent P. Tinerella, "Secret Sisters: Women Religious under European Communism: Collection at the Catholic Theological Union [Chicago]," *Theological Librarianship* 3 (2010): 8–15.

21. Karl Heinz Jahnke, *Partei und Jugend: Dokumente marxistisch-leninistischer Jugendpolitik* (Berlin: Dietz, 1986), 326.

22. Ulrich Wiegmann, *Pädagogik und Staatssicherheit: Schule und Jugend in der Erziehungsideologie und -praxis der DDR-Geheimdienstes* (Berlin: Metropole, 2007).

23. Chadwick, *Christian Church in the Cold War*, 21–22.

24. Ulrich Mähler, *Die Freie Deutsche Jungen, 1945–1949* (Paderborn: F. Schöningh, 1995).

25. Markus Anhalt, *Die Macht der Kirchen brechen: Die Mitwirkung der Staatssicherheit bei der Durchsetzung der Jugendweihe in der DDR* (Göttingen: Vandenhoeck and Ruprecht, 2016).

26. Noted in Applebaum, *Iron Curtain*, 261–62.

27. As quoted in Applebaum, *Iron Curtain*, 262.

28. Momchil Metodiev, "Bulgaria: Revealed Secrets, Unreckoned Past," in Lucian Turcescu and Lavinia Stan, eds., *Churches, Memory, and Justice in Post-Communism* (Cham, Switzerland: Palgrave Macmillan, 2021), 117.

29. Edwin E. Jacques, *The Albanians* (Jefferson, NC: McFarland, 1995), 447–60.

30. Peter Kenez, "The Hungarian Communist Party and the Catholic Church," *Journal of Modern History* 75 (December 2003): 865–89, and József Cardinal Mindszenty, *Memoirs* (New York: Macmillan, 1974), 83–210.

31. Kurz Hutten, *Christen hinter dem eisernen Vorhang*, vol. 1 (Stuttgart: Quell, 1962), 218–50.

32. Metodiev, "Bulgaria: Revealed Secrets, Unreckoned Past," in Turcescu and Stan, eds., *Churches, Memory, and Justice in Post-Communism*, 117.

33. Ramet, *Cross and Commissar*, 35.

34. Hans Hermann Dirksen, "Jehovah's Witnesses under Communist Regimes," *Religion, State and Society* 30 (2002): 235.

35. Pedro Ramet, *Cross and Commissar*, 21, and Bernard Wasserstein, *Vanishing Diaspora: The Jews in Europe since 1945* (Cambridge, MA: Harvard University Press, 1996), viii.

36. Quoted in Ramet, *Cross and Commissar*, 5.

37. Vladimir Tismaneanu, *Stalinism for All Seasons: A Political History of Romanian Communism* (Berkeley: University of California Press, 2003), 85–106.

38. Lucian Turcescu, "The Romanian Orthodox Church Rewriting Its History," in Lucian Turcescu et al., *Churches, Memory, and Justice in Post-Communism* (Cham, Switzerland: Palgrave Macmillan, 2021), 94–95.

39. Keith Hitchens, *A Concise History of Romania* (New York: Cambridge University Press, 2016), 256–57.

40. Vladimir Gsovski, ed., *Church and State behind the Iron Curtain* (New York: Frederick A. Praeger, 1955), 277–81, 292–93.

41. Quoted from the society's promotional literature in Gsovski, ed., *Church and State behind the Iron Curtain*, 277–81, 292–93.

42. See Magdó, "The Socialist Sacred."

43. Robert Royal, *The Catholic Martyrs of the Twentieth Century: A Comprehensive World History* (New York: Herder and Herder, 2000), 255–58.

44. Daria Klich, "La persecuzione degli ordini religiosi femminili: Le Suore Orsoline dell-Unione Romana," in Jan Mikrut, ed., *Testimoni della fede: Esperienze personali e collative dei cattolici in Europa centro-orientale sotto il regime comunista* (Rome: Gabrielli editori, 2017), 1020–27.

45. Quoted in Royal, *Catholic Martyrs of the Twentieth Century*, 266. See also Daniel Teodorescu and Gheorghe Boldur-Latescu, *The Re-Education Experiment in Romania: A Survivor's View of the Past, Present, and Future* (New York: Nova Science, 2013).

46. Christine Hall, "Human Freedom and the Enigma of Martyrdom in the Romanian Orthodox Church, 1944–1964," *Morality* 19 (2014): 151–75. The Pitești experiments were ended in 1951 and its perpetrators scapegoated and tried, but its methods lived on in other prisons. See Ion Cucliciu, "Romania: A Time of Yielding," in Jacob D. Lindy and Robert Jay Lifton, eds., *Beyond Invisible Walls: The Psychological Legacy of Soviet Trauma* (London: Routledge, 2001), 92–117. For Solzhenitsyn, see Jesse Kelly, *The Anti-Communist Manifesto* (New York: Simon and Schuster, 2023), 13.

47. "Communist Exploitation of Religion" (Richard Wurmbrand's Testimony before U.S. Senate, 6 May 1966), at www.avivamientos.net/en/books/Richard_Wurmbrand/exploitation

.html (accessed on 28 February 2022). On Wurmbrand generally, see Marian Eigeles, "Preaching Was His Life: Richard Wurmbrand," *Mishikan* 37 (2002): 96–103.

48. Wasserstein, *Vanishing Diaspora*, viii. See also Radu Ioanid et al., eds., *The Ransom of the Jews: The Story of the Extraordinary Secret Bargain between Romania and Israel*, 2nd ed. (Lanham, MD: Rowman and Littlefield, 2021).

49. Maclear, ed., *Church and State in the Modern Age*, 485–88.

50. Lavinia Stan, *Transitional Justice in Romania: The Politics of Memory* (New York: Cambridge University Press, 2013), 7–9.

51. *Religious Persecution in Romania* (Report Issued by the Romanian Missionary Society) (Wheaton, IL, 1985), 16.

52. "Romanians Bulldoze Holy Sites," *Chicago Tribune* (10 October 1985).

53. Judt, *Postwar*, 138–39.

54. Robert K. Evanson, "Political Repression in Czechoslovakia, 1948–1984," *Canadian Slavonic Papers/Revue Canadienne des slavistes* 28 (1986): 1–21.

55. Frank Cibulka, "Religion and Transitional Justice in the Czech Republic," in Turcescu and Stan, eds., *Churches, Memory, and Justice in Post-Communism*, 48.

56. Quoted in Trevor Beeson, *Discretion and Valour: Religious Conditions in Russia and Eastern Europe*, rev. ed. (London: Collins, 1982), 234.

57. Anna Remigie Češiková, "Gli ordini religiosi femminile: Vojtěcha Hasmandová," in Mikrut, ed., *Testimoni della fede*, 281.

58. Remembrance of St. Barbara Kovacoca, Sister of St. Francis (Slovakia), Women Religious Imprisoned under Eastern Communism Collection. Archives, Catholic Theological Union, Chicago.

59. Tom McEnchroe, "'Operation K'—How the Communists Wiped Out Czechoslovakia's Monasteries in One Brutal Stroke," *Radio Prague International* (13 April 2020), at https://english.radio.cz/operation-k-how-communists-wiped-out-czechoslovakias-monasteries-one-brutal-8103215 (accessed on 22 September 2022).

60. Katrin Bock, "Der Fall Babice," *Radio Prague International* (7 July 2001), at https://deutsch.radio.cz/der-fall-babice-8043648 (accessed on 22 September 2022).

61. Josef Skvorecky, *The Miracle Game* (Toronto: L&OD, 2002).

62. Peter Šturák, "La Chiesa greco-cattolica in Slovacchia," in Mikrut, ed., *La Chiesa cattolica e il comunismo*, 193–237.

63. Quoted material in this paragraph is taken from the February Report (1949) of the "Church Six," an advisory body subordinate to the Presidium of the Communist Party of Czechoslovakia's Central Committee; cited in Jaroslav Coranič, "The Liquidation of the Greek Catholic Church in Communist Czechoslovakia, 1948–50," *Journal of Ecclesiastical History* 72 (July 2021): 590–610.

64. Nadeje Hromàdkova, *Josef L. Hromádkova: Leben und Werk des tschechischen Theologen* (Mühlheim an der Ruhr: Evangelische Akademie, 1989).

65. From a speech in April 1949 as quoted in Sabrina Petra Ramet, "The Catholic Church in Czechoslovakia, 1948–1991," *Comparative Studies in Communism* 24 (1991): 386.

66. George Weigel, *The Final Revolution: The Resistance Church and the Collapse of Communism* (New York: Oxford University Press, 1992), 44.

67. Beeson, *Discretion and Valour*, 232ff.

68. Anonymous [translated by Gerald Turner], "The Church at the Crossroads," *Religion in Communist Lands* 13 (1985): 254-55.

69. Jan Tesař, *The History of Scientific Atheism: A Comparative Study of Czechoslovakia and the Soviet Union (1954-1991)* (Göttingen: Vandenhoeck und Ruprecht, 2019).

70. Quoted material taken from Ramet, "The Catholic Church in Czechoslovakia, 1948-1991," 381-84.

71. Ramet, "The Catholic Church in Czechoslovakia, 1948-1991," 379.

72. "Why the Czech Regime Fears God," *Times* (18 January 1983), 14.

73. Gordon H. Skilling, *Charter 77 and Human Rights in Czechoslovakia* (London: Allen and Unwin, 1981).

74. Quoted in Ramet, "The Catholic Church in Czechoslovakia, 1948-1991," 379.

75. "Why the Czech Regime Fears God," 14.

76. Blendi Fevziu, *Enver Hoxha: The Iron Fist of Albania*, trans. Majlinda Nishku (London: I. B. Tauris, 2016), 19-28, 47.

77. At the time of the Communist takeover, Catholics, located predominantly in the north, made up 10 percent of the population; the Orthodox made up 20 percent; the Muslims accounted for the remaining 70 percent.

78. Bernhard Tönnies, "Religionen in Albanien: Enver Hoxha and die 'nationale Eigenart,'" *Osteuropa* 24 (1974): 671, and Markus W. W. Peters, *Geschichte der katholischen Kirche in Albanien, 1919-1993* (Wiesbaden: Harrassowitz, 2003), 136ff.

79. Giacomo Gardin, *Banishing God in Albania: The Prison Memoirs of Giacomo Gardin, S.J.* (San Francisco: Ignatius, 1986), 15.

80. Joseph Ritho Mwanki, "La Chiesa in Albania," in Mikrut, ed., *La Chiesa cattolica e il comunismo*, 42.

81. Noted in Edwin Jacques, *The Albanians: An Ethnic History from Prehistoric Times to the Present* (Jefferson, NC: McFarland, 1995), 455.

82. Giacomo Gardin, diary from November 1950, reprinted in Gjon Sinishta, ed., *The Fulfilled Promise: Documentary Account of Religious Persecution in Albania* (Santa Clara, CA: H and F, 1976), 145-46.

83. See Zef Pllumi, *Live to Tell: A True Story of Religious Persecution in Albania, 1944-1951*, vol. 1 (New York: iUniverse, 2008), xv, 21. For the persecution of the Catholic Church in Communist Albania more generally, see Didier Rance, *Albanie: Ils ont voulu tuer Dieu: La persecution contre l'Église catholique (1944-1991)* (Paris: Bibliothèque AED, 1996).

84. See "Albania, Missing Persons from the Communist Era: A Needs Assessment," International Commission on Missing Persons (2 March 2021).

85. Francis Trix, "The Resurfacing of Islam in Albania," *East European Quarterly* 28 (1994): 1-9.

86. On Burrel and other prisons and work camps, see Rexhep Gashi, "Types of Prisons and Labor Camps and the Position of Convicted Persons in Albania during the Communist Dictatorship," *Thesis* 1 (2012): 27-50.

87. Janice A. Broun, "The Status of Christianity in Albania," *Journal of Church and State* 28 (1986): 50-51.

88. Archbishop Anastasios, *In Albania: Cross and Resurrection*, trans. John Chryssavgis (Yonkers, NY: Saint Vladimir's Seminary Press, 2016), 16.

89. Artan Hoxha, *Communism, Atheism, and the Orthodox Church of Albania: Cooperation, Survival, and Suppression* (London: Routledge, 2024), 9. Also see Beqja Hamit, "The Development of Atheistic Education in Albania," *Studime Historike* 3 (1983): 37–54. Translated in *Albanian Catholic Bulletin* 5 (1984): 35–43.

90. Barbara Frey, "Violations of Freedom of Religion in Albania," *Occasional Papers on Religion in Eastern Europe* 9 (1989): 1–6, and Finngeir Hiorth, "Albania: An Atheistic State?" *Occasional Papers on Religion in Eastern Europe* 10 (1990): 14–15.

91. Quoted in Frey, "Violations of Freedom of Religion in Albania," 6.

92. Giulio Cargnello, "Le persecuzioni religiose de regime comunista Albanese e la Chiesa cattolica," in Mikrut, ed., *Testimonie della fede,* 38, and Bernhard Tönnes, "Albania: An Atheist State," *Religion in Communist Lands* 3 (1975): 7.

93. Jacques, *The Albanians,* 486–87.

94. Fevziu, *Enver Hoxha,* 183.

95. Frey, "Violations of Freedom of Religion in Albania," 7.

96. Peggy Chutich et al., *Human Rights in the People's Socialist Republic of Albania* (Minneapolis: Minnesota Lawyers International Human Rights Committee, 1990), 82. In fact, beards in general were outlawed; even foreign visitors to Albania had to undergo a mandatory shaving until 1983.

97. Tönnes, "Religious Persecution in Albania," *Religion in Communist Lands* 10 (1982): 250.

98. Email interview with Thomas Qirjazi [translated by Sandra Allison] (5 January 2022).

99. Shannon Woodcock, *Life Is War: Surviving Dictatorship in Communist Albania* (Bristol: Hammeron, 2016), 132, and Joseph Ritho Mwaniki, "La Chiesa cattolica in Albania," in Mikrut, ed., *La Chiesa cattolica e il comunismo,* 50.

100. Personal conversation in Tirana, Albania (1 November 2021).

101. I am especially grateful to Roald Hysa of Tirana for sharing with me his recorded interviews with Muslim survivors of Communism for his book project, *Dëshmi nga e kalura* (Evidence from the Past).

102. Personal conversation in Tirana, Albania (2 November 2021).

103. Woodcock, *Life Is War: Surviving Dictatorship in Communist Albania,* 5ff.

104. Fevziu, *Enver Hoxha,* 183.

105. Archbishop Anastasios, *In Albania: Cross and Resurrection,* 100.

106. Anonymous, *History of the Party of Labor in Albania* (Tirana: Institute of Marxist-Leninist Studies at the Central Committee of the Party of Labor in Albania, 1971), 622–27.

107. Enver Hoxha, *Selected Works,* 1966–1973, vol. 4 (Tirana: Nentori, 1982), 791–92.

108. "Saint John Paul II: His Words to Albanians in 1993," *Vatican Radio,* at http://www.archivioradiovaticana.va/storico/2014/09/19/saint_john_paul_ii_his_words_to_albanians_in_1993_/en-1106870 (accessed 23 September 2022).

FIVE

1. Mao Zedong, *Mao Tse-Tung's Quotations: The Red Guard's Handbook* (Nashville: International Center, 1967), 6–7.

2. Julia Lovell, *Maoism: A Global History* (New York: Alfred A. Knopf, 2019), 7.

3. Arif Dirlik, "The Predicament of Marxist Revolutionary Consciousness: Mao Zedong, Antonio Gramsci, and the Reformulation of Marxist Revolutionary Theory," *Modern China* 9 (1983): 182-211.

4. Buddhism had a presence in Mongolia much earlier, but it only became fully entrenched in the sixteenth century. See Dominique Dumas, *Bouddhisme de Mongolie: Histoire, historiographie, et stéréotypes occidentaux* (Saint-Denis: Connaissances et savoirs, 2016), 147-77.

5. C. R. Bawden, *The Modern History of Mongolia* (New York: Praeger, 1968), 262-63.

6. Michael K. Jerryson, *Mongolian Buddhism: The Rise and Fall of the Sangha* (Chiang Mai: Silkworm, 2007), 65.

7. Christopher Kaplonski, *The Lama Question: Violence, Sovereignty, and Exception in Early Socialist Mongolia* (Honolulu: University of Hawai'i Press, 2014), 91-103.

8. Bawden, *Modern History of Mongolia*, 314.

9. Jerryson, *Mongolian Buddhism*, 69.

10. Quoted in Kaplonski, *The Lama Question*, 102.

11. Shagdariin Sandag and Harry H. Kendall, *Poisoned Arrows: The Stalin-Choibalsan Mongolian Massacres, 1921-1941* (Boulder, CO: Westview, 2000), 63.

12. Noted in Robert A. Rupen, *Mongols of the Twentieth Century*, vol. 1 (Bloomington: Indiana University Press, 1964), 228.

13. Quoted in Kaplonski, *The Lama Question*, 27.

14. Alan J. K. Sanders, *Historical Dictionary of Mongolia* (Lanham: Scarecrow, 2010), 159-61.

15. Jerryson, *Mongolian Buddhism*, 87.

16. Baabar (Bat-Erdene Batbayar), *Twentieth Century Mongolia*, trans. D Süjargalmaa et al. (Kent, CT: Global Oriental), 355.

17. Choibalsan to Nikolai Yezhov (specific date not provided); quoted in Baabar, *Twentieth Century Mongolia*, 360-61.

18. Rupen, *Mongols of the Twentieth Century*, vol. 1, 228, and Sandag and Kendall, *Poisoned Arrows*, 120.

19. See his speech from January 1938, partially reprinted in Rupen, *Mongols of the Twentieth Century*, vol. 1, 229.

20. Kaplonski, *The Lama Question*, 203.

21. Quoted in Jerryson, *Mongolian Buddhism*, 91.

22. Quoted in Baabar, *Twentieth Century Mongolia*, 364.

23. Sandag and Kendall, *Poisoned Arrows*, 125

24. Memorandum cited in Baabar, *Twentieth Century Mongolia*, 363.

25. See "Documentation of Mongolian Monasteries" (http://www.mongoliantemples .org/en/), a major research project, conducted between 2005 and 2007, to document the location and ruins of monasteries and temples destroyed in the 1930s and to record oral histories of those still living who remembered them.

26. Quoted material in Jerryson, *Mongolian Buddhism*, 90-93.

27. Krisztina Teleki, *Monasteries and Temples of Bogdiin Khüree* (Ulaanbaatar: Soyombo, 2011), 7.

28. Jerryson, *Mongolian Buddhism*, 96.

29. Quoted in Bawden, *Modern History of Mongolia*, 348.

30. Vincent Goossaert and David A. Palmer, *The Religious Question in Modern China* (Chicago: University of Chicago Press, 2011), 167.

31. Ian Johnson, *The Souls of China: The Return of Religion after Mao* (New York: Pantheon, 2017), 18.

32. Luke S. K. Kwong, "The Rise of the Linear Perspective on History and Time in Late Qing China, 1860–1911," *Past and Present* 173 (2001): 157–90.

33. Peter van der Veer, *The Modern Spirit of Asia: The Spiritual and the Secular in China and India* (Princeton: Princeton University Press, 2014), 140–53.

34. Quoted (without precise date) in Vincent Goossaert, "1898: The Beginning of the End of Chinese Religion?" *Journal of Asian Studies* 65 (2006): 316.

35. Goossaert and Palmer, *The Religious Question in Modern China*, 126, and Vincent Goossaert, "The Social Organization of Religious Communities in the Twentieth Century," in David A. Palmer et al., eds., *Chinese Religious Life* (Oxford: Oxford University Press, 2011), 182.

36. Vera Schwarcz, *The Chinese Enlightenment: Intellectuals and the Legacy of the May Fourth Movement of 1919* (Berkeley: University of California Press, 1986), 7.

37. Arif Dirlik, *Anarchism in the Chinese Revolution* (Berkeley: University of California Press, 1991).

38. Tu Wei-ming, "Destructive Will and Ideological Holocaust: Maoism as a Source of Social Suffering in China," *Daedalus* 125 (1996): 158.

39. Quoted in Schwarcz, *Chinese Enlightenment*, 123.

40. Cited in Rebecca Nedostup, *Superstitious Regimes: Religion and the Politics of Chinese Modernity* (Cambridge, MA: Harvard University Press, 2009), 191.

41. Fenggang Yang, *Religion in China: Survival and Revival under Communist Rule* (Oxford: Oxford University Press, 2012), 47.

42. Goossaert and Palmer, *Religious Question in Modern China*, 140–41, and Prasenjit Duara, "Knowledge and Power in the Discourse of Modernity: The Campaigns against Popular Religion in Early Twentieth-Century China," *Journal of Asian Studies* 50 (1991): 77–78.

43. Jonathan Spence, *Mao Zedong* (New York: Viking, 1999), 16–72.

44. Noted in Peter Dziedzic, "Religion under Fire: A Report on Religious Freedom in Tibet," *Tibet Journal* 38 (2013): 87.

45. Mao Zedong as quoted in Goossaert and Palmer, *Religious Question in Modern China*, 142.

46. Goossaert and Palmer, *Religious Question in Modern China*, 148–52. On the salvationist or redemptive societies, see David Owenby, "Redemptive Societies in the Twentieth Century," in Vince Goossaert et al., eds., *Modern Chinese Religion*, vol. 2 (Leiden: Brill, 2015), 685–727.

47. D. E. Mungello, "Reinterpreting the History of Christianity in China," *Historical Journal* 55 (2012): 546–49. To understand the contours and depth of anti-missionary sentiment, consult especially Ernest P. Young, *Ecclesiastical Colony: China's Catholic Church and the French Religious Protectorate* (New York: Oxford University Press, 2013).

48. Joseph Tse-Hei Lee, "Watchman Nee and the Little Flock Movement in Maoist China," *Church History* 74 (2005): 68–96.

49. Melissa Wi-Tsing Inouye, "Gospel Light or Imperialist Poison? Controversies of the Christian Community in China, 1922–1955," in Alan Baumler, ed., *Routledge Handbook of Revolutionary China* (London: Routledge, 2021), 126–30.

50. Johannes Schütte, *Die katholische Chinamission im Spiegel der rotschineschen Presse* (Münster: Aschendorffsche, 1957).

51. Cited in Paul Philip Mariani, *Church Militant: Bishop Kung and Catholic Resistance in Communist Shanghai* (Cambridge, MA: Harvard University Press, 2011), 5.

52. Johnson, *Souls of China*, 27.

53. On this system (*laogai*), see especially Jean-Luc Domenach, *Chine: L'archipel oublié* (Paris: Fayard, 1992), and Jean-Louis Margolin, "China: A Long March into the Night," in Stéphane Courtois et al., eds., *The Black Book of Communism: Crimes, Terror, Repression* (Cambridge, MA: Harvard University Press, 1999), 41–64.

54. Robert Royal, *The Catholic Martyrs of the Twentieth Century* (New York: Herder and Herder, 2000), 331–37.

55. In this context, one should also mention the Taiping Heavenly Kingdom that instigated the Taiping Rebellion (1850–64). This major challenge to state authority in the mid-nineteenth century weakened the Qing dynasty and helped ensure the future enmity between elite Chinese society and popular redemptive societies. See Thomas H. Reilly, *The Taiping Heavenly Kingdom and the Blasphemy of Empire* (Seattle: University of Washington Press, 2004).

56. S. A. Smith, "Redemptive Societies and the Communist State, 1949 to the 1980s," in Jeremy Brown and Matthew D. Johnson, eds., *Maoism at the Grassroots: Everyday Society in China's Era of Socialism* (Cambridge, MA: Harvard University Press, 2015), 340–63.

57. Of course, this legislation affected other landholding religious communities as well.

58. Holmes Welch, *Buddhism under Mao* (Cambridge, MA: Harvard University Press, 1972), 42–43, 72–73, 81–82, 232–37.

59. Holmes Welch, "Buddhism under the Communists," *China Quarterly* 6 (1961): 14.

60. Frank Moraes, *Report on Mao's China* (New York: Macmillan, 1953), 114–15.

61. Gregory Adam Scott, *Building the Buddhist Revival: Reconstructing Monasteries in Modern China* (Oxford: Oxford University Press, 2020), 39.

62. Xiaoxuan Wang, *Maoism and Grassroots Religion: The Communist Revolution and the Reinvention of Religious Life in China* (Oxford: Oxford University Press, 2020), 9.

63. Goossaert and Palmer, *Religious Question in Modern China*, 161.

64. Goossaert and Palmer, *Religious Question in Modern China*, 162.

65. Wang, *Maoism and Grassroots Religion*, 71.

66. Noted in Yang, *Religion in China*, 71–72.

67. Kenneth K. S. Chun, *Buddhism in China: A Historical Survey* (Princeton: Princeton University Press, 1964), 461.

68. Denise Y. Ho, *Curating Revolution: Politics on Display in Mao's China* (Cambridge: Cambridge University Press, 2018), 103–37.

69. One can view the posters, "Eliminate Superstition" (1965), at chineseposters.net. See also Richard Baum and Frederick C. Teiwes, *Ssu-Ch'ing: The Socialist Education Campaign, 1962–1966* (Berkeley: University of California Press, 1969).

70. "Decisions of the Chinese Communist Party Central Committee, concerning the Great Cultural Revolution on 8 August 1966," *India Quarterly* 23 (1967): 286.

71. David A. Palmer and Xun Liu, *Daoism in the Twentieth Century: Between Eternity and Modernity* (Berkeley: University of California Press, 2012), 11.

72. Quoted material in Wang, *Maoism and Grassroots Religion*, 77.

73. Wang, *Maoism and Grassroots Religion*, 105.

74. Henrietta Harrison, *The Missionary's Curse and Other Tales from a Chinese Catholic Village* (Berkeley: University of California Press, 2013), 164–65.

75. David Lester, "Suicide and the Chinese Revolution," *Archives of Suicide Research* 9 (2005): 99–104.

76. A. James Gregor and Maria Hsia Chang, "Anti-Confucianism: Mao's Last Campaign," *Asian Survey* 19 (1979): 1073–92.

77. James D. Frankel, *Islam in China* (London: I. B. Tauris, 2021), 112, and Michael Dillon, "Muslim Communities in Contemporary China: The Resurgence of Islam after the Cultural Revolution," *Journal of Islamic Studies* 5 (1994): 70–71, 85.

78. Yongyi Song, "Chronology of Mass Killings during the Chinese Cultural Revolution (1966–77)," *SciencesPo* (25 August 2011).

79. Isabelle Charleux, "Le patrimonie bâti dans la region 'autonome' chinoise de Mongole-Intèrieure: État actuel et avenir des architectures bouddhiques," in Maria Gravari and Sylvie Guichard-Anguius, *Regards croisés sur le patrimonie dans le monde à l'aube du XXI siècle* (Paris: Presses de l'université de Paris-Sorbonne, 2003), 225.

80. Dalai Lama, *My Land and My People* (New York: Potola, 1985), 158.

81. Tsering Shakya, *The Dragon in the Land of Snows: A History of Modern Tibet since 1947* (New York: Penguin, 1999), 185–211.

82. Tsering Woeser, *Forbidden Memory: Tibet during the Cultural Revolution* (Lincoln, NE: Potomac Books, 2020), 173. On the Tibet-China conflict generally, and its geopolitical context and stakes, see Carole McGranahan, *Arrested Histories: Tibet, the CIA, and Memories of a Forgotten War* (Durham, NC: Duke University Press, 2010).

83. Margolin, "China: A Long March into the Night," 543.

84. Barbara Demick, *Eat the Buddha: Life and Death in a Tibetan Town* (New York: Random House, 2020), 48.

85. Panchen Lama, *A Poisoned Arrow: The Secret Report of the Tenth Panchen Lama* (London: Tibet Information Network, 1997).

86. Quoted in Woeser, *Forbidden Memory*, 28.

87. The leaflet is quoted in full in Shakya, *Dragon in the Land of Snows*, 320–21.

88. Tubten Khétsun, *Memories of Lhasa under Chinese Rule*, trans. Matthew Akester (New York: Columbia University Press, 2014), 168.

89. Quoted in Woeser, *Forbidden Memory*, 48.

90. Gyurme Dorje, *Jokhang: Tibet's Most Sacred Buddhist Temple* (London: Hansjorg Mayer, 2010), 23–24.

91. Quoted materials from Woeser, *Forbidden Memory*, 92–93.

92. Peter Dziedric, "Religion under Fire: A Report and Policy Paper on Religious Freedom in Tibet," *Tibetan Journal* 38 (2013): 91.

93. Quoted in Woeser, *Forbidden Memory*, 159.

94. Woeser, *Forbidden Memory*, 292.

95. Margolin, "China: A Long March into the Night," 546, and Swaleha A. Sindhi and Adfer Rashid Shah, "Life in Flames: Understanding Tibetan Self Immolations as Protest," *Tibet Journal* 37 (2012): 34-53.

96. Shakya, *Dragon in the Land of Snows*, 347.

97. Jean-Louis Margolin, "Cambodia: The Country of Disconcerting Crimes," in Courtois et al., eds., *Black Book of Communism*, 577.

98. Philip Short, *Pol Pot: Anatomy of a Nightmare* (New York: Henry Holt, 2004), 47-84.

99. Margolin, "Cambodia: The Country of Disconcerting Crimes," 635.

100. Chanthou Boua, "Genocide of a Religious Group: Pol Pot and Cambodia's Buddhist Monks," in P. Timothy Bushnell et al., eds., *State Organized Terror: The Case of Violent Internal Repression* (Boulder, CO: Westview Press, 1991), 228.

101. Some persecution in so-called liberated areas, however, began well before 1975.

102. François Ponchaud, *Cambodge année zéro* (Paris: Julliard, 1977), 244.

103. Quotations taken from Ben Kiernan, *The Pol Pot Regime: Race, Power, and Genocide under the Khmer Rouge, 1975-79*, 2nd ed. (New Haven: Yale University Press, 2002), 55-56.

104. Henri Locard, *Pol Pot's Little Red Book: The Sayings of Angkor* (Chiang Mai: Silkworm Books, 2004), 171-72.

105. Quoted material taken from Boua, "Genocide of a Religious Group," 234-35.

106. Ian Harris, *Buddhism in a Dark Age: Cambodian Monks under Pol Pot* (Honolulu: University of Hawai'i Press, 2013), 72-89.

107. Kosal Path and Angeliki Kanavou, "Converts, Not Ideologues? The Khmer Rouge Practice of Thought Reform in Cambodia, 1975-1978," *Journal of Political Ideologies* 20 (2015): 305-32.

108. Charles P. Wallace, "Buddhism Rising Again from the Ashes of Cambodia," *Los Angeles Times* (19 June 1990).

109. Quoted in Harris, *Buddhism in a Dark Age*, 105.

110. Harris, *Buddhism in a Dark Age*, 110.

111. Quoted in Boua, "Genocide of a Religious Group," 238.

112. Karl D. Jackson, *Cambodia, 1975-1978: Rendezvous with Death* (Princeton: Princeton University Press, 1989), 212.

113. Marek Sliwinski, *Le génocide khmer rouge: Une analyse démographique* (Paris: Editions L'Harmattan, 1995), 76.

114. Margolin, "Cambodia," 594-95.

115. Ben Kiernan, "Orphans of Genocide: The Cham Muslims under Pol Pot," *Bulletin of Concerned Asian Scholars* 20 (1988): 33.

CONCLUSION

1. Hannah Arendt, *The Origins of Totalitarianism* (New York: Harcourt, Brace and World, 1966), and Mark Mazower, "Violence and the State in the Twentieth Century," *American Historical Review* 4 (2002): 1158-78.

2. Zoe Knox, "Russian Religious Life in the Soviet Era," in Caryl Emerson et al., eds., *Oxford Handbook of Russian Religious Life* (Oxford: Oxford University Press, 2020), 65.

3. Xenia Dennen, "The Lithuanian Memorandum," in Julie deGraffenried and Zoe Knox, eds., *Voices of the Voiceless: Religion, Communism, and the Keston Archive* (Waco, TX: Baylor University Press, 2019), 57.

4. Alan Knight, "The Peculiarities of Mexican History: Mexico Compared to Latin America, 1821–1992," *Journal of Latin American Studies* 24 (1992): 121–22.

5. Stella Rock, "'They Burned the Pine, but the Place Remains the Same': Pilgrimage in the Changing Landscape of Soviet Russia," in Catherine Wanner, ed., *State Secularism and Lived Religion in Soviet Russia and Ukraine* (New York: Oxford University Press, 2012), 159–89.

6. From a conversation with a guard at the pilgrimage site (5 November 2021).

7. Quoted in William W. Brickman, "Resistance to Atheistic Education in the Soviet Union," *Journal of Thought* 9 (1974): 26.

8. J. Pinkava, "Communists and Religion," *Tribuna* (February 1973), Czechoslovakia, box 12, C2, folder 18, Keston Archive and Library, Baylor University.

9. Amnesty International, *Prisoners of Conscience in the USSR: Their Treatment and Conditions* (London: Amnesty International, 1975), 101–37.

10. Wanner, ed., *State Secularism and Lived Religion in Soviet Russia and Ukraine*, 1.

11. George Weigel, *The Final Revolution: The Resistance Church and the Collapse of Communism* (New York: Oxford University Press, 1992).

12. Denise A. Austin and Togtokh-Ulzii Davaadar, "Pentecostalism in Mongolia," *Inner Asia* 22 (2020): 277–98.

13. Ian Johnson, *The Souls of China: The Return of Religion after Mao* (New York: Pantheon, 2017), 16. See also Yanfei Sun, "Reversal of Fortune: Growth Trajectories of Catholicism and Protestantism in China," *Theory and Society* 48 (2019): 267–98.

14. Pierre-Jean Luizard, *Laïcité autoritaires en terres d'Islam* (Paris: Fayard, 2008), 11.

15. Monica Duffy Toft, Daniel Philpott, and Timothy Samuel Shah, *God's Century: Resurgent Religion and Global Politics* (New York: W. W. Norton, 2011), 72–73, 79, and Sena Karasipahi, "Comparing Islamic Resurgence Movements in Turkey and Iran," *Middle East Journal* 63 (2009), 87ff.

16. Doug Bandow, "North Korea's War on Christianity: The Globe's Number One Religious Persecutor," *Forbes* (31 October 2016).

17. Richard Madsen, "Religion under Communism," in S. A. Smith, ed., *Oxford Handbook of the History of Communism* (Oxford: Oxford University Press, 2014), 597.

18. John Allen Jr., "Catholicism in North Korea Survives in Catacombs," *National Catholic Reporter* (16 October 2006).

19. Sandra Fahy, *Putting North Korea's Human Rights Abuses on the Record* (New York: Columbia University Press, 2019), 64–67.

20. Reginald E. Reimer, "Christian Responses to Persecution in Communist Vietnam and Laos," in Daniel Philpott and Timothy Samuel Shah, eds., *Under Caesar's Sword: How Christians Respond to Persecution* (Cambridge: Cambridge University Press, 2018), 298, and Jonathan Fox, *Thou Shalt Have No Other Gods Before Me: Why Governments Discriminate Against Religious Minorities* (Cambridge: Cambridge University Press, 2020), 178–81.

21. Human Rights Watch World Report (2021) available at https://www.hrw.org/world-report/2021 (accessed on 29 October 2022).

22. Pascal Fontaine, "Communism in Latin America," in Stéphane Courtois et al., eds., *The Black Book of Communism: Crimes, Repression, Terror,* trans. Jonathan Murphy and Mark Kramer (Cambridge, MA: Harvard University Press, 1999), 650–51.

23. Armando Valladares, *Against All Hope: The Prison Memoirs of Armando Valladares,* trans. Andrew Hurley (New York: Knopf, 1986).

24. Quoted in Paul A. Marshall, *Their Blood Cries Out: The Untold Story of Persecution against Christians in the Modern World* (Dallas: Word, 1997), 9.

25. Document 19 as reproduced in Donald E. MacInnis, *Religion in China Today: Policies and Practices* (Maryknoll, NY: Orbis, 1989), 8–26.

26. Freedom House, "Religious Revival, Repression, and Resistance under Xi Jinping" (2017), available at https://freedomhouse.org/article/new-report-battle-chinas-spirit-religious-revival-repression-and-resistance-under-xi (accessed on 20 October 2022).

27. Zhang Chunhua, "Religion at the Chinese Communist Party Congress [2022]," at https://bitterwinter.org/religion-at-the-chinese-communist-party-congress/ (accessed on 1 November 2022).

28. "Often their only crime is being Muslim," as the Council on Foreign Relations' report "China's Repression of Uyghurs in Xinjiang" bluntly puts it. See https://www.cfr.org/backgrounder/china-xinjiang-uyghurs-muslims-repression-genocide-human-rights (accessed on 20 February 2024). See also Sean R. Roberts, *The War on the Uyghurs: China's Internal Campaign Against a Muslim Minority* (Princeton: Princeton University Press, 2020), and Nury Turkel, *No Escape: The True Story of China's Genocide of the Uyghurs* (New York: HarperCollins, 2022).

29. See United Nations Human Rights Office of the High Commissioner, "OHCHR Assessment of Human Rights Concerns in the Xinjiang Uyghur Autonomous Region, People's Public of China" (31 August 2022), found at https://www.ohchr.org/sites/default/files/documents/countries/2022-08-31/22-08-31-final-assesment.pdf (accessed on 28 October 2022).

30. See especially Joseph Zen, *For the Love of My People I Will Not Remain Silent: On the Situation of the Church in China,* trans. Pierre G. Rossi (San Francisco: Ignatius, 2019).

31. Freedom House Report on Tibet (2022), at https://freedomhouse.org/country/tibet/freedom-world/2022 (accessed on 28 October 2022). See also Peter Dziedzi, "Religion under Fire: A Report and Policy Paper on Religious Freedom in Tibet," *Tibet Journal* 38 (2013): 87–113.

32. Amnesty International at https://www.amnesty.org/en/latest/press-release/2019/12/china-appalling-jail-sentence-outspoken-pastor-makes-mockery-religious-freedoms/ (accessed on 31 October 2022). See also "Religion in China," Council on Foreign Relations, at https://www.cfr. org/backgrounder/religion-china (accessed on 21 April 2022).

33. Tam T. T. Ngo and Justine B. Quijada, eds., *Atheist Secularism and Its Discontents: A Comparative Study of Religion and Communism in Eurasia* (New York: Palgrave Macmillan, 2015), 4–7.

34. Adeeb Khalid, *Central Asia: A New History from the Imperial Conquests to the Present* (Princeton: Princeton University Press, 2021), 220.

35. See, e.g., Michael Rectenwald et al., eds., *Global Secularisms in a Post-Secular Age* (Berlin: De Gruyter, 2015), and Craig Calhoun et al., eds., *Rethinking Secularism* (Oxford: Oxford University Press, 2011).

36. Sonja Luehrmann, "Was Soviet Society Secular? Undoing Equations between Communism and Religion," in Tam and Quijada, eds., *Atheist Secularism and Its Discontents*, 135.

37. Jeffrey Cox, "Secularization and Other Master Narratives of Religion in Modern Europe," *Kirchliche Zeitgeschichte* 14 (2001): 24–35.

38. José Casanova, "The Secular, Secularization, Secularisms," in Craig Calhoun et al., eds., *Rethinking Secularism*, 70.

39. Tzvetan Todorov, *Hope and Memory: Lessons from the Twentieth Century*, trans. David Bellos (Princeton: Princeton University Press, 2000), 91.

40. Courtois et al., eds., *Black Book of Communism*, 4.

41. Anne Applebaum, *Gulag: A History* (New York: Anchor Books, 2003), xviii–xix.

42. Tony Judt, "From the House of the Dead: On Modern European Memory," *New York Review of Books* (6 October 2003), 14.

43. Jeff Wood, *Black Struggle, Red Scare: Segregation and Anti-Communism in the South, 1948–1968* (Baton Rouge: Louisiana State University Press, 2004).

44. See, inter alia, Sonja Luehrmann, *Religion in Secular Archives: Soviet Atheism and Historical Knowledge* (Oxford: Oxford University Press, 2015); Antoine Wenger, *Catholiques en Russie d'après les archives du KGB, 1920–1960* (Paris: Descleé de Brouwer, 1998); James A. Kapaló and Kinga Povedák, eds., *The Secret Police and the Religious Underground in Communist and Post-Communist Eastern Europe* (London: Routledge, 2022); James A. Kapaló et al., eds., *Hidden Galleries: Material Religion in the Secret Police Archives in Central and Eastern Europe* (Zurich: LIT, 2020); and Felix Corley, ed., *Religion in the Soviet Union: An Archival Reader* (New York: New York University Press, 1996).

45. Ronald Grigor Suny, "The Left Side of History: The Embattled Pasts of Communism in the Twentieth Century," *Perspectives on Politics* 15 (2017): 455–64.

46. David Bentley Hart, *Atheist Delusions: The Christian Revolution and Its Fashionable Enemies* (New Haven: Yale University Press, 2009), 221.

Acknowledgments

Many are the people and institutions that help an idea become a book.

I thank Kevin Gary, Mark Schwehn, Nicholas Denysenko, Ronald Rittgers, Stephanie Wong, Slavica Jakelić, and Philip Jenkins. All read the initial essay/proposal, gave me helpful constructive criticism, and encouraged me to turn it into a book. I owe a particular debt to Mel Piehl for reading not only the initial essay but the entire manuscript, offering trenchant commentary and criticism on both. He greatly improved both the style and the substance of the book.

For assistance on this project and for so much else, I owe a special debt to Sara Shoppa, the interlibrary loan manager at Valparaiso University's Christopher Center Library. She kept the books and articles a-comin.'

I thank archivists at the Catholic Union in Chicago, the University of Notre Dame, and Baylor University. At the Catholic Union, I thank Derek Rieckens in particular. Seated at Baylor, the Keston Archives and Library, which holds a wealth of material related to the persecution of religious believers under Communist regimes, proved especially valuable. I thank there Kathy Hillman, Janice Losak, and especially Larisa Seago, who provided important materials and advice on numerous occasions. Anyone who works at Keston owes an abiding debt to the late Father Michael Bourdeaux, who made it his life's vocation to document Soviet-era religious repression in many countries. In addition, I am grateful to the staff at the Dominican Saulchoir library in Paris and the Library of Congress in Washington, D.C.

I thank the Allison family—David, Sandra, and Chris—who greatly facilitated my travels in Albania to learn more about persecutions there under the dictator Enver Hoxha. Sandra Allison also provided me with helpful translations of Thomas Qirjazi's reflections on growing up in Cold War Albania. In Albania, I am grateful to Ergest Biti, Sevin Serjani, Yilli Doci, Landi Jak Ofu, and Genti Kruja. Armandra Kodra of the Institute for the Study of Communist Crimes and Their Consequences in Albania and her husband, Roald Hysa, deserve a special word of thanks for providing me with information about the repression of Albanian Muslims.

I am thankful to Douglas Puffert and his colleagues at LCC International University for helping me before and during my travels related to this project in Lithuania and Latvia. In the former, I am also thankful for conversations with the historian Arūnas Streikus; in the latter, with the cultural anthropologist Solveiga Krumina-Konkova.

I am indebted to Timothy Samuel Shah, who read portions of the manuscript as it neared completion and offered helpful feedback drawn from his vast knowledge of global politics.

Students in my Communism and Religion seminar deserve a word of thanks. They read drafts of several chapters and offered their thoughts, questions, and feedback. These students include Conner Daehler, Megan Goff, Hogan Jackson, Emma Jacobs, Kevin Koenig, Brooke Koppang, Makayla Mann, Sylvia Schaffer, Samuel Starkenburg, and Amelia Tandy.

Additional people who deserve a shout-out include Eric Johnson, Heather Grennan Gary, Mark Biermann, Sharon Dybel, Pjerin Mirdita, Hope Biermann, Karen Palm, Joseph Creech, Joseph Goss, Mary Grace Swift, Jeni Prough, David Weber, Roman Van Meter, Lisa Driver, Gretchen Buggeln, Aaron Preston, Antonine Arjakovsky, and Tommy Howard, my father.

I thank editors at the online journal *Law and Liberty* for permitting me to reprint portions of my articles "God and the Ghosts of Communism," which appeared in July 2022, and "The Baltic Love of Freedom," which appeared in May 2023.

Visits to several museums stimulated thought related to this project, so let me thank personnel at Albania's National History Museum in Tirana and the Site of Witness and Memory in Shkodra, Albania; the Ukrainian National Museum in Chicago; the Balzekas Museum of Lithuanian Culture in Chicago; the National Museum of the Revolution in Mexico City; the Armenian Genocide Memorial-Institute in Yerevan, Armenia; and the Museum of Occupations and Freedom Fights and Project Homo Sovieticus in Vilnius, Lithuania.

I am grateful for funding provided by the Institute for Humane Studies at George Mason University and for the ongoing generous support provided by the late Richard and Phyllis Duesenberg.

This is my second book with Yale University Press under the editorial direction of Jennifer Banks. She and her colleagues model professionalism and good sense. I also thank the fine readers of the manuscript secured by the Press.

Not least and once again, I express my deep gratitude to Agnes R. Howard and our cherished family.

Index